SECURING YOUR PLACE AT A UK DENTAL SCHOOL

THE COMPLETE GUIDE FOR UNDERGRADUATES AND POSTGRADUATES

WRITTEN WITH SUCCESSFUL PAST
AND CURRENT DENTISTRY STUDENTS

Raza Ahmed
Dr. Kalpesh Prajapat BDS (Liverpool)

1st Edition

Copyright © 2020 I Want To Be A Dentist

Printed in the United Kingdom. First Printing, 2020 First Edition

ISBN: 979-86-74842-69-9

The information contained in this book reflects the views and opinions of its individual contributors and authors, and is in no way intended to be representative of the Universities, Dental Schools or associated official organisations.

While every effort has been made to ensure that this information is reliable and accurate with respect to the Dental School application process, it must be noted that this book is not an official document. We would encourage all individuals wishing to study Dentistry at university to seek guidance from UCAS and the respective official universities.

In order to protect the integrity of the dental school assessment process, the scenarios or questions in this book have been fabricated to be similar to those expected of a typical UK dental school interview. It is strongly suggested that you understand what the questions and scenarios are asking rather than regurgitating a pre-formulated answer.

In order to maintain the fairness of the interview, the examples we have created aim to give interviewees a broad base to think about the types of ways in which a scenario or topic could be asked, but in no way should be relied upon as what to expect in the interview. We advocate learning principles and applying them to the question to create a natural, honest answer. Most importantly, all applicants are advised to ensure that they have researched their career choice thoroughly to ensure dentistry is a suitable choice for them. The interview is ultimately a process to ensure the most appropriate candidates are selected, and should not be thought of as a test that should be passed. However, one of the aims of the book is to help you understand the assessment process and develop your interview techniques.

TABLE OF CONTENTS

CHAPTER 5: THE SELECTION PROCESS 157

CONTENTS

We really hope this book adds value in your application to study dentistry by giving you step-by-step guidance and a more in-depth understanding of how to prepare, from experienced applicants who have successfully gained entry to dental school.

All the best!
Kal & Raza

Co-founders of I Want To Be A Dentist

I WANT TO BE A DENTIST

What is I Want To Be A Dentist?

We are an educational platform created by current and former dentistry students. Our aim is to help applicants gain acceptance into university to study dentistry.

Why We Started I Want To Be A Dentist

As current and former students, we know how much it means to gain a place to study dentistry. We are also familiar with the process of getting into dental school, which we know is stressful and sometimes leaves you feeling deprived of support.

That's why we wanted to create a universal resource where dental school applicants can gather useful information that gives them confidence when applying for a place at a dental school, ultimately giving candidates the best chances of securing an offer.

We also wanted to create a network so those interested in studying dentistry could reach out to current dentistry students, creating an interconnecting union between applicants and those soon-to-be dentists.

Where We Can Help

Our book is the first stop for applicants to get advice and support. Find more free resources at *www.iwanttobeadentist.com.*

More About Our Services

Our website is packed with FREE resources to give you a head start.

Free Consultation For
Dentistry
Application Advice

Extra Free UK Dentistry
Interview Questions

Essential Third Party
Links

Free UCAT & BMAT
tutorials

Bursaries Available

You could be entitled to a 50% bursary for any package. Read more about eligibility later on.

Our Paid Services

We have teamed up with the UK's best current and former dentistry students, and UCAT and BMAT tutors to provide a valuable array of courses and services to help aspiring dentists maximise their chances of securing an offer at a dental school.

Choose from a range of different packages depending on your support requirements.

Why Choose Us?

These packages are designed to include everything you need to maximise your chances of securing a dental school interview. As current and former dental students, we know the types of things you need to boost your chances of gaining a dental school offer. That's why we developed these exclusive packages, giving you the support you need in one place.

Dental Applicant **Pre-interview Packages**

I Want To Be A Dentist

Courses & Mentoring

Ultimate Dentistry Interview Day Course

Dentistry Personal Statement Review Service

Online UCAT & BMAT Mastery Course

One-To-One UCAT & BMAT Tuition

Online Dentistry Interview Preparation Course

One-To-One Dental School Interview Mentoring

Tip: Use a mobile device to scan the QR and launch the website.

Services Included

☑ Personal Statement Review

☑ UCAS application help

☑ UCAT Online Mastery

☑ UCAT Online Mock Test

☑ BMAT Online Mastery

☑ BMAT Online Mock Test

☑ One-to-One 1Hr Tuition

☑ 1 Year Unlimited Access

Basic

£69

https://www.iwanttobeadentist.com/
pre-interview-preparation-package-basic

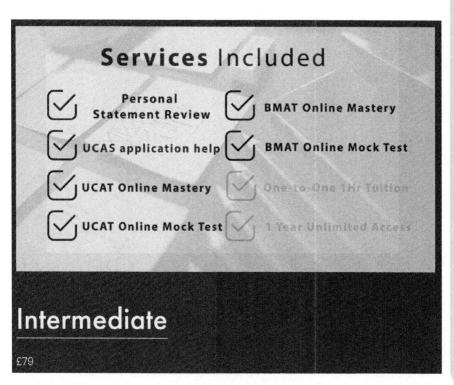

Services Included

- ✓ Personal Statement Review
- ✓ UCAS application help
- ✓ UCAT Online Mastery
- ✓ UCAT Online Mock Test
- ✓ BMAT Online Mastery
- ✓ BMAT Online Mock Test
- ✓ One-to-One 1Hr Tuition
- ✓ 1 Year Unlimited Access

Intermediate

£79

https://www.iwanttobeadentist.com/
pre-interview-preparation-package-intermediate

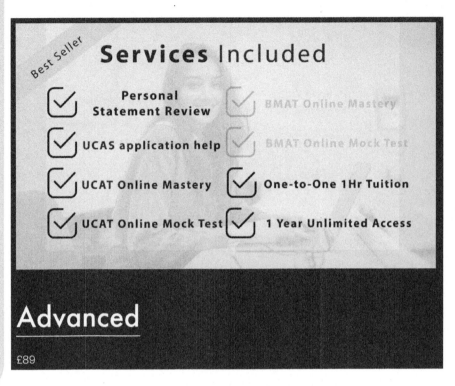

https://www.iwanttobeadentist.com/
pre-interview-preparation-package-advanced

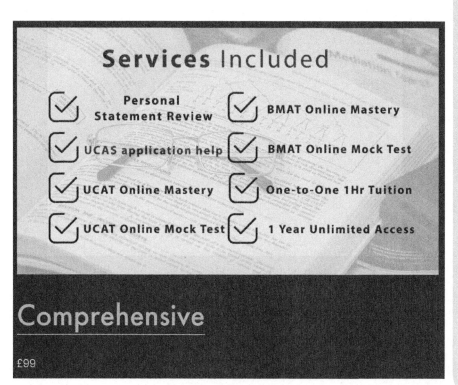

Services Included

- ✓ Personal Statement Review
- ✓ UCAS application help
- ✓ UCAT Online Mastery
- ✓ UCAT Online Mock Test
- ✓ BMAT Online Mastery
- ✓ BMAT Online Mock Test
- ✓ One-to-One 1Hr Tuition
- ✓ 1 Year Unlimited Access

Comprehensive

£99

https://www.iwanttobeadentist.com/
pre-interview-preparation-package-comprehensive

OUR PRE-INTERVIEW SERVICES IN DETAIL

Pre-interview Services	
Service	**What to expect**
Personal Statement Review	A full, detailed analysis of your personal statement with constructive feedback. 5 interview-style questions. Statement reviewed by current or former dentistry student or interviewer.
UCAS Application Support	24/7 advice, guidance and support with your UCAS application from beginning to end.
UCAT Online Mastery Course	An extensive in-depth UCAT course designed to boost your score and increase your speed. Designed in collaboration with top decile tutors, this course covers every section of the UCAT with 700+ questions, worked examples, strategies and confidence-boosting methods. We want you to score an average of 700+ and achieve Band 1 in SJT.
UCAT Online Mock Test	A unique, fully-timed UCAT mock test with mark scheme and explanations. Mock testing under timed conditions after completing the UCAT course modules.
BMAT Online Mastery Course	Aimed at those wishing to apply to Leeds Dental Institute, this exclusive BMAT course for dental applicants is designed by BMAT tutors and mentors who attained a score within the top 1%. The course covers every section of the BMAT with 200+ questions, worked examples, strategies and methods to boost your score.

Pre-interview Services

BMAT Online Mock Test	A full, simulated BMAT mock test with mark scheme and explanations. Designed for those wishing to apply to Leeds Dental Institute, the BMAT test has been developed to test your knowledge following our BMAT course.
One-to-One (UCAT / BMAT) Tuition	One-to-One UCAT & BMAT tuition with our top ranking tutors. Learn from those who attained a score within the top 1% of all candidates. Master every type of question style, boost your confidence and learn methods to improve your score.
One Year Access	We understand everyone needs time to learn. That's why, unlike other organisations, we offer access for a full year so you can learn at your own pace.

Our interview packages for dental applicants have been developed specifically to improve your confidence, enhance your interview technique and master the types of questions and scenarios you may expect at a typical UK dental school interview. Interview courses launching from October 2020.

Package Includes

 Online UK Dental School Interview Course

 Unlimited Access For 12 months

 200 + UK Dental Interview Questions

 Full Mock Interview Test

 1 hr One-to-One Interview Mentoring

 Dental University Matched Tutor

 Online In-person Mock Interview with feedback

Full Video Recording Of Mock Interview

[BASIC] £75 incl VAT

Dental Applicant **Interview Packages**

Best Seller

Package Includes

- ✓ Online UK Dental School Interview Course
- ✓ Unlimited Access For 12 months
- ✓ 200 + UK Dental Interview Questions
- ✓ Full Mock Interview Test
- ✓ 1 hr One-to-One Interview Mentoring
- ✓ Dental University Matched Tutor
- ✓ Online In-person Mock Interview with feedback
- ✓ Full Video Recording Of Mock Interview

[ADVANCED] £89 incl VAT

Package Includes

 Online UK Dental School Interview Course

 Unlimited Access For 12 months

 200 + UK Dental Interview Questions

 Full Mock Interview Test

 2 hr One-to-One Interview Mentoring

 Dental University Matched Tutor

 Online In-person Mock Interview with feedback

 Full Video Recording Of Mock Interview

[COMPREHENSIVE] £129 incl VAT

OUR INTERVIEW SERVICES IN DETAIL

Interview Services	
Service	**What to expect**
Online Dental School Interview Course	A highly bespoke, detail-packed dentistry interview preparation course for those wishing to gain a dental school offer. Covers essential information over 10 taught tutorials with in-depth advice from successful dentistry students. Covering MMI and panel interviews from all UK Dental Schools. Full simulated mock tests to attempt with answers. Over 200 + Dental School Interview questions covering the typical questions and scenarios giving you confidence and boosting your chances of gaining an offer!
12 Month Access	Enjoy 12 months unlimited access so you can learn at your own pace.
200+ Interview Questions	We have compiled typical questions likely to be expected at a UK Dental School interview. Cover different types of questions, MMI scenarios, panel interview questions and a full mock test.

Interview Services

Full Mock Interview	We have developed a full length MMI mock interview test with typical questions to be encountered at a UK Dental School interview. Developed for both MMI and panel interviews this test builds your confidence and maximises your chances of gaining an offer.
One-to-One Interview Mentoring	Exclusive one-to-one online interview sessions dedicated to help with areas you are struggling with, practising questions and receiving mentoring to boost your confidence and interview technique
Dental university Matched Tutor	We pair you with a current successful dentistry university student to ensure you receive the advice, guidance and support you require to succeed. Learn from those who have been through the process!
Online Mock Interview with feedback	This online mock-interview is conducted in exam conditions making it as close to the real interview as possible. Undertake a full MMI or Panel Interview with constructive feedback.
Full Video Recording Of Mock	Learn from your own eyes. We send you a video recording of your mock interview to help you see how you answer questions and your body language. This forms an invaluable tool to strengthen your interview technique and confidence.

BURSARY SCHEME

O ur philosophy is to help everyone along their journey to study dentistry at university. We have therefore launched a bursary scheme allowing anyone eligible to receive 50% off our package fees.

This bursary is valid for use on both pre-interview and interview packages and UCAT/BMAT e-lessons.

Who is eligible?

Use this table to determine whether you fulfil the criteria. You must provide supporting evidence for corresponding criteria.

Eligibility Criteria	Evidence Required
Free School Meals	Provide a recent letter from your school/college confirming that you receive free school meals (local authority funded only).
16 to 19 Bursary (England), or Education Maintenance Allowance (EMA) (Scotland, Wales or NI)	Please provide your official award letter for academic year 2019/20 or 2020/21. We do not accept evidence that relates to scholarships/bursaries at independent or fee-paying schools.

Eligibility Criteria	Evidence Required
Learner Support (FE 19+) or equivalent FE funding for Scotland, Wales or NI	Please provide your official award letter for academic year 2019/20 or 2020/21.
Student Finance England Maintenance Grant or Maintenance Loan* (full-rate), or Student Awards Agency Scotland (SAAS) Young Students'/Independent Students' Bursary (full-rate), or Student Finance Wales or Northern Ireland Maintenance Grant (full-rate)	Please provide your Student Finance or SAAS award letter for academic year 2019/20 or 2020/21. Please ensure you include the pages that show the means tested grant/bursary element. You must be in receipt of a full-rate means-tested award. *If your course started after August 2016, we will accept evidence of a full-rate means-tested Maintenance Loan from Student Finance England. Please ensure you check what qualifies.
Income Support, or Job Seeker's Allowance (JSA), or Employment and Support Allowance (ESA)	If you or a parent/guardian you live with are in receipt of one of these benefits please provide an award letter (all pages) from the UK Jobcentre Plus, dated 2020. If your parent/guardian is the person in receipt of JSA or ESA then it must be the income-based benefit (e.g. means-tested) and not contribution-based.
Universal Credit	If you or a parent/guardian you live with are in receipt of Universal Credit (income used to calculate the award must be less than 35k) please provide a recent statement (current or previous month) from 2020. We must be able to see the name of the claimant, the date, and the take-home pay for the period.
Working or Child Tax Credit	If you or a family member you live with are recipients of Tax Credits please provide an award letter from 2019/20 or 2020/21. You must be named on the award and the household income used to calculate the award must be less than 35k. Please ensure you provide both the pages that show this or your application will be rejected.

Eligibility Criteria	Evidence Required
EU State Benefit	If you or a parent/guardian you live with are in receipt of an equivalent means-tested benefit from another EU state you may be eligible. Please provide an award letter from a relevant government agency, plus a translation into English, both dated 2020.
Being in care for at least 13 weeks during period of secondary education.	Evidence of being looked after in care with dates coinciding with those of your secondary education years.
If your home address is within quintiles 1 or 2 of POLAR3 Neighbourhood - based on the classification of postcodes by the Higher Education Funding Council for England (HEFCE). Postcodes in quintiles 1 and 2 of the POLAR3 Low Participation Neighbourhood	Proof of home postcode with bill or letter address to you at this address.
Asylum Support	If you or a parent/guardian you live with are in receipt of this support please provide an official award letter, dated 2020.

We DO NOT accept any of the following as evidence: P60 (end of year certificate); annual accounts; council tax/housing/child benefit letters.

HOW DO I CLAIM FOR A BURSARY?

I f you have determined that you are eligible and have the correct evidence follow these steps to apply for your claim by email:

Step 1. Address the email to *hello@iwanttobeadentist.com* with the subject line: IWTBAD Bursary

Step 2. Attach scanned or clear photographs of the documents you submit as evidence and include the criteria category, i.e Universal Credits.

Step 3. Include the name of the service/package you would like to purchase (i.e. pre-interview BASIC) and send the email.

Step 4. If you fulfil the criteria we'll send you a response email containing a unique link to claim 50% off the package purchase.

Which packages can I get bursary for?

Anyone eligible is entitled to 50% off both one pre-interview package and one interview package.

FREE BONUS RESOURCES

As a thank you for purchasing this book we'd like to give you free access to these bonus resources.

1. Free 'Dental School Checklist' Spreadsheet

This downloadable checklist helps you decide which university is best for you. Although you only have four choices, making the final decision is tremendously challenging. Use this table to objectively score each criteria to help your decision making process when selecting a Dental School.

Dentistry University Open Day Checklist Dental School Selection Criteria								
University Name	Location	Course Structure	Entry Requirements	Success Rate	Opportunities	Ranking	My Overall Score
Belfast							
Birmingham							
Bristol							
Cardiff							
Dundee							
Glasgow							
Leeds							
Liverpool							
London – King's College							
London – Barts							
Manchester							
Newcastle							
Plymouth							
Sheffield							
Aberdeen							
Preston (university of Central Lancashire)							

2. Free Access to UCAT & BMAT online module

We understand that you are committed to maximizing your chances of gaining an offer to study dentistry at university.

As part of our pre-interview resources, we have developed a unique online UCAT & BMAT mastery course. Developed with the UK's leading tutors and mentors, these courses help you achieve scores of 700 + in UCAT and gain top marks in the BMAT.

Here's your link to access each course now for FREE (scan QR code)

UCAT FREE module (*https://www.iwanttobeadentist.com/ ucat-free-module-sign-up*)

BMAT FREE module (*https://www.iwanttobeadentist.com/ bmat-free-module-sign-up*)

3. Free PDF - Personal Statement Mark Scheme

We want to do everything we can to make a beneficial impact on your application. A key determinant of the UCAS application is the personal statement. With a well-structured, well written and cogitative statement you can drastically strengthen your application in its entirety.

We've designed this useful mark scheme to help you think like an assessor. Using this you can see where your statement can be strengthened.

4. 10% OFF CODE for our online courses

In addition to this book, you can also benefit from our online pre-interview and interview packages discussed earlier.

All our book readers can get a gift voucher for a 10% discount for any of our packages on our website *www.iwanttobeadentist.com*.

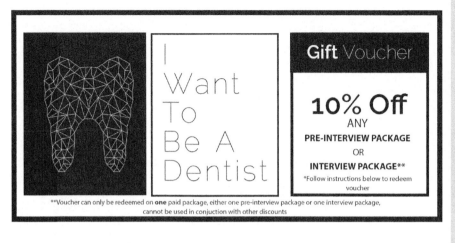

What Can I Use The Voucher On?

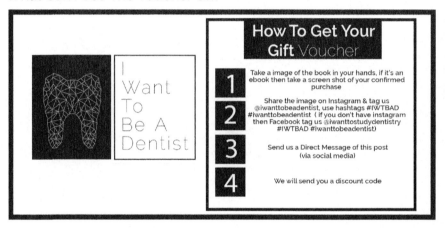

You can get 10% off the total fee on any of our pre-interview or interview packages*.

Find out more about our packages below:

Pre-interview Packages

https://www.iwanttobeadentist.com/
pre-interview-dentistry-applicant-preparation-packages

*Please note that this voucher cannot be combined with any other offers.

How To Get The Discount

Get your unique voucher code in 4 easy steps.

Step 1: Take a photograph of this book in your hands. For an ebook take a screen shot of your confirmed purchase.

Step 2: Share the image on Instagram and tag us @iwanttobeadentist. Use hashtags #IWTBAD #iwanttobeadentist.

If you don't have an Instagram account tag us on Facebook instead @iwanttostudydentistry #IWTBAD #iwanttobeadentist.

Step 3: Send us a direct message on Instagram or Facebook with the photo or screenshot.

Step 4: We'll send you your discount code to use.

PREFACE

Securing a place to study dentistry is for many like winning a 'golden ticket'. Gaining acceptance into a university to study dentistry is one of the most difficult application processes compared to other course subjects.

Strict entry criteria and a greater desire to study dentistry have made it tougher than ever to achieve a dentistry offer.

Due to strict government capping on the numbers of training places in dentistry to prevent oversupply of dentists, there is great demand for each position. As such, entry to study dentistry is facilitated by competitive selection rather than recruitment.

It's estimated that there are more than 10 applicants for every single training post in dentistry, compared to training in medicine, where there are four times more available spaces and twice as many medical schools.

Furthermore, each dentistry school's admission process is carefully designed and scrutinised to be a universally fair process so candidates are assessed on their motivation, communication and core values as well as academic achievements.

In addition, owing to the exceptional academic achievements of the high calibre dentistry candidates, universities make the entry process even more challenging by insisting that candidates complete aptitude tests such as BMAT and UCAT.

This book is therefore intended to be of value to those wishing to apply to study dentistry, particularly those who may not be familiar with the application process or how the interviews are conducted.

By the end of this book you will be well informed about the exact selection process, how to go about selecting your position at your desired university, and you'll be fully equipped with the tools to secure your training post!

ACKNOWLEDGEMENTS

We are extremely grateful to the current and past dentistry applicants and newly graduated dentists that have contributed their anecdotal experience and knowledge towards making this a valuable, fact-based resource for our readers.

Special gratitude to our key contributors:

Nafi Iftekhar

Currently transitioning into his second year at Leeds Medical School, Nafi was a straight-A scholar in Maths, Further Maths, Physics and Chemistry. Previously gaining multiple STEMM awards for his academic extracurricular activities, he is one of the youngest premium tutors online, teaching prospective medical professionals how to achieve high scores in entrance exams; having achieved one of the highest BMAT scores in the country himself.

Dr. Michael Denny BDS BSc (hons)

Since qualifying from Liverpool University, Michael has worked in a variety of settings, including general dental practice and urgent dental care. He now works full-time at Carisbrooke Dental Practice – a private specialist referral practice in Leicester. He is currently part way through his MSc in restorative dentistry at UCL Eastman Dental School and is also currently finishing a post graduate certificate in Endodontics. Before studying Dentistry, Michael gained a first-class honours degree in Physiology at the University of Liverpool.

Dr. Amit Dattani DMD MFDS RCPS(Glasgow) MBChB

Dr. Amit Dattani is a qualified dental surgeon and medical doctor. He qualified in dentistry in 2013 from the internationally renowned university of Debrecen in Hungary. Amit also completed a medical degree from the University of Birmingham in 2019 and is following a pathway to specialise in Oral and Maxillofacial Surgery.

Fadheelah Nadeem Yaseen

Having secured A-Levels in Biology, Chemistry and English Literature, Fadheelah is currently in her second year of study at the University of Leeds. Some of her present endeavours include mentoring prospective dental students, working with MIND charity as a mental health advocate and playing a key role in the "Open Wide" committee; an initiative set up by Leeds Dental Students to educate under-represented individuals in dentistry.

Rohan Gandhi

Rohan is a third year dental student at the University of Birmingham after completing A-levels in Biology, Chemistry and Maths. After applying to Birmingham, Bristol, King's and Cardiff, Rohan gained a place at Birmingham.

Rishi Daggar

A second-year dental student, the combination of an altruistic community and wide range of learning opportunities available made dentistry a clear choice for Rishi, who undertook A-Levels in Biology, Chemistry, Maths and Economics before studying dentistry.

Outside of clinics, Rishi spends his time involved with charitable initiatives, is a member of numerous societies, tutors prospective university students, and he plays for and helps manage the university hockey teams. Away from university, Rishi enjoys kicking back with a good movie in the company of his three dogs.

Zahraa Maiter

A London dental student, Zahraa is currently completing an intercalated BSc in Regenerative Medicine and Innovation Technology. Zahraa has also been involved with numerous dental societies at the college, including the student council, for which she organized a dental student wellbeing conference, and the Smile Society. She is a strong advocate of mental health awareness, including those who suffer from burnout at university, and for the representation of women in dentistry in all specialities, including leadership roles. In her free time, she enjoys spending time with friends, meditating and also volunteering in the UK and abroad.

Adam Moosa

Currently a fourth year dental student at Barts and the London, Adam studied A-Levels in Biology, Chemistry, Physics and Drama. He applied to Barts and the London, Liverpool, Newcastle and Sheffield universities. He is especially interested in Oral Surgery and Dental Public Health. In his spare time he enjoys running, playing guitar and watching movies.

Dr Alex King BDS

Alex graduated from University of Manchester Dental School in 2020. Alex is starting foundation training in South East Manchester. He has a keen interest in Minimally Invasive Ethical Cosmetic Dentistry and hopes to provide Smile Make-overs and Implant treatment in the near future.

Alex's runs Instagram podcast 'The Bulk-Fill Podcast' (@akingdental), which is aimed at young dental professionals.

Simran Khambay

Simran is currently a fourth year dental student at the University of Manchester. After completing A levels in Biology, Chemistry and Maths, she received offers from Manchester and Liverpool. Simran is interested in pursuing a career in Restorative, Cosmetics and Oral Surgery. She is a foodie and loves to bake.

Karolina Sadauskaite

Karolina is a fourth year dental student at the University of Dundee and the current Student's Union Vice President of the Dental School. She studied advanced biology, chemistry and physics, among other subjects, in school and graduated from the European Baccalaureate program. Since joining the university she has won awards for the highest grades in her year for the 2nd and 3rd year.

Brinder Singh Shergill

Brinder is a fifth year dental student at the University of Glasgow. He previously graduated with a 2:1 (Hons) in Biomedical sciences. Thereafter he worked as a Territory Manager within the NHS and private healthcare sector. During his dental degree he has been selected to be a peer mentor as well as represented the University of Glasgow in many organisations such as the British Association  of Cosmetic Dentistry and as is chair of the undergraduate group of the British Society of Periodontology and Implant Dentistry.

Jasleen Batra

Currently a fourth year dental student at Plymouth University (Peninsula), Jasleen studied A-levels in Biology, Chemistry and Psychology. She also took a gap year before beginning dental school. She enjoys sports and volunteers in her spare time.

Amrish Rajdev

Currently a third year dental student at the University of Bristol, Amrish studied Biology, Chemistry, Maths and German at A-level before going on to study Dental Material Science at Queen Mary university of London, where he obtained a Bachelor of Engineering with First Class Honours, before securing a place at Bristol.

Harriet Beaty

Current fourth year dental student at New-castle University, Harriet has a First Class Honours in Biomedical Sciences (Newcastle university, 2016) and 4 A-Levels in Art, Biology, Maths and Chemistry. She was the British Academy of Cosmetic Dentistry (BACD) Rising Star 2018 and the current BACD student representative for Newcastle university. Harriet is also a study club director  for Dentinal Tubules, an online learning platform for dentists and dental students, and a product specialist for Bryant Dental, one of the leading dental loupes providers in the UK.

Kathryn Eccles

Kathryn is a fourth year dental student at Newcastle University. After completing A-Levels in Maths, Chemistry and Biology, she went on to apply to Newcastle, Sheffield, Bristol and Cardiff – receiving offers from all 4 universities. Throughout dental school she has been heavily involved with rowing, train-ing with the high performance programme at the university, trialling for team GB, and achieving several national wins.

Dr Anam Chaudhry BDS

Anam has recently qualified from the University of Birmingham. Gaining a distinction in clinical dentistry, she is now due to begin her DFT year. Anam applied and received offers from Birmingham, Kings and Manchester and subsequently began her studies at the University of Birmingham in 2015.

At university Anam was involved in several organisations. She was the events lead of the Islamic Medical Society, through which she organised several events, such as the annual charity dinner. She has organised workshops in collaboration with medical societies in an effort to improve dental care in hospital settings. Above all, she is passionate about making dentistry accessible to everyone, regardless of their background. She also volunteers with the various Widening Access to Medicine and Dentistry schemes.

Adetayo Ayorinde

Adetayo is a fifth year dental student studying at Newcastle University. She studied Biology, Chemistry and Maths at A-level. At University, she has enjoyed getting involved with many societies, while also being a peer mentor and student representative for her dental school. She has an interest in cosmetic dentistry, and would also like to explore facial aesthetics in the future. Outside of dentistry, Adetayo enjoys playing her musical instruments, playing archery and spending time with her friends and family.

Jenna Angle BSc (hons)

Jenna is a current fourth year dental student at Newcastle University. She previously achieved first class honours in Biomedical Science from Oxford Brookes University, where Jenna was awarded the Biomedical Scientist's President's prize and the Micro-biology society prize in 2016. Jenna is an international student from Australia, and studied Art, Biology, English, Economics,  French and Maths for her International Baccalaureate (IB) in the Middle East. She has gained an interest in prosthodontics during her clinical time at dental school.

Thanks you to our additional contributors

Dr Kasim Butt BDS MJDF RCS Eng PgCert Dent Ed
Dr Mohammed Ali-Abbas Hussain BDS BSc (hons)
Dr Laurie Stumper BDS
Dr Andrew El-Khanagry BDS
Khushbu Morar BSc MSc
Rohan Jadav
Simran Chahal
Areej Mehdi

COMMON ACRONYMS & DEFINITIONS

We'll start by first covering a few common terms that you are likely to come across when researching further into Dentistry. Some of the terms highlighted are highly relevant to the Dentistry field. Having a good understanding of them can be valuable in an interview or when creating your personal statement.

UNDERGRADUATE
A university student who has not yet taken a first degree, i.e. a sixth form leaver

POSTGRADUATE
A postgraduate student is anyone who has completed an undergraduate degree and is studying for a *postgraduate course.*

UCAS UNIVERSITIES AND COLLEGES ADMISSIONS SERVICE

https://www.ucas.com/

The centralized service used by students use to apply for a place at university.

UCAT University Clinical Aptitude Test
https://www.ucat.ac.uk/

UCAT is an admissions test used by a number of UK university dental degree programmes as part of their selection criteria.

BMAT BioMedical Admissions Test
https://www.admissionstesting.org/for-test-takers/bmat/

The BioMedical Admissions Test is an aptitude test used as part of the admissions process for Medicine, Biomedical Sciences and Dentistry. The test results are intended to be used as a component of the selection decision in conjunction with other information available to admissions tutors.

Multiple Mini Interview (MMI)

The MMI format consist of a series of stations whereby the candidate is assessed on different theoretical and practical challenges. These may range from role-play or practical scenarios to traditional panel interview questions.

GDC General Dental Council
https://www.gdc-uk.org/

As the regulatory body for the dental profession, the GDC sets standards for the dental team to protect patients and the general public.

CQC Care Quality Commission
https://www.cqc.org.uk/

The CQC is an independent regulator for health and adult social care services in England, monitoring, inspecting and regulating health and social care services, including dental services.

The aim of the CQC is to ensure health and social care services provide people with safe, effective, compassionate, high-quality care. It also encourages improvements in care services.

BDA British Dental Association
https://bda.org/

The BDA is the professional association and registered trade union organisation for dentists in the United Kingdom.

DCP DENTAL CARE PROFESSIONAL

The term dental care professional refers to members of the wider dental team, which includes: dental hygienists, therapists, nurses, technicians and orthodontic therapists.

UDA UNIT OF DENTAL ACTIVITY

Dentists in England and Wales performing treatments under a general dental services contract are paid in Units of Dental Activity (UDA). Each UDA has a set value as per the practice contract.

UOA UNIT OF ORTHODONTIC ACTIVITY

Dentists in England and Wales performing orthodontic treatment under an orthodontic services contract are paid in Units of Orthodontic Activity. Each UOA has a set value as per the practice contract.

DENTIST WITH A SPECIAL INTEREST (DWSI)

This refers to a dentist being accredited by an external body in a specific field of dentistry and then being contracted to deliver specific, more complex NHS treatment in practice outside the mandatory services of the General Dental Services contract. This is usually just one part of the dentist's overall work in practice. The term has now been replaced with Dentist with Enhanced Skills (DES).

Dentist with Enhanced Skills – NHS England Commissioning Guides in 2015 set out a concept of more complex "Level 2" services to be performed by Dentists with Enhanced Skills rather than all General Dental Practitioners. A "Level 2" enhanced practitioner provides specific treatments on referral in general dental practice. These treatments are deemed more complex than normally provided by a primary care dentist under a general dental services contract but not sufficiently complex for a specialist or consultant. This service is commissioned by the NHS for specific treatments.

Tier 2 Dentist – This term is synonymous for a dentist with Enhanced Skills.

GDP GENERAL DENTAL PRACTICE

A general dental practice provides patients with ongoing continuing general dental care. Some general dental practices offer both NHS and private treatment, whilst some are exclusively private practices.

CDS COMMUNITY DENTAL SERVICE

The CDS provides dental care for patients with special needs – for example, those with mental or physical disabilities. They also provide care for paediatric patients who are unable to be treated in general dental practice due to anxieties or complex comorbidities. CDS dentists are salaried employees.

DO – DENTAL OFFICER WITHIN THE CDS

A dental officer within the community dental service usually provides care to patients with special needs, or paediatric patients referred from general dental practice due to anxieties or complex comorbidities.

SDO – SENIOR DENTAL OFFICER WITHIN THE CDS

A senior dental officer within the community dental service usually specialises within a particular area of special care, or paediatric dentistry.

DFT – DENTAL FOUNDATION TRAINING

Dental Foundation Training, previously called Vocational Training (VT), was introduced in 2012 as a training scheme for new dental graduates.

PRACTICE PRINCIPAL

In Northern Ireland, the term principal is used for a dentist that is on the Health and Social Care Board's dental list.

PRACTICE OWNER

The practice owner is the person who owns and runs a general dental practice. Practice owners can be single-handed practitioners, a partnership comprising two or more dentists, or a limited company.

PARTNER
Partners are two or more dentists that jointly own and run a dental practice.

PERFORMER
In England and Wales, those who carry out primary dental care under an NHS contract must be registered as performers with their name included on a Primary Care Organisation's Performers List.

DENTAL ASSOCIATE
Self-employed dentists working in a practice owned by another dentist, dental professional or company.

LOCUM
A locum dentist works in a dental practice on a short-term basis, covering absences or temporary gaps in recruitment, as well as assisting practices that may be falling behind in their contract delivery.

DENTAL CORPORATES
A dental practice can be owned by a corporate body. Approximately 13% of NHS contracts in England are held by the ten largest corporate providers (2015–2016 data).

KEY RESOURCES & LINKS

In order to help you stay organised, this section features key information related to the application process.

DENTISTRY SCHOOLS

There are sixteen dental schools in the UK. Out of the sixteen, two are graduate entry. There are an additional two postgraduate entry dental institutes that only accept graduated Dentists. Therefore this resource focuses on individual (undergraduate and postgraduate) students wishing to study Dentistry.

Undergraduate schools

Belfast
Queen's university Belfast School of Dentistry
Grosvenor Road
Belfast
Northern Ireland
BT12 6BP
Tel: 02890 972215
Web: *qub.ac.uk/schools/mdbs/*

Birmingham

School of Dentistry
5 Mill Pool Way
Birmingham
B5 7EG
Tel: 0121 466 5472
Email: dentadmissions@contacts.bham.ac.uk
Web: *www.birmingham.ac.uk/schools/dentistry/*

Bristol

Bristol Dental School
University of Bristol
Lower Maudlin Street
Bristol
BS1 2LY
Tel: 0117 394 1649
Email: choosebristol-ug@bristol.ac.uk
Web: *bristol.ac.uk/dental/*

Cardif

Wales College of Medicine
Dental School
Heath Park
Cardiff
CF14 4XY

Tel: 029 2074 2470
Email: dentalhos@cardiff.ac.uk
Web: *cardiff.ac.uk/dentistry*

Dundee

University of Dundee
Dental School
Park Place
Dundee
DD1 4HN
Tel: 01382 381 600
Email: asrs-dentistry@dundee.ac.uk
Web: *dentistry.dundee.ac.uk/*

Glasgow

Dean of the Dental School
Glasgow Dental Hospital and School
378 Sauchiehall Street
Glasgow
G2 3JZ
Tel: 0141 211 9703
Email: med-sch-dental-ug@glasgow.ac.uk
Web: *gla.ac.uk/schools/dental*

Leeds

School of Dentistry
University of Leeds
Leeds
LS2 9JT
Tel: 0113 343 9922
Email: denadmissions@leeds.ac.uk
Web: *medicinehealth.leeds.ac.uk/dentistry*

Liverpool
School of Dentistry
University of Liverpool
Pembroke Place
Liverpool
L3 5PS
Tel: 0151 794 2000
Web: *www.liverpool.ac.uk/dentistry/*

London – King's College
Faculty of Dentistry
Guy's Tower
Guy's Hospital
London
SE1 1UL
Tel: 020 7118 1164
Web: *kcl.ac.uk/dentistry*

London – Barts and The London School of Medicine and Dentistry
Queen Mary university of London
Royal London Dental Hospital
Turner Street
London
E1 2AD
Tel: 020 7882 2240 / 2243
Fax: 020 7882 7206
Email: *dentistry@qmul.ac.uk*
Web: *qmul.ac.uk/dentistry/*

Manchester
Faculty of Biology, Medicine and Health
Oxford Road
Manchester
M13 9PLH

Tel: 0161 306 0211
Email: *ug.dentistry@manchester.ac.uk*
Web: *bmh.manchester.ac.uk/study/dentistry/*

Newcastle
School of Dental Sciences
Framlington Place
University of Newcastle
Newcastle upon Tyne
NE2 4BW
Tel: 0191 208 8245
Web: *ncl.ac.uk/dental*

Plymouth
University of Plymouth
Peninsula Dental School
Portland Square
Drake Circus
Plymouth
PL4 8AA
Tel: 01752 600600
Web: *plymouth.ac.uk/schools/peninsula-school-of-dentistry*

Sheffield
School of Clinical Dentistry
University of Sheffield
Claremont Crescent
Sheffield
S10 2TA
Tel: 0114 215 9304
Web: *sheffield.ac.uk/dentalschool*

Graduate Entry Schools

Graduate entry schools formally accept individuals who have previously completed an undergraduate degree.

Kings College London also offers a fast-track (4 year) dentistry programme for graduates.

Plymouth and Barts and the London School of Medicine and Dentistry also accept graduates into their 5-year Dentistry programme.

More information on which schools consider graduates can be found later in this chapter.

Aberdeen
Institute of Dentistry
University of Aberdeen
Cornhill Road
Foresterhill
Aberdeen
AB25 2ZR
Tel: 01224 551 901
Email: *dentistry@abdn.ac.uk*
Web: *abdn.ac.uk/dental/*

Preston (University of Central Lancashire)
School of Dentistry
University of Central Lancashire
Preston
Lancashire
PR1 2HE
Tel: 01772 892 400
Web: *uclan.ac.uk/schools/dentistry/*

Postgraduate Only Dental Institutes

These schools only accept dentists who have graduated and wish to pursue further post-graduate dental studies.

UCL Eastman Dental Institute
256 Gray's Inn Road
London
WC1X 8LD
Tel: 020 3456 1092
Web: *ucl.ac.uk/eastman/*

Edinburgh Dental Institute
University of Edinburgh
Lauriston Building
Lauriston Place
Edinburgh
EH3 9HA
Tel: 0131 536 3979
Web: *ed.ac.uk/dentistry*

KEY LINKS

iwanttobeadentist.com

Free Work Experience Template

How I Gained Four Dentistry Offers (Article)

Dental School Council Website

GAMSAT Advice

Roles Of A Dentist

Standard Entry Table

Graduate Entry Table

CHAPTER 1

IS DENTISTRY FOR ME?

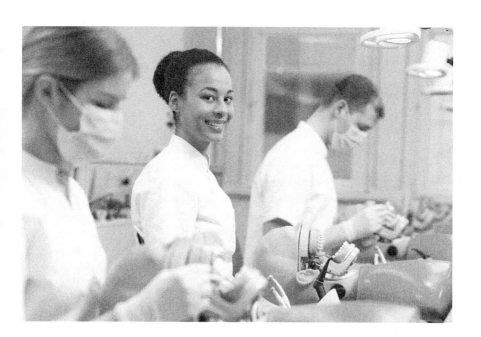

INTRODUCTION

This chapter 'sets the scene' for the endless possibilities that a career as a dentist can offer you.

In this chapter we will cover:

- Dentistry as a career
- General Dental Practitioner
- Hospital dentistry
- Dental specialists
- The wider dental team
- Jobs as a dentist you may not have known
- Salary
- Challenges
- Benefits
- Graduate prospects and Dental Foundation Training
- Life as a qualified Dentist

At this point you may be in one of two predicaments. You may be absolutely certain that dentistry is the career choice for you (hence buying this book) or you may still be undecided. This chapter will, I hope, provide some clarity to help make your decision more definitive.

Dentistry As A Career

Dentistry as a career provides a very unique opportunity to work in society as a healthcare professional; diagnosing, treating and managing a variety of oral and dental health issues, including aesthetic issues affecting patients.

As a Dentist you will ideally have a personable nature, a desire to help others, strong manual dexterity and the ability to use sound judgement to help make clinical decisions in the patient's best interests.

Of course, oral and dental health play a significant role in overall health and wellbeing. Dentists are privileged to be skilled at helping improve aesthetics of an individual's dentition, enhance function for speech and eating and alleviate dental pain caused by disease using their range of technical skills and knowledge.

Importantly, all dentists work as part of a wider team in caring for a patient. More on the dental team will be discussed later in this chapter.

General Dental Practitioner

Most dentists work as General Dental Practitioners also termed GDPs.

GDPs have a broad range of skills and usually work in 'high street' practices providing a variety of routine and complex treatments. GDPs are self-employed and work under an associateship agreement with the practice owner. A GDP may work solely under the NHS, be a mixed NHS and private practitioner or solely provide private treatments. This would often be based upon the practice he or she works within. Most practices in the UK are mixed practices providing contractual NHS services and private dental treatments.

A GDP can enhance their scope of practice by undertaking structured learning and additional postgraduate training to develop skills.

Examples of these include, but are not limited to, dental implant placement and restoration, non-surgical facial aesthetic treatments and intravenous conscious sedation. Therefore, a 'general' dentist may undertake formal postgraduate training, for instance an MSc in Implant Dentistry to enhance their skill set.

Furthermore, GDPs have the flexibility in their career to work full time or part time (depending on their contractual agreement). This offers great possibility to work part time in hospitals or other practices, to undertake lectureship or teaching positions, or to conduct personal non-dental activities.

A GDP typically sees between 10 and 40 patients per day for routine oral health checks, fillings and extractions and other treatments. The more time a GDP spends treating individual patients, the fewer patients can be seen on a daily basis.

Hospital Dentistry

Hospital dentistry comprises of four service deliveries:
1. Dental consultant led treatment planning and management – often patients referred from a GDP in primary care practice. These may include, but are not limited to, oncology, hypodontia, cleft-lip and palate patients.
2. Complex dental care for in-patients such as head and neck cancer patients in oral and maxillofacial departments or orthognathic (jaw) surgery patients.
3. Emergency dental care for out-patients such as acute dental pain or dental trauma
4. Medically compromised out-patients requiring treatment under a hospital setting when treatment is too complex for primary dental care. Examples include patients taking intravenous bisphosphonates for cancer who are at risk of Medication Related Osteonecrosis of the Jaw following dental extraction (tooth removal).

Dentists working in a hospital may fall under these job categories:

1. Dental Consultant
   - A Dental Consultant is a Dentist who has undertaken a formalised accredited training pathway to attain high level, specialist skills in their chosen discipline. A Dental Consultant, by definition, has achieved the highest level of training in their specialisms. Using their skills, they help with NHS service delivery for patients requiring the most advanced care. From a clinical aspect, NHS Dental Consultants provide advice, guidance and treatment to patients with complex needs, these may include oncology, hypodontia, cleft lip and palate and other patients with complex dental and medical conditions. Typically, an NHS dental consultant will have undergone several years of core training post-graduation, to then enter a five year NHS funded speciality training pathway to lead to a consultant position. Most NHS dental consultants work in dental teaching hospitals or district hospitals managing complex dental care, but also have time dedicated to teaching, managerial tasks and governance duties.

2. Specialty Registrar (StR)
   - An StR is a dentist who is undertaking an accredited formalised training pathway to gain specialist status in one or more disciplines of dentistry. Typically StRs have undertaken several years of core training (DCT/SHO) roles prior to entering into a formal training pathway. Many StR posts are NHS funded pathways where the trainee works in a dental or district hospital providing advanced care under the guidance of a Dental Consultant.

3. Specialty Dentist / Staff Grade (SpD)
   - An SpD works in a dental or district hospital in one of the sub-specialties such as Oral and Maxillofacial

Surgery, Oral Surgery, Paediatrics, Restorative, Ortho-dontics etc. Their role is not as a 'specialist' as they have not technically completed a formal accredited pathway to allow them to use this title. However, many SpDs have undertaken several years of core training roles that have provided them with vast amounts of experience within that specialty. SpDs may work full-time or part-time allowing them to also work in other dental settings such as a general dental practice.

4. Dental Core Trainee/ Senior House Officer (DCT/SHO)
   o DCT is a structured pathway and typically occurs following Foundation Training (although this is non compulsory). For some, DCT is the stepping-stone to specialty training (StR). For others, it may be an additional period of training to enhance or learn valuable practical competencies for exit into primary dental care or secondary care posts such as Specialty Dentist roles. The purpose of DCT is to enable recent dental graduates an opportunity to gain additional skills and competencies in particular dental specialisms.

5. Academic Clinical Fellow/ Lecturer (ACF/ACL)
   o ACF/ACL are dentists who have embarked on developing an aptitude for academia through research opportunities to support academic career progression. These dentists often teach undergraduate and post-graduate dentists in their chosen field.

Departments found in a hospital include:

1. Oral and Maxillofacial Surgery (not found in Dental Hospital)
2. Restorative Dentistry (includes periodontics, endodontics, prosthodontics)
3. Oral Surgery
4. Orthodontics

5. Paediatrics
6. Oral and Maxillofacial Radiology
7. Oral Medicine
8. Special Care Dentistry

Hospital dentists are salaried employees so they have a fixed work pattern and less flexibility than GDPs. The hospital facilitates a pathway for NHS postgraduate training for dentists to gain specialist status and attain a consultant position. Dental hospitals also facilitate university training for dentistry students on NHS patients.

Community Dentist

Community Dental Services are provided to ensure that everyone can have access to dental health care. Some patients due to physical disability or medical conditions are unable to be treated in a general dental practice.

A community dentist is salaried and may work in a variety of locations including an outreach centre, patient's own home, nursing homes, community clinics and mobile clinics.

Patients who may need community dental services include:

1. High decay risk children requiring anxiety management control with inhalation sedation
2. Children with learning difficulties such as autism spectrum disorder
3. Adults who have difficulty accessing general dental services such as those with learning difficulty or mental health problems
4. Adults requiring home visits (domiciliary care)

‖Dental Specialties

Dentists may further their training to gain specialist status. The General Dental Council grants entry to the specialist list through the practitioner evidencing their training and experience. Only those on the list can call themselves a 'specialist'.

The lists of specialists exists to (taken directly from GDC website):

1. Ensure high standards of training
2. Indicate those dentists who possess recognised specialist knowledge, skills and attitudes
3. Protect patients against unwarranted claims to be a specialist
4. Facilitate appropriate referrals of patients
5. Promote high standards of care by dentists qualified to use a specialist title
6. Encourage postgraduate education

There are 13 dental specialties, the route to each specialty has been determined by European and GDC regulations

1. **Dental and Maxillofacial Radiology**
   Involves all aspects of medical imaging which provide information about anatomy, function and diseased states of the teeth and jaws.
2. **Dental Public Health**
   A non-clinical specialty involving the science and art of preventing oral diseases, promoting oral health to the population rather than the individual. It involves the assessment of dental health needs and ensuring dental services meet those needs.
3. **Endodontics**
   The cause, diagnosis, prevention and treatment of diseases and injuries of the tooth root, dental pulp, and surrounding tissue.

4. **Oral and Maxillofacial Pathology**
   Diagnosis and assessment made from tissue changes characteristic of disease of the oral cavity, jaws and salivary glands. This is a clinical specialty undertaken by laboratory-based personnel.

5. **Restorative Dentistry**
   Involves replacing missing teeth, repairing damaged teeth and extends to rehabilitation of the whole mouth, based on the three monospecialties; prosthodontics, periodontics and endodontics.

6. **Oral Medicine**
   Oral health care of patients with chronic recurrent and medically related disorders of the mouth and with their diagnosis and non-surgical management.

7. **Oral Microbiology**
   Diagnosis and assessment of facial infection, typically bacterial and fungal disease. This is a clinical specialty undertaken by laboratory-based personnel who provide reports and advice based on interpretation of microbiological samples.

8. **Oral Surgery**
   The treatment and ongoing management of irregularities and pathology of the jaw and mouth that require surgical intervention. This includes the specialty previously called Surgical Dentistry.

9. **Orthodontics**
   The development, prevention, and correction of irregularities of the teeth, bite and jaw.

10. **Paediatric Dentistry**
    Comprehensive therapeutic oral health care for children from birth through adolescence, including care for those who demonstrate intellectual, medical, physical, psychological and/or emotional problems.

11. **Periodontics**
    The diagnosis, treatment and prevention of diseases and disorders (infections and inflammatory) of the gums and other structures around the teeth.

12. **Prosthodontics**

    The replacement of missing teeth and the associated soft and hard tissues by prostheses (crowns, bridges, dentures) which may be fixed or removable, or may be supported and retained by implants.

13. **Special Care Dentistry**

    The improvement of the oral health of individuals and groups in society who have a physical, sensory, intellectual, mental, medical, emotional or social impairment or disability or, more often, a combination of these factors. It pertains to adolescents and adults.

More information on the dental specialist list can be found at *https://www.gdc-uk.org/registration/your-registration/specialist-lists*

The Wider Dental Team

As mentioned above, the dental team work with patients to manage, treat, diagnose and prevent oral and dental disease and problems.

The team consists of many valuable members without whom dentists could not do their job.

Remember it is important to note that in order to undertake the tasks mentioned, the registrant must be suitably trained, competent and indemnified.

DENTAL NURSE/ASSISTANT

The dental nurse's role is critical in the success of the operating dentist. The roles and responsibilities of the dental nurse are varied and include:

1. Infection control and decontamination of dental instruments
2. Maintenance and stock control of dental operating equipment

3. Set up of specific, relevant dental equipment, materials and patient laboratory work
4. Storing and recording patient clinical notes including dental charting
5. Assisting the dentist with clinical procedures such as suctioning saliva, mixing dental biomaterials, holding cheek retractors.
6. Administration tasks including clinical bookings, answering calls, managing patient concerns and complaints.
7. Reassurance, advice and emotional support for anxious patients
8. Processing of dental radiographs

Additional skills can be acquired through training, allowing the nurse to take on more responsibilities that can certainly help the dental team. These may be carried out on prescription from or under the direction of another registrant.

1. Radiography (taking x-rays for diagnostics)
2. Taking clinical photographs for patient records, tracing cephalographs
3. Take dental impressions and shade taking
4. Taking study models of teeth or bleaching trays
5. Application of fluoride varnish to prevent tooth decay
6. Oral health education – training to allow the dental nurse to provide specific dental advice to patients
7. Treatment coordinator – here the dental nurse has a role in providing a brief consultation to help offer the patient more information. Here the nurse can undertake a non-clinical consultation with the patient to establish their dental desires. The trained nurse can discuss options that may be available for the patient and provide generic advice. Following this initial consultation, if the patient wishes, a clinical consultation can be booked with a clinician. It is not uncommon for the dental nurse, who is trained, to undertake a 3D scan of the teeth and take clinical images prior to the patient's treatment.

8. Conscious sedation nurse – providing assistance with the dentists for treatment under intravenous or inhalation sedation as an adjunct to the clinical dentistry for anxious adults or children
9. Placing rubber dam
10. Measuring and recording plaque indices
11. Removing sutures after the wound has been checked by a dentist
12. Constructing occlusal registration rims and special trays
13. Repairing the acrylic component of removable appliances
14. Applying topical anaesthetic to the prescription of a dentist
15. Constructing vacuum formed retainers to the prescription of a dentist

Dental nurses do not diagnose disease or plan treatment.

Dental hygienists work in all sectors of dentistry from the community to hospitals but are commonly placed in general dental practices, forming a key component in the pathways of managing periodontal (gum) diseases.

Dental Hygienist

Dental hygienists can carry out treatments directly on patients and under a dentist's prescription. Key tasks undertaken by a dental hygienist include:

1. Dental hygiene care to a wide range of patients
2. Obtaining a detailed dental history from patients and evaluating their medical history
3. Conducting a clinical examination within their competence
4. Completing periodontal examination and charting and use indices to screen and monitor periodontal disease
5. Diagnosis and treatment planning within their competence
6. Prescribing radiographs – taking, processing and interpreting various film views used in general dental practice
7. Planning the delivery of care for patients
8. Giving appropriate patient advice

9. Providing preventive oral care to patients and liaising with dentists over the treatment of caries, periodontal disease and tooth wear
10. Undertaking supragingival and subgingival scaling and root surface debridement using manual and powered instruments
11. Using appropriate anti-microbial therapy to manage plaque related diseases
12. Adjusting restored surfaces in relation to periodontal treatment
13. Applying topical treatments and fissure sealants
14. Giving advice to patients on how to stop smoking
15. Taking intra and extra-oral photographs
16. Giving infiltration and inferior dental block analgesia
17. Placing temporary dressings and re-cement crowns with temporary cement
18. Placing rubber dam and taking impressions
19. Maintaining care of implants and treatment of peri-implant tissues
20. Identifying anatomical features, recognising abnormalities and interpreting common pathology
21. Carrying out oral cancer screening
22. If necessary, refer patients to other healthcare professionals
23. Keeping full, accurate and contemporaneous patient records

A hygienist may also undertake further skills to perform tooth whitening (under a dentist's prescription), administering inhalation sedation and removing suture after wounds checked by dentist.

The dental hygienist cannot restore teeth, carry out treatment on the nerve of the tooth, extract or adjust unrestored teeth.

Dental Therapist
Dental therapists are able to conduct treatment direct to the patient and under the prescription of the dentist.

The dental therapist can undertake those tasks capable of the dental hygienist and additional tasks including:

1. Direct restorations (fillings) on primary (baby) and secondary (adult) teeth
2. Pulpotomies (removal of the tooth nerve) on primary teeth
3. Extract primary teeth and place pre-formed crowns on primary teeth

A therapist may also undertake further skills to perform tooth whitening (under a dentist's prescription), administering inhalation sedation and removing sutures after wound are checked by the dentist.

DENTAL TECHNICIAN

The dental technician works as part of the wider team often, off-site, in their own laboratory. However, there are some laboratory technicians who work on-site in a location within a dental practice or hospital.

The main role of the technician is to make dental devices to the prescription of the dentist or the clinical dental technician (we will touch on what a clinical dental technician is after this).

A dental technician can undertake the following tasks:

1. Review cases coming into the laboratory to decide how they should be progressed
2. Work with the dentist or clinical dental technician on treatment planning and outline design
3. Give appropriate patient advice
4. Design, plan and make a range of custom-made dental devices according to a prescription
5. Modify dental devices including dentures, orthodontic appliances, crowns and bridges according to a prescription
6. Carry out shade taking

7. Carry out infection prevention and control procedures to prevent physical, chemical and microbiological contamination in the laboratory
8. Keep full and accurate laboratory records
9. Verify and take responsibility for the quality and safety of devices leaving a laboratory
10. Make appropriate referrals to other healthcare professionals

Additional skills which dental technicians could develop include:

1. Working with a dentist in the clinic, assisting with treatment by helping to fit attachments at chair side.
2. Working with a dentist or a clinical dental technician in the clinic, assisting with treatment by:
    1. Taking impressions
    2. Recording facebows
    3. Carrying out intra-oral and extra-oral tracing
    4. Carrying out implant frame assessments
    5. Recording occlusal registrations
    6. Tracing cephalographs
    7. Carrying out intra-oral scanning for CAD/CAM
    8. Taking intra and extra-oral photographs.

Dental technicians do not work independently in the clinic to:

1. Perform clinical procedures related to providing removable dental appliances
2. Carry out independent clinical examinations
3. Identify abnormal oral mucosa and related underlying structures
4. Fit removable appliances

Clinical Dental Technician (CDT)

A CDT is a qualified dental technician who provides complete dentures and other dental devices on prescription from a dentist.

A CDT can undertake the following:

1. Prescribe and provide complete dentures direct to patients
2. Provide and fit other dental devices on prescription from a dentist
3. Take detailed dental history and relevant medical history
4. Perform technical and clinical procedures related to providing removable dental appliances
5. Carry out clinical examinations within their scope of practice
6. Take and process radiographs and other images related to providing removable dental appliances
7. Distinguish between normal and abnormal consequences of ageing
8. Give appropriate patient advice
9. Recognise abnormal oral mucosa and related underlying structures and refer patients to other healthcare professionals if necessary
10. Fit removable appliances
11. Provide sports mouth guards
12. Keep full, accurate and contemporaneous patient records
13. Vary the detail but not the direction of a prescription according to patient needs

Additional skills which CDTs could develop include:

1. Oral health education
2. Re-cementing crowns with temporary cement
3. Providing anti-snoring devices on prescription of a dentist
4. Removing sutures after the wound has been checked by a dentist
5. Prescribing radiographs

6. Replacing implant abutments for removable dental appliances on prescription from a dentist
7. Providing tooth whitening treatments on prescription from a dentist

ORTHODONTIC THERAPISTS (OTs)

OTs are registered professionals who effectively conduct orthodontic related treatments under the prescription of the dentist or orthodontist.

Responsibilities:

1. Clean and prepare tooth surfaces ready for orthodontic treatment
2. Identify, select, use and maintain appropriate instruments
3. Insert passive removable orthodontic appliances
4. Insert removable appliances activated or adjusted by a dentist
5. Remove fixed appliances, orthodontic adhesives and cement
6. Identify, select, prepare and place auxiliaries
7. Take impressions, pour, cast and trim study models
8. Make a patient's orthodontic appliance safe in the absence of a dentist
9. Fit orthodontic headgear
10. Fit orthodontic facebows which have been adjusted by a dentist
11. Take occlusal records including orthognathic facebow readings
12. Take intra and extra-oral photographs
13. Place brackets and bands
14. Prepare, insert, adjust and remove archwires previously prescribed or, where necessary, activated by a dentist
15. Give advice on appliance care and oral health instruction
16. Fit tooth separators
17. Fit bonded retainers

18. Carry out Index of Orthodontic Treatment Need (IOTN) screening either under the direction of a dentist or direct to patients
19. Make appropriate referrals to other healthcare professionals
20. Keep full, accurate and contemporaneous patient records
21. Give appropriate patient advice

Additional dental team members

(not registered with GDC, but must follow their ethical standards)

RECEPTIONIST

The dental receptionist is often the first person to greet the patient so they play a critical role giving patients a good first impression.

Their duties include:

- Welcoming patients as they enter the practice and answering telephone and email enquires
- Arranging, booking and cancelling patient clinic appointments
- Taking and monitoring payments for treatment
- Minimising and managing patient complaints
- Office duties such as handling sensitive and confidential information
- Registering new patients

PRACTICE MANAGER

A practice manager is often found in 'high street' dental practices in primary care. Hospitals tend to have departmental managers and a broad team of management.

The practice manager oversees the non-clinical and business aspect of the practice, allowing the dentists to focus on the clinical aspects of the practice. Facilitating an efficient, highly profitable, ethical and positive environment is their utmost goal. Their duties and responsible can be divided into these main areas:

- General management
  - Management of debt, patient complaints, keeping up-to-date with policies, clinical government, management of staff rota and leave, partaking and leading staff meetings.
  - Handling patient complaints

- Health and Safety
  - Undertaking risk assessment, keeping updated with first aid, RIDDOR, COSHH, fire safety and waste disposal

- Financial planning and management
  - Monitoring cash flow, stock control and Units of Dental Activity count, collection of data for end of year accounts

- Human resource and staff
  - Ensure staff have correct induction, receive contract of employment, manage PAYE, sickness and holidays, deal with disciplinary and grievances

- Marketing and strategic plans
  - Develop strategies to help improve the uptake of services

- Administration and IT
  - Ensure practice IT is fully operational and maintained

- Physical resource management
  - Maintenance and serving existing equipment and facilities

Jobs as a dentist you may not have known

As touched upon earlier in this chapter, there are multiple career avenues a dentist may take. Below are some other career options which are not often discussed.

ARMED FORCES DENTIST

Become a 'dental officer' in the Royal Army Dental Corps. Here, you will work with the Army, Royal Navy and Royal Air Force providing dental care. The army offers unique benefits such as a minimum starting salary following training of £70,000 and funds dental degrees for prospective army dentists. However, you are usually committing 4 years to the Royal Army Dental Corps in return.

As part of your training you are taught basic military survival and weapon handling. The role offers varied travel to different locations. Although not for everyone, this maybe for you if you enjoy the adventure.

TEACHING ASSISTANT OR CLINICAL TUTOR

If you enjoy and are passionate about helping others learn, you may wish to take up a teaching role. Many GDPs are 'visiting tutors' at dental teaching schools and work with undergraduate dental students to help with their clinical practice.

Working part-time as a teaching dentist, whilst also working in practice the remaining days, can help to create a varied working week.

Alternatively, there are full time teachers who have dedicated their career to helping undergraduates.

RESEARCHER WITHIN DENTISTRY

Dentistry is a vast field with 13 dental specialties. With a continuous drive for further new evidence and information, research and development is key to ensuring that the best available evidence is delivered to patients. Research is often conducted within dental teaching universities in collaboration with professors, senior academic staff, postgraduate students and specialty registrar and consultants.

Dental Forensics

Forensic dentistry deals with obtaining identifiable information of individuals for legal purposes, through examination and handling of dental evidence of deceased patients. It is likely that forensic dentists will work with a wider team of professionals including pathologists, anthropologists and the police.

Forensic dentistry was used in the tragic disaster of the Grenfell tower fire to help identify victims.

Business Ownership

Become a Dental Practice Owner

You may have a burning desire within you to be your own boss. For many dentists, owning a practice is their end goal and forms part of their career pathway. Ownership of a dental business is a definitive possibility should you wish for it. With many perks such as increased flexibility of treatment, having your own set-up, owning your own asset and an increased income, it is not surprising many dentists choose this option. However, ownership is not for everyone and many dentists are content working for a practice owner as an associate or being a salaried dentist.

Portfolio Career

The term 'portfolio career' has been drawing more traction in dentistry - but what is this? Effectively this is a career which consists of several part-time jobs at once, rather than one full time role.

The term can be given to those clinicians who wish to work at different clinics or hold more than one 'title'. For instance, working part-time at two dental clinics whilst also holding a clinical tutor role at the dental teaching hospital.

Salary

Below is a table of the typical salaries for UK dentists in different roles.

Role	Average salary (£)
Dental Foundation Trainee	31,992
Dental Associate	69,130
Dental practice owner	120,000
Hospital Dentist (staff grade/ specialty dentist)	50,000
Specialty registrar	47,000
Consultant	90,000

Table 1: Average salaries of UK Dentists

Challenges

No career is without its challenges. Dentistry is no different. Despite having many positives, which certainly outweigh the challenges, here are the most commonly discussed challenges:

PATIENT DEMANDS VERSUS REALITY

Patients are becoming increasingly drawn to particular trends in society, often influenced by media coverage. Composite veneers, bleached shaded porcelain veneers and 'Kylie Jenner lip fillers' – to name a few.

It is extremely important for the treating clinician to be aware of the ethical obligation they have to their patients and the relative limitations of dental treatment. Patients may wish for a certain treatment or procedure, without fully knowing what it is, just because of something they've seen or heard about but are not fully informed.

In such cases, the role of the clinician is one of an educator and gatekeeper, safeguarding the dental and oral health of the patient; not simply following their commands. The best result is often a compromise but sometimes there's disagreement between the dentist and patient. Nevertheless, it is essential that the dentist always provides treatment that's in the patient's best interest.

STRESSES OF WORKING IN DIVERSE TEAM WITH MANY PERSONALITIES

A dental team is often very diverse with many different personalities. As with any successful team, good morale is crucial to stimulate a positive team culture. In reality, differences of opinion mean this isn't always possible when individuals don't see eye to eye, sometimes disrupting a positive culture. In closely-knit teams, differences of opinion can cause greater harm than good. However, this occurs rarely, and the majority of dental teams work very well together as a professional team in a clinical environment.

DEMANDS TO HIT 'TARGETS'

This is mainly a subject for dental practices, however, hospitals also have 'waiting time' targets to reduce. Many practices in the UK treat NHS patients under a UDA (Units of Dental Activity) General Dental Services contract. Thus the practice, and each of its dentists, is required to fulfil the practice's UDA quota or face a penalty.

To this end, dentists treating NHS patients are usually bound by their associate contract to perform a specified number of UDA, i.e. 4,000. As the closing date (1st April) draws near, stress levels are often higher if this figure has not been fulfilled. Worst still, if the practice as a whole has a low UDA count, all of the dentists might have to work together to achieve the UDA target. This of course can increase stress for the clinician.

STRINGENT REGULATIONS

Dentistry is strictly regulated profession with a plethora of requirements and procedures for record keeping, radiation, risk management and infection control (especially in light of COVID-19). Whilst the regulations are beneficial, dealing with all of them can sometimes feel overwhelming.

ADMINISTRATION

A crucial part of the daily workflow for dentists involves maintaining contemporaneous records. This can be highly demanding for the dentist, who has to accurately type complete and concise notes which provide a factual account of the discussion had with the patient. Finding the time to write up patient records in a busy clinic can be difficult during working hours so the dentist might do these administration tasks during breaks or after the clinic closes.

Another admin task is going through referral letters received, which must be read by the dentist. New referrals must be completed by the dentist to the referring clinician, all of which is done outside normal clinic hours and can be tedious.

PATIENT LITIGATION

The biggest cause of stress for many dentists is the fear and anxiety of patient litigation. Unfortunately the UK has one of the highest dental litigation rates amongst all countries. Some experts suggest that young dentists are likely to be sued at least once during their career. The increased patient demand coupled with the proliferation of 'no win, no fee' claims is a source of slight fear in the eyes of younger dentists.

Benefits

Although we have discussed many of the challenges and drawbacks that come with dentistry, there are far more uniquely attractive benefits for a dentist.

REWARDING

There are not many careers that are as rewarding as dentistry. The role of a dentist allows a very personal level of satisfaction to be attained. Whether this be relieving pain for a patient, or transforming a neglected dentition into a state of optimal oral health, the rewards can really be life changing. Of course, the salary is beyond the average for most graduate jobs, and almost unlimited for entrepreneurial dentists with multiple dental practices.

ENJOYMENT

As a field of medicine, dentistry offers the practitioner a vast range of clinical disciplines to practice, allowing a unique level of variety to their working day. As such, clinicians can limit their practice or skill set to an area or skill that they thoroughly enjoy. This freedom offers unrivalled job satisfaction – doing something worthwhile that you love.

FLEXIBILITY

As mentioned earlier, dentists can choose to follow a 'portfolio career', working multiple part-time roles as opposed to one full-time role. This facilitates great flexibility, allowing dentist to have a fantastic and unique work-life integration.

STABILITY

For any graduate, job security is a significant factor. Dentists have one of the lowest unemployment rates in the country. Dentists form an essential component of the health care service. Most UK dental graduates can be certain of getting a 'Dental Foundation' position as a dentist for their first year out of university. Statistics from Health Education England in 2019 suggested that from the 1,041 dental 5th year students interviewed for jobs, there were approximately 954 places for Dental Foundation Training positions. More on Dental Foundation Training is discussed later.

SOCIAL LIFE

A career as a dentist can mean a lot of socializing. As well as working within a team, you meet a diverse array of patients daily. There are also many networking and educational conferences where the dental community meet and socialise.

RESPECT

As a dentist, you are uniquely positioned in society and highly respected due to the contributions made for improved oral and dental health. With this respect and status, it is important that clinicians maintain and uphold the integrity of the profession.

Another interesting point is that the British Dental Association and the General Dental Council advocate the use of the honorary tile of 'Dr', meaning you can change your title after graduating as a dentist – a very humbling experience.

Graduate Prospects and Dental Foundation Training (DFT)

Dental Foundation Training, previously called Vocational Training (VT), was introduced in 2012 as a training scheme for new dental graduates. This NHS training programme is designed to allow a smooth transition into working life from dental school, giving newly qualified dentists broad exposure and a sound understanding of dentistry in the NHS. It is intended as a year of employment for graduates to train and learn. Each graduate works in a protected environment under an 'educational supervisor'. The recruitment process for dental graduates is very competitive, the details of which are beyond the scope of this resource, and unlikely to be asked at interview. In addition, the recruitment process may well have changed by the time you approach this stage.

MORE INFORMATION CAN BE FOUND HERE

https://www.copdend.org/postgraduate-training/dft-recruitment-2019/

Life As A Qualified Dentist

Learn more about life as a qualified dentist on our website. We have interviewed several qualified dentists who have all taken different pathways following graduation. Each dentist discusses their background and what led them to their current roles today.

CHAPTER 2

THE DENTISTRY
UCAS APPLICATION

INTRODUCTION

In this chapter, we aim to help you maximise your chances of getting into dental school by giving you some useful tips that have been used successfully by previous and current applicants. This chapter covers the following topics:

- All You Need to Know About UCAS
- Timeline of Key Events
- UCAS Application Assistance
- Extenuating Circumstances
- Mastering the Personal Statement
- Real examples from Accepted & Rejected Candidates
- Graduate Personal Statements
- Competitive Landscape and Statistics

All you need to know about UCAS

All university applications in the United Kingdom are sent through a service called UCAS, which stands for "University and Colleges Admissions Service". UCAS is a gateway and portal for your application to be sent to your chosen dental school. UCAS forms the online intermediary between yourself and your chosen university.

Your UCAS application plays a crucial role for selection.

It is critical for you to understand the entry requirements for each dental school. Learn more about the university entry requirements via the official UCAS website and use our *standard entry table* to see a summary of these criteria (QR code available in 'key links' section).

We strongly advise anyone interested in dentistry to fully research the career to ensure that it's a suitable choice for you. As part of this, we advise *learning more about the role of a dentist* (see link in 'key links section) in society and seeking dental work experience and insight into the role of a dentist to learn more about this career option. We'll discuss more about dentistry work experience and how to gain greater insight into the career in Chapter 4.

Your UCAS application plays a crucial role in candidate selection. The university admissions team goes through each application thoroughly to select the most suitable applicants for the year. It's a nerve wracking time for students but you can be assured that you are in safe hands with this guide.

To start your application you first need to register. You will be asked to fill out personal details, create a password and answer a few security questions. The next stage varies, depending on whether you are applying from your school, college, a private centre or independently. If you are registering through an educational institution then you will be provided with a buzzword from your teachers or the centre. This simply allows UCAS to identify you with the correct organisation. However, if you're applying independently you will be required to answer additional questions to complete your registration. Please note that an independent applicant is not at a disadvantage compared to other candidates.

Once registration is completed you will be provided with log in details which you should keep safe and secure. The application will then require you to add further information regarding your background. For example, whether you have had any criminal convictions, or any disability needs that the university can help you with.

Remember, it's important to be completely honest while completing your application as it is a chance for the university to get to know you better.

Universities welcome applicants with disabilities but it is strongly advised that individuals contact their prospective dental school for advice before submitting an application, if the applicant believes that their health could affect their ability to practise dentistry safely.

While a disability may not make a career in dentistry impossible, the Dental School has a responsibility to ensure that the student satisfies the 'Fitness to Practise' requirements of the General Dental Council at the point of qualifying. These include a range of factors to ensure the individual is able to communicate clearly, sensitively and effectively, able to undertake examination and treatment of patients and perform certain practical clinical procedures.

It is also critical to take your time with the application and plan ahead to ensure the information you put down is free from error. You can save your progress in each part of the application so there's no need to rush.

The next stage is to provide details regarding ethnicity, sexual orientation, national background and religious beliefs. As well as any widening participation opportunities that you have had. This information is not disclosed to the university unless they offer you a place. This helps the university set up additional support programmes for students once they begin attending.

Once all the details are filled out, it's time to choose your courses. You get the option to select up to 5 universities where you would possibly like to study your chosen subject. The other universities will not be able to see where else you have applied. UCAS advises that you select 4 choices for dentistry and select one course as a backup. This is due to the competitive nature of the course, although ultimately it's your choice. We cover the universities which offer dentistry in more detail in Chapter 3, so do refer to that as well.

The next stage is the finer details. Providing previous examination results such as GCSEs or any other examinations you have taken or are about to take. It's important that you make this information as accurate as possible. Use your previous certificates as references if needed.

A major part of your application is the Personal Statement. This is a fundamental document allowing universities to see your ambition, career insight, cogitative skills and traits you exercise that will help in preparing you to become a dentist. The statement has a word limit of 4,000 characters in 47 lines of text. You can be under the word limit but going over will mean that you won't be able to submit the statement and it will have to be cropped. The UCAS tool under the Personal Statement section allows you to check whether your personal statement is over or under the limit. If over the limit, you can see by how much.

Your personal statement is all about you and will go to all of your chosen universities. Articulated in the correct way, a dental personal statement will highlight many important and salient points, including: reasons for choosing to study your subject; what you have learnt from your work experience or your research into the career and any hobbies or additional skills that you have. A well-devised strategy for constructing an outstanding statement is covered later in this chapter.

Your personal statement should strictly be your own work. As UCAS uses a software plagiarism tool, any similarities between previous and current statements would be quickly and swiftly identified, rendering your application void and likely compromising your chances of entering into a career in dentistry at all. We strongly recommend that you have a look at our guidance on writing the strong statement for dentistry, ensuring that you use this to compile a basic infrastructure to then flesh out with your own personal touch.

Every application requires a referee, who will need to submit their own statement about you and fill out a section, so that the university can know you a little better. The referee will also be required to give you predicted grades on any pending qualifications. A referee can be one of your teachers if you are applying from a school or college. If you're an independent candidate the referee can be a tutor or even a previous employer if you have been out of education. Once this is complete you can then pay and send off your application. The UCAS fee is £25 if you are applying for multiple university choices. If you make just one choice your application the fee is £20.

After your application is sent off you will receive a UCAS track number, which enables you to follow the progress of your application in regards to receiving offers. The next step would be to wait for any offers from universities. For dentistry, before you can receive an offer, you will be required to attend an interview. You will hear from all universities regarding interviews through email and you will be able to check your offers on UCAS track. Once you have received a response from all of your chosen universities, you can make a firm choice and an insurance choice. Your firm choice is the university at which you want to be immediately accepted if you meet the grade requirements or 'conditions'. Your insurance choice is the university you want to keep your offer for in case you don't meet the requirements of your first choice. If your offer is conditional, this would mean that the university needs you to meet entry requirements (i.e. AAA) before accepting you. However, if your offer is unconditional, this allows you to progress regardless of you meeting these entry requirements. In the case of conditional offers, you will need to wait until results day to find out whether you have been accepted or not on UCAS track.

‖ Timeline of Key Events

KEY DATES AS OF 2020

15th October – Deadline for all Medicine and Dentistry applications for UCAS. You must submit before this date as UCAS does not accept late entries!

UCAT DATES

Candidates must only attempt the UCAT exam once per application cycle. Almost all dental schools require this as part of their criteria. To determine if UCAT is needed, we have compiled information in our standard entry table, which is in the 'Key Links' section at the start of this book. All those wishing to study dentistry are advised to visit the official university for the latest updated information.

The test usually runs between July and October in the UK. Registration typically opens in May.

However, there may be exceptions and this is subject to change. For example, in 2020, dates have shifted due to the outbreak of Covid-19.

More information on the UCAT update can be found here: https://www.ucat.ac.uk/

The pricing varies, depending on when in the year you sit the test, but it's typically around £55-80 in the UK and £115 if you're outside the EU.

BMAT DATES
For those wishing to apply for a place at Leeds Dental School, the BMAT is mandatory.[1]

There are usually two sittings for the BMAT exam, however, for 2020 there are only November test dates. Candidates must only sit the BMAT once per application cycle.

BMAT 2020 NOVEMBER EXAM:
- 1st September – Registration begins
- 1st October – Standard registration closing date
- 15th October (5pm) – Late registration closing date (late fee BMAT applies)
- 4th November – BMAT 2020 test day
- 27th November – BMAT results released
- 4th December – Deadline for BMAT results enquiry

---

1 For 2020 the BMAT September Exam is not going ahead due to COVID-19

‖ UCAS Application Assistance

Now that you know what UCAS is and what to expect, this chapter aims to provide you with some tips to come out with the best application possible.

Make sure to have a separate email address to enter into UCAS. Do not use a school email address, because you may not receive updates through that email, as schools often remove email addresses of school leavers.

You also have the option to prevent sharing of updates about offers or rejections with your school or college. This option is found on the UCAS Track section under preferences. Some students may not want to share this information with their school or colleges. This is a personal choice and it would be recommended to discuss how your school or college utilises this data before making this decision.

You also have the opportunity to start off early with the UCAS applications opening around September. Take your time with the application. Don't leave it until the last minute. Have someone double check your applications just to make sure that all the information and details are correct and that you are happy with your application.

The personal statement is the chance for your universities to get to know you better before they invite you over for an interview. Take this opportunity to put forward everything about yourself and remember to be clear and concise in your wording. There is further advice on writing your Dentistry Personal Statement in this chapter.

EXTENUATING CIRCUMSTANCE
Sometimes in life we are faced with events or experiences that may take us off our usual 'routine' pathway and can result in negative consequences to our mental, psychological and physical health.

Extenuating Circumstances can be described as serious and exceptional factors outside your control which adversely affected your performance during your study.

If you have been negatively impacted through extenuating circumstances it is absolutely within your right to voice this to the appropriate individuals and organisations. Although you may be resilient, if your examination results have been compromised then informing the school, examination officer and the examination board is prudent.

Aside from disability or prior ill health, significant extenuating circumstances could also be adverse personal circumstances such as bereavement or other difficult home or family circumstances.

For potential students who may have narrowly missed entry requirements due to such significant extenuating circumstances, we advise you to contact the prospective university to discuss your individual circumstance further before UCAS applications are finalised.

INTERVIEW STAGE

If you have been invited to a dental school interview but due to extenuating circumstances your performance may be negatively affected, it's best to contact the school ahead of this date.

For obvious reasons, schools are unlikely to accept any retrospective notifications regarding pre-existing extenuating circumstances.

‖ Mastering Your Personal Statement

Remember the personal statement is something that you have full control over and is one of the key information tools used by admissions teams to determine whether you should be invited to an interview. As such, you should aim to invest time and focus on ensuring this document does justice to your application.

In this section we will discuss how to write an impactful and relevant personal statement for dentistry. The aim is to provide you with all the material needed to write your own. We will also be exploring some personal statements and evaluating them.

Give yourself plenty of time to write a correct personal statement. As mentioned earlier, the personal statement should consist of a maximum of 4,000 characters in 47 lines of text, which equates to about 500 words. However, you are not expected to do all of it in one go. It will take many drafts and attempts for you to complete your own statement to a high standard. Structuring your statement based upon the advice and information in this chapter should aid you with creating a framework to expand. Lastly, once you have your final draft, get tutors, academics and trusted peers to read your statement. This will give you broad feedback and allow you to eradicate any errors, further improving your statement.

‖ Essential Structure

INTRODUCTION

The layout of your statement is vital in allowing you to construct an impactful and well written statement, ultimately capturing the reader's attention. Typically this will be the university's dental admissions tutors. Imagine being part of the admissions team and having to filter through hundreds of statements each day. In your introduction, aim to captivate your reader by explaining the truthful and motivational reasoning for your decision to pursue dentistry and your honest rationale for why you are suited to this career. It is of utmost importance that your reasoning is genuine and not just because you are attracted to the earning potential. To stimulate your thoughts, here are a few questions that you can ask yourself to get started.

1. Why do you want to study dentistry?
2. What experience inspired you to apply for dentistry?
3. What do you find interesting about dentistry which no other career has to offer?
4. If other careers are similar, what is it about dentistry, i.e. medical surgery, which really attracts you?
5. What was your most insightful incident?
6. What traits or characteristics make you suited to dentistry over other candidates?

Hopefully, answering some of those questions will allow you to continue to the next stage of your statement.

MAIN BODY

One factor that often troubles students with their personal statement is the limitation of the word count. Our advice is to first get started by actively working to create a statement that you can later refine and reduce the number of words. There are many things to include in the main body of your statement which are crucial to building a successful statement. You may wish to begin by listing these in bullet points, which can then later be expanded to create more detailed paragraphs.

In the main body, you should aim to demonstrate the efforts you have made to gather career insight and work experience and the cogitative accounts from your research and observations. Your reflection and learning should be powerful discussion points, giving clarity and reinforcement to the reader that this is a well-founded career decision based upon your proactive thought process.

Selecting or highlighting key events, such as those from your career research or experience can be useful in generating salient factors leading to your decision. For instance, is it the combination of hands-on skill, scientific acumen and patient management skills that you witnessed, or was it the technology and equipment utilised that fascinated you? The key here is to portray your genuine desire to pursue dentistry as a career based on realistic and justified reasoning.

Use this as your opportunity to really discuss how these factors intertwine with your characteristics and traits which make you well suited to the career.

To maximise your work experience and to gain a deeper career insight learn more in Chapter 4.

The main body of the personal statement also allows you to highlight your personal achievements and non-academic endeavours, especially in relation to team work and leadership. Remember that as a dentist, your role is within a diverse team and your aim should be to link how your achievements make for a good dentist. For example, if you play a team sport, this can be used to illustrate your strength of working as part of a wider team, similar to the way a dentist works with their own team consisting of dental nurses, technicians and receptionists.

Through the personal statement, universities will aim to determine and extract qualities that coincide with those of aspiring dentists. As such, it is important to demonstrate traits of altruism. Altruism can be defined as 'the selfless concern for others wants'. Excellent examples of this include partaking in regular volunteering commitments, or helping with community or religious initiatives. By discussing such topics you can create a highly personalised statement whilst also exhibiting caring and selfless characteristics – factors relevant to a career in dentistry.

As mentioned above, the way you relate these activities to the behaviour expected of a competent dentist allows the reader to understand how you are a suitable candidate.

Among the many traits of a dentist, communication and interpersonal skills could be considered one of the most important of all. Due to this, the personal statement should certainly address how you have mastered these important characteristics. Candidates are advised not to simply list activities or responsibilities but to specify and explain how these have enhanced their communication and personal skills. Linking these factors to how they integrate well with a career in dentistry is beneficial for the individual to optimise their points.

Something which many applicants feel dubious about is the topic of manual dexterity. To clarify this confusion, it is not necessary to possess high level of dextrous skills prior to entering the course. Developing them will be part of the degree course and those applying should refrain from implying that they possess these skills.

Instead the personal statement should enthuse your appreciation for the learning process and your readiness to learn clinical skills. It is also prudent to dedicate a few lines or a short paragraph to concisely reflect on the importance of manual dexterity in dentistry, and perhaps to demonstrate what activities or skills you have undertaken to enhance your skills.

Here are a few questions you can ask yourself to get started:

1. What are your relevant work experiences or career insights?
2. What difficulties have you overcome?
3. What can you bring to the university?
4. What responsibilities have you taken?
5. What personal characteristics do you possess which makes you think you will be a good Dentist? Give examples and evidence of this.

CONCLUSION

One quality of a good personal statement is that it flows seamlessly from one section to another and is easy to read. The conclusion of the personal statement should leave a good impression on the reader and make them want to invite you over for an interview to get to know you further. Try to avoid clingy finishing statements or from using quotes overall. It makes the statement feel less genuine and can put the reader off. You want to come across as a professional well-rounded individual. To ensure that you can make a final impression on the reader, see if your conclusion answers these questions:

1. Does your conclusion indicate that you are aware of the demands of a dental student?
2. Does your conclusion represent your own genuine views?
3. Does your conclusion summarise your main points from the statement?
4. Does your conclusion fit into the statement well?
5. Is your conclusion going to make the reader want to get to know you more?

HOW PERSONAL STATEMENTS ARE ASSESSED

Genuine Desire	Life Skills	Interests Other Than Academia	Altruism	Communication & Interpersonal Skills
Truthful Motives Rationale Career Insight Ambition	Team Player Organisation Leadership Dexterity	Sports Music Hobbies Community/ Religions	Regular Volunteering Community Initiative	Debating public speaking Customer services

The personal statement functions as a key to help you secure your dentistry interview. Each university will have its own admission criteria, with the personal statement being a key determinant in this. Whilst each School will assess the statement uniquely, we have devised these questions to help when creating your personal statement. Although these factors may not be exactly the criteria that schools use, these cornerstones form the foundations of an impactful statement. By critiquing your statement and partaking in your own statement analysis you will more easily be able to identify how your statement can be strengthened. The diagram below highlights the five broad aspects a dentistry personal statement can be categorised into when reviewed.

After each successive draft, undertake an in-depth review, asking yourself these questions as you read through your statement.

Does the applicant have a realistic interest in Dentistry?

> Tip: The statement should show your ambitious interest in dentistry. You should demonstrate an excellent insight with reflection and relevant reasoning for your decisions. Use the statement to discuss how these stimulated your interest and led you to seek further information.

Is the applicant informed about a career in Dentistry?

> Tip: The statement allows you to display your truthful motives to study dentistry. The rationale should be well explained and you should evidence how and where you have derived your insight from. If you have been unable to gain work experience, you should show what other avenues you have sought dentistry career insight. Proactively engaging and partaking in online courses, actively speaking to dentists, reading related article are all plausible.

Does the applicant have life skills?

> Tip: Can you evidence being a team player; being organised; showing leadership; having dexterity; demonstrate time management; possessing problem-solving ability?

You should be able to demonstrate having an excellent range of skills, abilities and responsibilities and link these to how they will benefit you being a dentist.

Is the applicant involved in interests other than academia?

> Tip: It is very likely that most applicants will have the required academic entry requirements, therefore it's important to focus on your non-academic interests and link these to how they will benefit you with a career in dentistry.

With dentistry being a stressful career, work-life integration is key. You should reveal varied interests such as being part of a sports team, music involvement, hobbies or community and religious activities. Highlighting these shows you have commitment to areas other than academia and have good time management.

Does the applicant show altruism?

> Tip: Altruism is showing a selfless desire to help others. If you are committed to a particular voluntary role or are involved in regularly helping others at college or school or as part of a community initiative this is important to mention. This demonstrates self-motivation, leadership and organisational skills

Is there evidence of strong communication and interpersonal skills?

> Tip: Communication is a fundamental aspect of day to day dentistry. If you are involved in activities related to communication such as a job in customer services, or have a role involving good verbal interaction such as in debating societies, lecturing, acting or public speaking, these are worth mentioning.

Aim to create a well written account with excellent reflection of how this will benefit you as a dentist.

Real example personal statements from accepted and rejected candidates

This section gives you some examples of Dentistry Personal Statements. Please note that these are examples and should not be copied in any way as the UCAS software will detect this as obvious plagiarism and you risk compromising your entire application. Use these examples for inspiration and to fabricate an infrastructure to then expand upon.

We have included personal statements which have both been rejected and accepted by universities. The aim is to provide you with an in-depth understanding of how to improve your personal statement by making a few changes. To maintain confidentiality specific names have been removed from these example statements

Undergraduate Statements

PERSONAL STATEMENT 1

Dentists can save lives. I was told this when I asked a professor at the end of a Summer Residential at the university of Birmingham. My naive question was: "Why are dentists paid so much?". Usually when people go to a dentist they are most concerned about whether they have cavities. However, the dentist is not only looking for signs of tooth decay. They are also looking for signs of oral cancer, which can be as simple as a sore feeling at the back of the throat. This fascinated me as I understood how dentistry can enhance longevity, not just the quality of life.

My interest grew further for the career as I began by volunteering every Saturday at an elderly care home. This is where I assisted with hygiene and helped elderly disabled patients. I feel grateful for having spent time with patients with dementia, Alzheimer's or stroke, to name a few. This experience made me appreciate life whilst focusing on patient care through engaging in conversations and being there for patients whenever they needed assistance, replicating for me the roles of a dentist. I continued my work experience in a practice where I shadowed a dentist for three weeks. Each day I observed the fluent communication between the dentist and the nurses whilst providing personalised care for each patient and delivering a quality experience. Manual dexterity was another skill often illustrated by the dentist whilst conducting surgical extractions in a small work space. Through playing the ukulele I have improved my motor skills, as the instrument is smaller in size and requires focus and stability to play. As well as conducting titrations in chemistry which require fine measuring ability.

Working in a ceramic dental laboratory gave me the opportunity to produce a crown and a bridge, giving me invaluable insight into the efficiency of a multidisciplinary team communicating together through different departments. I witnessed how technicians, dental hygienists and dentists all assisted one another through teamwork with the joint dental practices being below the laboratory. This display of teamwork gave each member of staff confidence and trust in each other. In 2018, I visited Pakistan for two weeks to provide aid for those affected by the devastating effects of the earthquake. Working for the community appealed to me as I made a difference to people's lives, which gave me a sense of gratification that I one day wish to achieve as a dentist.

During my gap year I have taken active steps to arrange hospital placements as well as working at the optician chain Specsavers on my weekends. From greeting patients and doing pre-tests, answering phone calls and communicating with the optometrists, I am able to improve on my independent skills whilst gaining experience in a healthcare environment. I wish to evaluate my previous weaknesses and improve as an individual in this year, I hope that this shows my devotion towards this course.

The book 'The Smile Stealers' showcased to me the development of dentistry throughout different stages of history. One of the most interesting themes for me was the changes in social and cultural attitudes towards the mouth and disease. This was explored along-side the more clinical aspects of dental history, such as the role of anaesthesia and the invention of the dental drill. I was interested in solved cases like the 'malevolent tooth worm', considered to be the cause of tooth pain for hundreds of years, before the advent of germ theory. This led me to subscribe to the "Oral health Foundation".

In high school, out of 65 applicants I was selected to be the Head Boy. I was entrusted with the responsibility of holding weekly student meetings. By enhancing my leadership, communication skills and confidence, I have been able to develop my persona to meet the demands of a good dentist so I am able to make a difference to people's lives. As a mentor in my school, I took responsibility for a group of younger students to help them realise their priorities so they could fulfil their potential. By doing so, I was able to improve my own organisational skills and successfully motivate others and myself.

For sport, I play for a local cricket team and am always involved with the club's fundraising events. My cricket team gives me a healthily balance between academia and personal life whilst promising commitment; an attribute required for a good dentist.

Dentistry is rewarding yet a laborious career requiring dedication. However, my experiences thus far have shaped me into a caring, well-rounded and self-motivated individual that is capable of embarking on this exciting journey.

Undergraduate Dental Surgery Personal Statement 2019 – Rejection

STATEMENT EVALUATION

This introduction of the statement starts off a cliché. The student refers to the paycheck that dentists receive. Regardless of context, money can come across as being their initial motivation to study dentistry. This immediately comes across as an unappealing reason, hence, the student was rejected. Although the student mentions that dentistry allows them to save lives, they do not go into depth about their reasoning, which is why the introduction does not flow as well, because they are trying to mix two points into one.

The main body of the personal statement is focused on their work experience as well as what they are doing in their gap year. This was the correct format to use but the phrases they used do not correctly elaborate on any of their experiences in detail. They have also tried to allow the reader to get to know them better through explaining their hobbies such as playing cricket and their previous achievements.

The conclusion finishes off strong. The student does understand the demanding nature of the course but nevertheless the ending does not accompany its surrounding chapters well enough and therefore could be improved further.

Below we have included examples of personal statements to show you how you can develop yours further, whilst also including everything you wish to write.

PERSONAL STATEMENT 2

I see dentistry as the perfect opportunity to combine my passion for science with my ambition to help others. The prospect of working within a community, on a daily basis, whilst exploiting my meticulous motor skills, inspires me. My decision to pursue dentistry was reinforced through several weeks experience at NHS-run practices, during year 12. Shadowing numerous dentists at three varied practices opened my eyes to this multi-faceted career. These experiences taught me the fundamental dentist-patient relationship was key to establishing the most successful and fulfilling treatment, whether it was a check-up or a complex restorative procedure. In addition, I observed that the dentist's level of manual dexterity and skill to communicate was crucial for delivering successful treatment, especially in lengthy and complex procedures such as root canal surgery.

Through talking to all members of the dental team, in addition to helping at Reception, I noticed organisation, close relationship and trust united them in giving their patients the best possible clinical experience. I also noticed all dentists, regardless of speciality, employ advanced leadership skills and problem solving capability.

After witnessing a multiple tooth extraction, the sound of a decayed tooth cracking in forceps really highlighted the grit needed by a dentist. As I shadowed scale and polish procedures and more intricate endodontic treatments, I witnessed the dentist encouraging and educating their patients into the prevention of various oral diseases; a vital aspect of modern day dentistry.

To understand how a simple impression, taken from the boy with broken front teeth, was transformed into a lustrous set of central incisors, I sought experience at a dental laboratory. This gave me knowledge of the technical aspects that are not often seen. Whilst viewing the making of crowns and dentures, tasks of immense expertise, I appreciated the dentist's need to produce incredibly accurate instructions for the technician. As a technology student I too must complete work to an exact tolerance, whether it is perfecting a weld joint or using CAD software, resembling the accuracy of a dental surgeon. My discussion with a dental graduate on vocational training highlighted the demands of the course and the complexities that may arise from some cases. It did not deter me in the least, only strengthening my choice of career. Gaining one of the 200 prestigious National Engineering Arkwright Scholarships, in Year 12, shows I have the academic resilience and problem solving capacity to handle the complexities of this demanding course. As a senior prefect I have enhanced my ability to make difficult decisions under pressure whilst acting responsibly. Whilst achieving all three Duke of Edinburgh awards, I have demonstrated that my commitment, individual leadership and communication skills are important for keeping a team well organised and supported – qualities essential to becoming a proficient dentist. By providing weekly assistance for children with learning difficulties, I have built a close, ongoing relationship with both colleagues and pupils. This has educated me to be patient, empathetic and communicate with people from a variety of ages and ethnic backgrounds – helpful attributes for patient care. Studying A-levels in Biology and Chemistry, I have been introduced to the fascinating topics of anatomy and biochemistry whilst sharpening my practical skills through dissections and laboratory experiments. I am now eager to explore the various dental related sciences during the five-year course. Whether captaining the squash team or shooting for the RAF, I have excelled at new challenges whilst demonstrating the ability to work within a team or by myself. While I know, from discussion with undergraduate students, the pathway to dentistry is an ever challenging one, I believe I am armed with the confidence and eagerness to enter the stimulating world of dentistry.

Used in 2010 – Offers from the University of Liverpool

STATEMENT EVALUATION

This student has done a great job linking back how their attributes would make them an excellent candidate for the course. In the introduction they mention their motor skills, indicating that the individual is well informed of skills needed by a dentist. The introduction also states why they have chosen this as a career, making it clear to the reader where their initial interest for studying dentistry has come from.

The main body of the statement is very well laid out where the student has mentioned how they have gained further understanding of the course requirements. The candidate has made a good use of this opportunity to show what they have learned from their experiences while sharing their own achievements and goals.

Towards the end of the statement, the student also mentions their A-levels. This is a good way of incorporating their current study into the statement whilst also indicating that they are able to replicate the qualities of a dental student.

PERSONAL STATEMENT 3

Seeing the importance of dental surgeons during the recovery of victims of life-threatening accidents in a presentation by the West Midlands Fire Service made me aware of how dentistry can make a positive impact on people's lives. After researching the field, I became fascinated by the variation of working environments and the precise, intricate style of work that dentistry offers. Undertaking seven weeks of work experience, five of which were in Pakistan, at three practices reinforced my decision to follow dentistry as a career path, as it has enriched my understanding of dental procedures and the benefits dentists can bring to their patients. During the five weeks I spent in Lahore, Pakistan at Ideal Dental Surgery, I witnessed a wide range of procedures; such as root canal treatment and surgical extractions. Observing how dentists performed complex treatments in short windows of time, whilst maintaining impeccable standards, displayed how versatile and skilful a good dentist must be in order to satisfy their patients' needs. After seeing interactions between dentists and their patients, I gained an understanding of how dentists should balance clear communication, time efficiency and excellent service to maintain strong customer relations, to ensure they thrive as a business as well as a practice. This, paired with knowledge acquired through GCSE Business Communication, has increased my perception of the business aspects of running a practice. A further two weeks of shadowing at two cosmetic clinics, Dental Works and Aesthetics Dental, allowed me to observe the use of advanced equipment, such as intra-oral cameras and CEREC 3D instruments, and understand their benefits to the quality of the patient's treatment. Over the past 12 months, I have provided weekly care to two patients at "x" Care Home. Volunteering in this pastoral role has shown me how to put people at ease, in addition to developing my attention to detail whilst completing tasks. Further-more, it has highlighted the importance of balancing professionalism and personality. Studying Biology has enabled me to manage, and organise, a large workload. I have developed time management skills which will prove to be paramount when undertaking dentistry as a profession. Additionally, I plan to actively practise prior knowledge by becoming a Biology Mentor for year 12. In secondary school, I joined the Debate Mate program. In this I developed my ability to speak formally and coherently with members of my team by presenting a logical argu-ment on a given motion. I enjoyed the challenges debating brought, as you have to speak with conviction on a topic, sometimes contrary to your own beliefs or moral judgement. Furthermore, doing so enabled me to think with an open mind, and consider both sides in order to arrive at conclusive decisions. In my final year, my team won all three debates in the regional final. Whilst working as an Executive School Councillor, I had the opportunity to develop my interpersonal skills, allowing me to help bridge the lack of student communication with management. My dexterous abilities have been refined through stress relieving activities, like knitting, sewing and table tennis. I became a Table Tennis Ambassador in year 11. This role held me responsible for the maintenance of equipment, and provided the opportunity to teach a class. I have also spent four years within Sea Cadet Corps and RAF

Cadets. Progressing through the ranks taught me how to delegate and use initiative to complete tasks effectively.

Dentistry is an advancing sector providing countless opportunities for further study, making it a rewarding and fulfilling career prospect. I believe my drive, diligence and experiences make me an excellent candidate for the challenges dentistry will present, and will enable me to flourish, not only as a member of a university's community, but also as a committed student of dentistry.

Used in 2017- Offers from The University of Birmingham

STATEMENT EVALUATION

The introduction makes it clear for the reader to understand where the student had the inspiration for studying dentistry. The statement then explains what the individual has done to follow up from the presentation and find out more; in this case undertaking work experience. Through using technical and correct vocabulary, such as root canal, indicates that the student has engaged well in their work experience, showing commitment to the reader. This is a good way to link the introduction to the first paragraph which goes in depth to explain what the student has attained from their work experience.

A positive aspect from the statement is that it does not simply focus on work experience but also allows the reader to engage with the candidate. This is done through explaining personal achievements such as becoming a table tennis ambassador. This may seem small in the hindsight of things but is crucial to indicate that the student has a life outside of academia.

PERSONAL STATEMENT 4

I have always been fascinated by how advances in technology have increased our understanding of the human body and how the world around us works. This stems from a keen interest in studying the sciences from a young age. I am attracted to the field of dentistry as it will provide me with opportunities to combine my interests, skills and experiences to improve community healthcare.

My understanding of the dental profession has been greatly increased by four weeks of work experience in contrasting dental practices. During my work experience at NHS practices I recognized that as well as being highly skilled surgeons, dentists are leaders of small teams. I observed how the dentist managed their team, for example by delegating treatments such as scale and polish to the dental hygienist. This gave the dentist more time to see another patient who required root canal treatment; a more complicated and extensive procedure.

I believe dentists are an important symbol of local healthcare provision, and I became aware of a correlation between poor oral hygiene and a patient's social status. I would like to have the opportunity to investigate this pattern, in order to help identify and improve the oral health care of people from disadvantaged groups. My work experience has fuelled my passion to learn more, and so I have continued to pursue my interest in dentistry. I have attended the "Dentistry Show", which emphasised to me how dentistry really is a constantly evolving field of healthcare. I found technology such as "Digital Radiography" very fascinating as it could replace conventional X-ray films, and greatly reduce patient radiation exposure.

An aspect of dentistry that has particularly intrigued me is the materials used in dental treatments and I have attended a dental materials taster day at Queen Mary University. This opportunity gave me a thorough insight into why specific materials are used in certain dental treatments, filling in gaps in my knowledge.

I regularly carry out volunteer work to help and support my local community. I have cared for young children at a local nursery. This has given me invaluable experience in working with children and allowed me to develop skills in gaining children's trust, thus being able to help them.

I also have experience of shadowing a Housing Officer in re-housing homeless people. This experience helped me to empathise with the homeless and to appreciate the problems and discrimination they face on a daily basis. I have raised money for charity by applying patterns using henna at local community events. A similar intricacy and manual dexterity is required to be a dentist. I believe my community volunteer work has also developed my communication skills. During my time at "x", I have tried to give something back to the school and was honoured to be chosen to represent my peers in the Student Council. This allowed me to make my school a more enjoyable environment to learn, embarking on projects to build new facilities, such as a Sixth Form study area. This has improved my skills in communication and respecting and representing the views of others. I also organise a weekly dental society within my school. A number of students attend from two schools and this has given me the opportunity to provide prospective dentists a chance to be able to discuss current and ethical issues.

I maintain a good work life/balance by playing in the school's XI football team, and I am captain of a school chess team. Playing matches for the football team has given me valuable team work skills. I enjoy competing in the chess team because I find it stimulating, as I relish problem solving. Captaining this team demonstrates my leadership, teamwork, planning, and problem solving abilities. I firmly believe my strong academic ability, passion for dentistry, social skills, commitment to community wellbeing, and good manual dexterity make me well suited for an exciting yet demanding career in dentistry.

Used in 2010 – Offers from University of Bristol

STATEMENT EVALUATION

A good personal statement will always show the candidates personal development and their journey from choosing to study dentistry, to learning further about it and then applying. The introduction is well composed and underlines the student's main interest for choosing dentistry.

The student is reflective upon their work experience, whilst recognising the main qualities of being a dentist and making links to their own journey which mirrors the same qualities. The student uses their volunteering as a way to replicate how dentists also give back to their community and this is done even when they mention helping contributing to their sixth form.

By including their hobbies they are able to show the reader that they have a life outside of studying. This not only displays their personality but also indicates that they are ready to cope with a career in dentistry because it can be stressful at times.

PERSONAL STATEMENT 5

If it weren't for my crowded teeth, I might not have found my fascination to pursue a career in dentistry. As a child I suffered from crowding and an overbite requiring extensive orthodontic work and several tooth extractions. During the treatment I marvelled at the precision, intricate skill and multifaceted approach required by the dentist and I was inspired to become a dental practitioner. My desire to help others combined with my genuine enthusiasm for science makes dentistry an ideal career to pursue. This aspiration was reinforced during numerous work experience placements covering a variety of dental fields.

Working with a community dentist allowed me to spend time at an open access centre and witness the higher prevalence of oral disease in people with social deprivation and the challenges this poses. I also spent time at a special needs paediatric clinic where I realised the importance of building rapport with children and parents. The caring nature required here was similar to that I had used whilst teaching first aid weekly at school to 11-12 year olds.

During a week with an NHS dental surgeon, I saw the importance of educating and encouraging patients to improve oral health. Shadowing him made me aware of the dentists' holistic approach, ability to listen and understand the patients' healthcare needs and to act professionally.

I spent a week at a private general practice observing various treatments from routine check-ups to complex procedures such as root canal preparation. I noted how vital good communication skills and empathy are in reassuring the patient regardless of the complexity of treatment. Two days at a dental lab demonstrated to me the importance of teamwork between the technician and the dentist. Here I recognised techniques and skills I have acquired through model car making, that were used to produce a ceramic crown, which replicated the original tooth.

My enjoyment in the construction of model cars has developed my ability to handle small tools with precision in order to achieve fine detail. Whilst shadowing an orthodontist for a week I was particularly intrigued by Invisalign, which used a CAD-CAM virtual 3D treatment plan as well as a series of plastic retainers to accurately move the teeth. This was very different to when I had fixed braces. The challenge of keeping up with constantly advancing dental technology makes it a rewarding career to pursue. I spent a day with an implantologist and saw how implants could replace dentures, emphasising the remarkable impact specialist dentists can have in changing patient's lives.

'The Mouth as a Global Window to Systemic Health' was one of the seminars I enjoyed whilst at the prestigious AAAS science meeting in Vancouver. It further fuelled my fascination for dentistry and gave me an insight into factors linked to oral health.

I am caring, compassionate and committed to helping others; characteristics that are essential in a career in Dentistry. Volunteering at Oxfam for two years has taught me about communicating with the public, good time management and ways of coping with stressful situations that I will encounter in dentistry.

My ability to work as part of a team was highlighted by completing my Gold Duke of Edinburgh Award, which involved hard work, commitment and conviction. During three years in the Cadet force I was responsible for my section requiring me to be supportive, encouraging and work closely with other cadets in order to achieve our goals. Competing in cricket and hockey at club and school level shows I am a team player and have good hand-eye coordination. Being a member of debating society and playing team sports has developed my ability to communicate and work well with others. Achieving my LTA Tennis Leadership Award, Lifeguard Qualification and captaining the school hockey team have all developed me as an effective leader. I am fully aware that dentistry will be a demanding path to follow, however I feel I have the necessary attributes, motivation and enthusiasm to rise to the challenge.

Used in 2013- Offers from University of Sheffield

STATEMENT EVALUATION

This is another example of a very well organised personal statement. The student is able to use their personal experiences for choosing a career in dentistry. This makes the statement relatable and genuine.

The individual also describes what they have learned from their work experience in different dental settings. The candidate mentions what they have observed in the practice which interest them such as the use of CAD-CAM. This shows that the candidate has demonstrated the initiative to research further into this topic.

PERSONAL STATEMENT 6

My interest in dentistry was sparked by exposure to the profession combined with a natural curiosity for science and an aspiration to help others. From my 2 weeks experience at "x" Dental Surgery and 3 days at "x" Dental Care, I gained a deeper and more accurate insight into what day-to-day dentistry involves.

I found work in general practice more diverse than I expected. An example of this was when an autistic woman came into the surgery. She was nervous and reacted badly on seeing the dental nurse. We took the time to talk to her and distract her to calm her down. This experience showed me the importance of adapting to a wide variety of people and situations, working together as a team to ensure comprehensive treatment whilst maintaining professional and ethical standards.

I observed a range of procedures, including denture fittings, root canals and extractions. By the end of my work experience I could differentiate between decay and healthy tissue using x-rays. I was enthralled by the proficiency and intricacy involved and the wide variety of specialist equipment used.

After observing several root canal treatments, I was inspired to learn more. Through research on websites such as the BES, I learnt that it is an inflammation of the pulp, requiring cleaning, shaping, disinfecting and obturating to preserve and achieve healthy periapical tissue.

Further research on the NHS website exposed me to cutting-edge developments, for instance, the recent discovery that pluripotent stem cells from human urine cells can produce teeth-like structures and has the potential to form human teeth. Although this advancement is promising, the current consensus is that patients should focus on prevention rather than cure.

Moreover, from my work experience I ascertained that dentists, as well as often diagnosing serious conditions such as oral cancer, also work with hygienists to teach patients oral hygiene and give associated advice on topics such as diet and smoking, which improves general health.

Across my work experience at a GP, Pharmacy and Primary School, I found that the ability to explain complex procedures concisely was essential alongside the need for empathy, patience and respect to develop a warmer and more personal patient relationship. For the past year I have volunteered at "x" Preparatory School as a Sport Teacher's Assistant, where I had to plan and teach lessons, augmenting my time-management and organisation skills whilst utilising my Level 1 Sports Leadership Award.

I have also been working with a charitable organisation called Sikh Connections for 3 years and have recently had the privilege of working with the charity. I interacted with a broad range of people, from teaching children at camps to feeding the homeless, improving my communication and interpersonal skills.

In addition, I am completing my Duke of Edinburgh Silver award. As map reader in my expedition, I proved my ability to pragmatically handle challenging and stressful situations as well as coordinating a team. At school, I am a Year 7 Senior Prefect, head of the Prefect Team and an Individual Needs Mentor.

I am approachable and compassionate when supporting students who are vulnerable or have learning difficulties. My manual dexterity has been established through cross-stitching, playing the piano and the ukulele.

My self-motivation has driven me to participate in many school sports teams including netball and rounders. Playing basketball across the country at a national level has highlighted my dedication and teamwork skills. I have a realistic understanding of the ongoing education and demands associated with being a dentist but I also perceive it to be both tremendously rewarding and a huge responsibility. I am confident that I have the passion, stamina and skills to pursue a career in dentistry and would be honoured to be a member of this profession.

Used in 2016 – Offers from The University of Sheffield & the University of Plymouth

STATEMENT EVALUATION
In the statement, the applicant goes in depth with their extracurricular activities. The candidate shows their well suited abilities for dentistry

through their volunteering and care for the community. The statement is written with a consistent flow and addresses why the applicant has chosen dentistry as a career. This makes the statement stand out, as the candidate does not only list factors, but explains the reasoning behind their choices for choosing dentistry.

The conclusion finishes off well with a summary of what the student can also bring to the university and that they understand the demands of becoming a dental student.

Personal Statement 7

In my younger years, the level of care I received during my own orthodontic treatment and the impact it had on my confidence made me start to hone in on dentistry as a career choice. I found that dentistry incorporates everything I strive for in a career: elements of science, employing manual dexterity, building a rapport with patients and working in a team.

During a six-week work experience shadowing clinicians, I witnessed the level of precision required in procedures such as root canal treatment. Sitting in on a consultation between a dentist and a patient made me realise how the dentist ensured patient input; going through the procedure and answering any misunderstandings. It fascinated me how an individual with so much in-depth knowledge about this area adapted himself effectively to communicate in laymen's terms so the patient felt contented and knew potential outcomes.

In the time spent with the hygienist, she stressed the importance of prevention in preference to restoration when she educated patients on oral hygiene, diet and tobacco. It was surprising to realise how hygienists have taken on many roles of a general practitioner and how the dentist will have to become more of a specialist.

Accompanying the domiciliary service, I was impressed by the teamwork required between dentist and supportive specialists. One reluctant elderly dementia sufferer agreed to have her dentures fitted only after gentle persuasions and encouragement by the team.

At a private clinic, I was fortunate to observe dental implant surgery and bone grafting. Radiographs taken pre-surgery allowed me to see how the patient's occlusion is determined and post-surgery to confirm implant positioning.

During the two weeks spent in a dental laboratory I witnessed the production of dentures from the impressions taken and casting. Whilst completing the Discovering Dentistry MOOC, I discussed issues involving water fluoridation; weighing the prevention of cavities against potential fluorosis. This enabled me to consider different viewpoints and see how theory is linked to potential advantages and ethical issues raised.

As a tutor at 'x', I led classes of GCSE to A-level students of biology and chemistry. I worked with individuals to surpass their targets and created question packs. Volunteering with the Sterling Dental Foundation team this year, I have been tasked to help organise three fundraising events. I have taken part with dentists and dental students in social action projects where local primary schools attend the dental surgery for a day packed full of activities with an emphasis on learning about maintaining good oral health.

Volunteering for two years at Mencap, caring for individuals with learning disabilities, I built strong relationships with visitors by listening to their stories and socialising with them. Through empathising with individuals and instilling in them the confidence to be more open about experiences, benefitting both them and myself immensely. This is similar to how a dentist could build trust through careful consideration with a patient. Completion of my Duke of Edinburgh Bronze award encouraged me to pursue a more challenging expedition in Morocco. This involved ascending Mt. Toubkal and assisting in the construction of local roads for villages. These experiences challenged my physical and mental commitment and I would like to think, strengthened my character. I received acknowledgement as Honorary

Student of the Year in academic achievement. Having initially only played the piano socially, I went on to achieve Grade 5.

As captain of the school hockey team, in addition to playing for county, I was given the opportunity to both lead and be a team player. Reflecting upon all my experiences, I have found that Dentistry is the career for me. With a realistic appreciation of the academic, physical and emotional demands required in undertaking a dental degree programme and career I would welcome the opportunity to embark on the course and am looking forward to participating in all aspects of university life.

> **Used in 2017- Offers from The University of Plymouth, King's College London University, The university of Bristol & The university of Sheffield**

STATEMENT EVALUATION
A great aspect of this statement is the use of accurate terminology. Not only does this show the reader that the candidate has done their research but also displays their commitment to pursuing a career in dentistry.

The statement explains in great detail how the candidate has developed as an individual as well as how their experiences so far have driven them towards this career. Their commitment is shown through volunteering implying that they would suit a career which gives back to the community.

PERSONAL STATEMENT 8
To me, dentistry not only includes the understanding of learned theory but also has the aspect of working hands-on. The ability to communicate, be empathetic and build rapport with patients to improve their general wellbeing in a caring manner is something I admire. The dental environment will offer me the opportunity to develop such skills to contribute to society as well as keep my mind sharp and active.

I consolidated my desire to study dentistry when I shadowed dentists at a local practice. I noticed how strong interpersonal skills were

SECURING YOUR PLACE AT A UK DENTAL SCHOOL

essential in enabling the dentist to explain treatment options in a way the patient could understand, as well as listen to their concerns. I was intrigued by the delicate management of a root canal. This procedure required concentration and patience as the dentist worked in such a confined space; demonstrating the versatility of skills the dentist requires.

I was introduced to the concept of universal precaution where the health care professionals consider all patients to be carriers of infectious blood borne diseases thus handling all patients equally, keeping the dental team and public safe. I had an opportunity to carry out an amalgam restoration on a model extracted tooth. Initially this was challenging however, on completion it was rewarding to see the result. I observed the dental nurse sterilising equipment, which taught me the importance of sterilisation and prevention of cross-infection. This allowed me to appreciate the significance of the multidisciplinary team within the practice.

For three years I volunteered as a weekly teacher's assistant at a Saturday school. This demonstrated my commitment in giving back to my local community and developed my professionalism, which is an important characteristic of an efficient dentist.

Currently, I am a tutor for young children, which has enhanced my sense of empathy and patience, which I can use when dealing with younger patients. I also held a part-time job in retail, which enabled me to build professional communication skills with customers and work well within my team of colleagues.

To further my knowledge in the field of dentistry, I have been committed to my school's medical society where presentations are given about the latest medical news, such as new dental research linking gum disease with increasing chances of developing Alzheimer's disease. Additionally, I have attended dental lectures at King's College London, which emphasised the ever-changing dental field and the vastness of research and its constant integration into dentistry.

Through my various experiences, I have worked with people of different abilities, backgrounds and ranging age groups. As a dentist, interacting with the public involves dealing with patients of diverse cultures and communities. I appreciate the promotion of prevention, education and treatment to raise awareness on oral health to all patients. I enjoy being part of my school's community and take part in extra-curricular activities such as sports and drama. I had a main role in the Christmas pantomime, which developed my acting skills.

Being a confident public speaker allows me to take part in debates on controversial issues, where I respect opinions of my peers whilst challenging them with my own views. My current role as senior prefect has helped my time management and organisational skills. To relax, I enjoy playing the ukulele which advances my manual dexterity. I like baking and decorating my bakes with neat and elegant designs. I understand from talking to dentists and dental students how intense and challenging studying dentistry is and how committed one must be to become successful. Listening to lectures specific for aspiring dental students has exposed me to both the pros and cons of studying dentistry. From this I have concluded that the rewards of treating patients undoubtedly outweigh the difficulties associated, which is why I genuinely believe no other career is more suited to me.

Used for 2018 -Offers from King's college London University & Barts

STATEMENT EVALUATION
This personal statement highlights the major qualities within dentistry such as manual dexterity, working within a multidisciplinary team, and giving back to the community. The statement shows realistic views about dentistry as it still indicates that there is hard work involved in becoming a dental student but nevertheless they are ready to embark on this journey.

PERSONAL STATEMENT 9

When someone is happy they smile. Therefore, isn't it important that a smile is not only aesthetically pleasing, but also increases self-confidence?

Becoming a Dentist and possessing the skills necessary to improve the confidence of patients by giving them the teeth of their dreams would give me a huge sense of satisfaction and fulfilment.

My interest in Dentistry blossomed when I spent my GCSE work experience at my local dental practice. I quickly realised the close relationship a dentist develops with each patient. I was fascinated by the manual dexterity of the dentist and his ability to quickly diagnose a problem.

My desire to pursue a career in Dentistry was further stimulated by Year 13 work experience. I observed the dentist do fillings, extractions and a complex treatment plan. I gained an understanding of patient confidentiality, informed decision making and the trust a patient places in their dentist. I shadowed an Orthodontist for a day, giving me an insight into the different specialities associated with dentistry. My interpersonal skills were enhanced last year when I became my school's first Social Peer Mentor, spending lunchtimes with a child with Autism. Helping out in the Learning Support Centre has made me more caring and patient.

As Deputy Head Boy and the President of the St. Vincent de Paul Group, I have become an effective leader and motivator. I have addressed the student body many times to present our fundraising plans and together as a group, we have achieved much success. I help my peers with A-level Maths and tutor a Year 12 student with Biology; I often envisage myself teaching young patients about the importance of oral hygiene. My life was changed when I participated in School Aid Romania, organising fundraisers and then taking my funds to Romania to help those in need. It was moving to see the delight of the children when they received something as simple as a toothbrush and toothpaste. My honesty is exemplified by the responsibility placed on me to collect and be responsible for the Friends of Lima Money. Volunteering regularly in the charity shop and working part-time in a pharmacy illustrates my ability to interact with the general public and work effectively in a small team.

I am a volunteer at the Carefully Yours Project, a scheme promoting the independence for over 55s, allowing them to make new friends. I developed an understanding of the general public as there are elderly people with many different needs and conditions at the project; therefore I gained an insight into the range of different patients I would see as a dentist.

Being a Dementia Friend to a man with dementia further demonstrates my ability to form bonds, work with people and empathise. Forming relationships that will span many years make a career in dentistry so appealing.

Last summer I was a leader at a Summer Scheme for children with disabilities. Enjoying an amazing two weeks, I got the chance to improve my communication skills with children with Autism and Down's Syndrome. As I calmed the children down when they became unsettled and agitated, I felt optimistic that I would be able to reassure patients on a dental chair.

For relaxation, I play the flute and I have passed Grade 3. I play Gaelic Football and as a member of a sports team, I have gained an appreciation for the value of teamwork. On Fridays, I coach Under 6s Football and I find it so fulfilling to know that the young boys look up to me.

I was Bank of Ireland Student of the Year 2014, showing that I will be able to cope with the academic demands of the Dentistry course. My good manual dexterity is shown by my love of origami and playing the flute. I am enthusiastic about a career in Dentistry as it provides the opportunity for further specialisation, whilst being a very rewarding career. I know that with hard work I will be an asset to your university and a competent dentist.

Used in 2016- Offers from University of Glasgow, University of Birmingham, University of Liverpool & Queens University Belfast

STATEMENT EVALUATION

This statement includes unique experiences that the candidate has undergone. A descriptive account has been given to the reader, which is what a good personal statement should do. The candidate manages to describe situations which they themselves could imagine becoming a dentist. This creates a good impression on the reader as it shows that the candidate is ready for the challenges at dental school.

PERSONAL STATEMENT 10

During childhood visiting the dentist was a highly daunting and intimidating experience for me; not knowing why it was so imperative for me to attend was always an ongoing thought. However, after reading an article stating that "almost a third of five year olds suffer from tooth decay and it is the most common single reason why five to nine year olds are admitted to hospital", I was astonished, and this led me to read further about the significant link between poverty and poor oral health in children. It was this that initially motivated me to pursue a career in dentistry.

I now wish to participate in a leading role that enables me to educate people about the importance of oral health, ensuring that good habits are firmly established and I would ultimately be a credit to the NHS. It was upon carrying out work experience at 'x' Dental Care for eight weeks that confirmed my passion for dentistry. This experience allowed me to witness procedures such as tooth extractions and root canal treatments.

I was most impressed by the impact that dentists had on an individual's wellbeing. During this time I observed many examinations with children and learnt the techniques dentists used in order to explain the importance of oral hygiene. This was a revelation and left me inspired about the value of good oral health and the social impact it has.

Additionally, I learned that people do not regularly visit the dentist due to not being able to easily access an NHS dental practice and I strongly feel that I would like to have a position in promoting the importance of good oral health to the population and improving the access to NHS dental care in deprived areas of the UK.

To supplement my ongoing development, I have secured employ-ment at The 'x' Dental Group to assist with their decontamination procedures. Here I have been able to understand the importance of infection control and also the significance of working as part of a team within a practice.

In 2014, I travelled to China for ten days, during which time I volunteered at an orphanage, where I lead a group of children through various activ-ities. In addition, I also helped out at a homeless shelter and worked coherently within a team to distribute food to those in need.

The trip to China allowed me to develop my personal integrity and improve both my leadership and teamworking skills, as well as high-lighting the importance of working within a team to be an effective dentist. I have also volunteered at the British Heart Foundation's store for a total of 6 months. This was a positive experience as it enabled me to develop a great deal of confidence in interacting with new people on a daily basis, as well as building relationships with regular visitors.

Additionally, I have volunteered at a retirement village, where interacting with people of a different generation ensured that my interpersonal and communication skills adapted accordingly.

Furthermore, I have also completed a course provided by Future-learn entitled "Discover Dentistry", which allowed me to understand the importance of each member of the dental team as well as enlightening me into the development of dental related technology. Moreover, I participated in LAMDA for 8 years, which has developed my ability to communicate effectively with people of different ages and learning abilities. Also, I have played the violin and recorder since the age of 8 which required good hand-eye coordination and manual dexterity.

In my spare time I enjoy to cross stitch which requires extreme precision and has ensured that my manual dexterity has been able to develop and has increased my ability to focus on intricate detail for extended periods of time.

I am excited to have the opportunity to be able to apply my love of biomedical science coupled with a practical application in serving the community and is something I look forward to enhancing further during my time at dental school and when I enter the dental profession.

Used in 2017- Offers from University of Plymouth & Barts

STATEMENT EVALUATION
A great part about this personal statement is that the candidate is completely honest. It's okay to say that dentistry wasn't what you always had in mind, but what's important is the journey you encountered which made you choose dentistry as your career. Mentioning non-academic activities, such as your hobbies is crucial. This will allow the reader to know that you will be able to cope during stressful periods within the course. This is something that this personal statement does really well.

PERSONAL STATEMENT 11
Dentistry is a profession of science and art. Its diverse demands and challenges, from academic rigour to physical craftsmanship and patient interactions, make it a highly attractive profession. Exploring dental healthcare and practice through reading, qualifications and work experience has confirmed and intensified my desire to pursue a career in dentistry.

Two weeks of work experience at an NHS and private clinic, and a week at a separate private clinic, provided me with important insights into dental healthcare, highlighting the diversity of skills required and the value of the NHS. Furthermore, this contrasting experience demonstrated the ways in which dental care is influenced by a range of factors such as patient demographics and socioeconomic factors.

Observing dental consultations underlined the importance of good communication, both within the dental team and with patients. A consultation with a deaf patient highlighted just how challenging this can be. I enjoyed the exciting opportunity to perform composite fillings on extracted teeth and noticed that the physical intricacies involved in dental practice share many similarities with my silver-smithing experiences.

I look forward to taking the same care and pride in practical dental work as I have done when producing jewellery. Additional experience in primary and secondary orthodontics reinforced the relationship between dental health and overall physical, psychological and social wellbeing. It was pleasing to witness self-confidence being restored through the correction of malocclusion.

Observing maxillofacial practice provided further insight into specialisation opportunities and first-hand experience of the ways in which technological advances, such as the 3D printing of models from CT head scans, affect the dental profession. Completing Sheffield University's Discover Dentistry MOOC provided me with a grounding in the history of the profession and likely future developments.

Researching the work of Fauchard and reading Breiner's Whole-Body Dentistry have expanded my interests and underlined the importance of holistic approaches to patient care. In particular, I am interested in the importance of preventative treatment as a means of minimising invasive interventions.

After reading NICE guidelines from 2014, I explored prevention of caries in children with my own in-depth, independent research, in my

EPQ. In Biology, I particularly enjoy studying the processes of human function, from a cellular to system level. Chemistry has honed my practical skills and understanding of scientific method, whilst Maths continues to advance my logical thinking.

Weekly volunteering at a local hospice proves to be both a rewarding and challenging commitment, emphasising the fundamental role of empathy in healthcare and the importance of equality irrespective of social standing.

At school, my leadership roles as a Prefect and House Captain provide further teamwork opportunities, such as when organising school open days. With Grade 8 qualifications in both acting and verse and prose, I regularly participate in and direct school productions. I also fence at Silver Award level and look forward to completing my Gold Duke of Edinburgh award.

As a keen musician, I play the flute in the school orchestra and as a member of my school's Medical Society, I enjoy discussions on current ethical issues. My work experience has demonstrated the rewarding nature of dentistry, not only through helping others, but also encouraging on-going personal and professional development. Although aware of its demands, I remain passionate about and look forward to pursuing this career.

> **Used in 2017 - Offers from King's College London University, Barts, University of Birmingham & Queens University Belfast**

Statement Evaluation

This statement informs the reader what has interested the candidate for applying to dentistry. This can be any extra reading the candidate has done, courses which the applicant has attended or even any personal experiences. It is a great way to make the statement seem more authentic.

THE DENTISTRY UCAS APPLICATION

PERSONAL STATEMENT 12

Having my braces removed changed my life irrevocably, I became more confident and more outgoing. I have now realised that our appearance has a big influence on our social life, increasing our self-esteem drastically. It became clear to me that dentists have a large impact on individuals and I was determined to find out more about this career.

My interest in dentistry was further fuelled when I undertook clinical work experience at a dental surgery for 2 weeks. The most comfortable patients were the ones who had visited the dentist regularly and had established a strong bond with her. This highlighted the dentist's need for strong interpersonal skills and the ability to explain diagnostics in a simple way that patients could understand.

The aspect of continuity in dentistry was something that struck me as it cannot be achieved in another medical profession to the same extent. The harmonious way that the dentist and the nurse worked together inspired me. They were in perfect synch, allowing them to deliver treatment quickly and effectively.

The most memorable moment was when I came across a worried patient whose brother suffered from mouth cancer. The dentist's heart-warming approach eliminated his concerns of suffering the same fate. This opened my eyes to the emotional challenges a dentist may have to face in their career and how important it is to show professional integrity while also being empathetic.

Whether it was a filling, extraction or root canal, it was inspiring to observe the change in emotion from when a patient entered the room to when they left. I have shown my philanthropic nature by volunteering as a patient befriender in the orthopaedics ward at King's College Hospital, learning how to deal with concerned individuals, offering them comfort and a listening-ear for their troubles and worries.

My curiosity about how living organisms function and how our world works led me to study the sciences. Being one of the founding members of the medic society, debating ethical issues, only further increased my passion. In particular, my enthusiasm for embryonic stem cells led me to complete an EPQ regarding the ethics surrounding them.

Through additional research, I discovered stories of people whose lives were saved due to the remarkable potential of embryonic stem cells. This made me appreciate modern medicine and the scientists behind this research. It also made me question whether we can use embryonic stem cells to treat dentofacial deformities or if it could ever be possible to use them to regrow teeth.

Studying media developed my creative, technical and project management skills. In a world where technology is rapidly advancing, we can employ the influential power of the media into our career. For example, we can educate children on the importance of dental hygiene through media platforms and this will ensure they take better care of their teeth from a young age. Certainly, prevention is the key to oral hygiene. My decision to pursue this career was consolidated after the 'Evolution's Bite' talk at the Royal Institution. It was fascinating to me how much information can be gathered from a single tooth, such as the diet of an animal as well as how they have evolved. Completing a Discover Dentistry online course further confirmed my choice as I enjoyed learning about the history of dentistry and its progression. Tutoring has strengthened my communication skills and belonging to the local girls' football team taught me the importance of effectively working in a team.

Participating in the Duke of Edinburgh Bronze Award challenged my ability to stay calm under pressure whilst also using specialist equipment. SFX makeup has enhanced my manual dexterity, a skill that is essential when working with the intricate details in dentistry. I have no doubt that I want to be part of this community that is always in a state of development and is proud of what they do.

Used in 2018- offers from Queen Mary University of London

STATEMENT EVALUATION

This statement highlights the candidate's accomplishments really well. An important aspect of the personal statement is telling the reader your personal achievements. You should be proud of what you have accomplished, no matter how small or insignificant those accomplishments may seem. This statement also draws connections between the candidate's unique skills and how they will make them a good doctor in the future. Overall a very well composed personal statement.

PERSONAL STATEMENT 13

What first fascinated me about dentistry was the fact that it is an art form in its own right. The combination of clinical knowledge, practicality and near perfectionist side to the career is what motivates me to pursue a degree in it. Given that teeth are something we use every day and smiles are the first thing we notice about people, the role of a dentist in society is vital to the upkeep of public oral health.

Dentists are also responsible for educating the public on how they themselves can prevent damage being done to their teeth. This makes it a valued and noble profession, in my eyes. To expand on my interest, I undertook work experience at x Dental Practice for 4 weeks, where I observed treatments such as fillings, root canals and extractions. I saw the teamwork between the dentist, receptionist and dental nurse and how it was crucial to efficiently run a practice when working towards the common goal of giving patients the best possible care.

I have developed teamwork skills from my role as a prefect, where I worked with the student body to create a safer and friendlier environment, as well as playing rugby for the school team, where we all worked as a cohesive unit. I observed that dentists often have to be comfortable with taking the lead within the team during testing situations. For instance, during my work experience it was the dentist who had to calm an angry patient due to an endodontic file breaking in the root canal. This also helped me to understand that dentists need to be honest and integral when owning up to mistakes.

I myself developed excellent leadership skills through the role of charities officer at school when organising an event for Macmillan Cancer Support. I noticed from my placement that communicating both clearly and empathetically was vital for a dentist when explaining treatments in detail, especially when reassuring anxious patients.

Working as a lifeguard at X Leisure has refined my communication skills as I often had the responsibility of explaining certain rules to members for their safety. Volunteering with vulnerable children at Norwood, a charity for people with learning disabilities, was really humbling. The voluntary work I undertook has also made my communication more creative as I regularly had to explain information to children with varying disabilities.

Helping out at my school's Key Stage 3 science clinic furthered these skills. I had to convey complex ideas as simpler ones in order for students to grasp difficult concepts. I saw that this is quite similar to a dentist explaining a procedure or treatment to a patient. I was motivated by the intricacy of the manual dexterity that I saw during certain procedures such as fillings and root canal treatment. This led to me playing the flute more frequently, achieving grade 5, as well as attending dental courses, where I practised suturing and carving molars out of wax. They helped me to appreciate the extent of manual dexterity that dentists require as well as refining this skill at the same time.

During my free time, I love to swim and also have an enthusiasm for photography. For the past 11 years I have been practising karate and have achieved a first dan black belt in the martial art. As a result, my discipline and commitment have greatly improved, both of which are fundamental to a career in dentistry.

I appreciate the demands and challenges that come with a career in dentistry. However, I believe that with my mature, responsible attitude, tenacity and commitment, I have what it takes to become a dental professional. I am eager to experience life at university and the many challenges to come.

Used in 2017 – Offers from University of Birmingham

STATEMENT EVALUATION
Giving examples of what you actually witnessed during your work experiences is really useful. That is something that's written really well in this statement. The statement also includes what that particular event during their work experience then led them to do, which is a great inclusion as dentistry is a career which requires reflection.

PERSONAL STATEMENT 14
"Missing, false, decayed, crowned…" These were some of my thoughts as I peered inside my grandmother's mouth. You see, I come from an Egyptian background, where dentists are a luxury for the rich. Growing up, I have realised the importance of regular dental care and hygiene, especially after receiving orthodontic treatment. These experiences instilled in me the desire to help others, not only by treating dental diseases and pain but also by amplifying patients' confidence through improving their dental aesthetics.

My passion for dentistry was enhanced through my work experience in a hospital orthodontic department, which inspired me to observe the different branches of dentistry. Consequently, I spent a further 3 weeks in a general NHS dental practice, an orthodontic dental laboratory and in the maxillofacial department during my HOSPEX course in the Royal Derby Hospital. This was enlightening, as I saw the different types of dentistry and the distinction between work in NHS hospitals and clinics. Effective teamwork, communication and the caring attitude of a MDT became evident in theatre where the surgeons took a biopsy on a patient who had a malignant tumour in her mouth. This encouraged me to research articles in the BDJ about reducing the risk of cancer. One article showed how ethanol in mouthwashes had little benefit to the active ingredients for plaque control yet increased the risk of oral cancer. I found this shocking and it highlighted the importance of cancer research.

During my A-levels, I enjoyed studying the theoretical aspects of biology and chemistry, as well as developing a range of practical skills: from dissections in biology to precise titrations in chemistry. Studying mathematics has enhanced my knowledge of mechanics and developed my problem solving skills which are vital for a dentist, who must choose the right treatment and perform it correctly. Having excellent time management skills enabled me to conduct my independent study and achieve bronze in the physics and chemistry Olympiads.

Furthermore, my role as House Captain gives me the opportunity to motivate pupils from all year groups to succeed in both sports and academia. This summer I spent a month in Tanzania as part of a community based project. We raised over £5,000 prior to the trip, which helped us to build a classroom and install both running water and electricity. I felt privileged to teach the children English, mathematics and P.E. as well as supporting nervous children in becoming more confident. This proved challenging, as we overcame language barriers in Swahili, but rewarding, as my empathy towards the children grew. This eye-opening experience contrasts greatly with my ongoing volunteering at Broom Lane Care Home since Year 9, where I am learning how to care for the elderly holistically. It is humbling to see their confidence in me grow through the years. This bears direct relevance to the long-term patient care and trust that the profession involves.

Through my involvement in the Silver Duke of Edinburgh Award, I gained a sense of mental toughness. This helped me greatly when climbing, and summiting, Mt. Kilimanjaro in Tanzania this summer, where I discovered the importance of teamwork, especially in challenging situations.

Hobbies such as playing rugby for the first XV in Year 11 and tennis training on a weekly basis are an important part of my life to balance my academic work. In addition, practising my grade 5 keyboard pieces allows me to relax and reflect, as well as developing my manual dexterity, which is essential for a dentist.

Pursuing a career in the field of dentistry is my ambition. The mouth is an intimate and vital part of an individual's anatomy and through my academic and extra-curricular pursuits, I have developed the character traits required to care for this essential part of the human body. Dentistry beautifully intertwines science, dexterity, and my enjoyment of problem solving, making it the ideal profession for me.

Used in 2015- Offers from University of Leeds, University of Liverpool, Bristol University & the University of Birmingham

Statement Evaluation

Mentioning what you are currently doing allows the reader to have an insight to your current life. This personal statement mentions how their A-level subjects have also allowed them to develop some useful skills which the candidate has linked back to how they will be useful as a dentist. This demonstrates to the reader that the candidate has the ability to cope with the demands of the course making them a suitable applicant.

Personal Statement 15

I would like to pursue a career in dentistry as I am a scientist as well as an artist. Dentistry will allow me to make a real difference to people's lives by applying Science in an artistic manner. I have seen how dentists can enhance an individual's well-being by improving cosmetic appearance and reducing suffering. In addition, the never-ending developments in dentistry will feed my inquisitive mind.

A career in dentistry event enhanced my enthusiasm for the profession, and covered topics such as medical ethics. Speaking to both students and clinicians, I learnt that although practising dentistry can place high demands on practitioners, the job satisfaction is substantial in terms of patient gratitude.

My two-week work experience enabled me to see many procedures, and I appreciated the benefit of patient education, the value of team work and of being compassionate towards patients. I observed how dentists detect patient anxiety and use light conversation to put the patient at ease. I enjoyed handling impression materials and shaping brace wire. Shadowing nurses, technicians and receptionists, I learnt about patient care and data protection. I was introduced to the stresses of being a dentist, such as emergency cover.

To find out how dentistry is practised abroad, I travelled to America for further work experience, and in doing so realised the importance of the NHS in the UK. Visiting the BDIA showcase and reading the BDJ online has been an enjoyable experience and has expanded my knowledge. An article of interest was on the impact of dental phobia on consent, which highlighted the importance of patient education.

Academically, my A-levels show my enthusiasm not only for science, but also for performing arts. Studying chemistry has given me an insight into substances such as amalgams, which I observed being used during my work experience. Biology has improved my precision skills through carrying out procedures like dissections, which is an essential skill for a dentist. Physics has improved my ability to approach problems in a logical fashion, which I believe will help me in systematically diagnosing pathologies.

My keen interest in theatre inspired me to take Drama, which helps me unwind and has vastly improved my confidence in facing the public. This will be useful in communication with both patients and my team in order to deliver the best possible care.

My job at Specsavers has improved my dexterity using fine tools as well as my communication skills. I was trained to greet patients with a smile, a key quality of a complete dentist.

Recently I played the lead role in "The 39 Steps" for my theatre group and was given an "Outstanding Actor" award. Fitting in rehearsals alongside my studies reflects my time management skills, which is essential for a busy dentist. My role in the school basketball and cross-country teams has moulded me into a strong and positive team player, which will help me to work with my team to make clinics efficient.

A first aid course taught me of the importance of triage, and how to react and take charge in unforeseen situations. I set up a health screening team to raise funds for the charity FOCUS, where I measured blood pressure and BMI. This sharpened my organisational, data recording, listening and leadership skills as we strived to make the clinic more efficient. It was also highly rewarding to help out those in need.

I am a Lieutenant of the Ismaili Volunteers, who organise cultural gatherings. My tasks include serving food and helping the elderly use the restrooms. Through this I became a more patient and understanding individual, which is vital to be a good dentist. It also led me to receiving a citizenship award for my efforts.

I want to be an outstanding dentist, and as I believe I have the required attributes of leadership, communication and team working, a strong academic foundation and an insight into life as a dentist, I am in no doubt that dentistry is the career for me.

Used in 2016 – Offers from Barts, Newcastle University, University of Sheffield & University of Liverpool

STATEMENT EVALUATION

The candidate demonstrates why they would be a good dental student through their commitment to not just their academics but also their hobbies and things they have passion for. This enables the candidate's personality shine through. This is a useful part to include within the statement as it allows the reader to get to know the candidate more and can really impress the reader and allow them to see that the applicant is a hardworking and motivated individual.

PERSONAL STATEMENT 16

Having experienced significant orthodontic care from a young age, I was grateful for the impact it had on my appearance and self-esteem. The ability to restore such confidence within someone is what strengthens my motivation to study dentistry. The various roles of my dentist as a restorer of oral health and an oral aesthetician, who concerned himself with my wellbeing and satisfaction as a patient which truly enlightened me.

What I find most alluring about this course is how creative, hands-on, and ever-changing it is. Moreover, being able to build a strong rapport with patients as you help to see them through their journey is captivating to me.

To understand what a career in dentistry entails, I spent 2 weeks shadowing a variety of dentists, nurses and admin staff at different dental practices, where I appreciated the individual skills and interpersonal relationships of the multidisciplinary team. I observed an array of different procedures; from bridges to crowns, to more complex procedures such as implants.

I noticed how easily the dentist changed their tone of voice to show compassion and accommodate people with different problems, ages, and genders, with the ultimate aim being to provide the best patient care. A crucial moment I recall, was when a nervous non-English speaking patient came for a surgery and the dentist impressively calmed them down using his empathetic speech. It is here I saw dentistry not only helps patients physically but emotionally too.

Witnessing the work of a domiciliary dentist at a care home outside a regular practice taught me how dentistry also reaches out for the less able in our community and is in good position for our aging population.

A placement at a practice in India gave me an idea of the approach of dentistry abroad, where I learnt the differences in professionalism and how people are less aware of dental hygiene. Seeing this compelled me further to pursue dentistry.

Volunteering at St. Luke's Hospice shop for the past year gave me crucial time management skills while also studying for my A-levels, which was also valuable experience in communicating with various personalities, like that of a dentist.

I attended several taster courses, open days, lectures on digital dentistry, where I spoke to a variety of dentists about dental past and future. Intrigued by the variety of dental tools, I visited a dental museum where I explored the evolution of dental equipment and procedures, presenting dentistry as a career of cutting-edge science that's constantly developing.

Having recognised the level of repetition involved in this profession and the need for patience when delivering care to challenging patients as demanding aspects of this career, I too have had similar exposures like this such as tutoring my cousin.

In high stress environments, it is important to have an outlet for stress. For me it is playing cricket and football at school and local clubs, whilst also serving my community. Captaining my local cricket team for the past 3 years pushes me to work effectively under pressure alongside others, yet still express my own ideas as a leader. It has also enabled me to work efficiently in a team and learn to prioritise tasks in a fast-paced environment, similar to that of a dental practice. Practicing taekwondo and badminton has greatly refined my tactile abilities, which is a key skill in performing intricate tasks such as root canals.

Moreover, I take great interest in knitting at my school club and sketching, involving complex gestures and manual dexterity which is helpful as dentists need to work on a small scale with meticulous flair. These experiences have allowed me to identify many parallels with my skills and that of a dentist and can picture no other profession to express my facets as a good communicator with an artistic nature and the love for the interaction with people. I appreciate the hardships of this course, both physically and mentally, but my desire to learn has strong potential to overcome this.

Used in 2019 – offers from University of Plymouth & Barts

STATEMENT EVALUATION
This statement demonstrates what the candidate has learned from their work experience with a really professional outlook. The statement includes what interested the candidate to pursue a career in dentistry. This allows the reader to understand and follow the journey of the applicant, from first considering dentistry to learning through experience and applying it to dentistry.

The conclusion summarises really well why the candidate believes they will be suited for a career in dentistry. Their extracurricular activities have linked back to how that will allow them to become a successful dentist in the future.

Graduate Entry Personal Statement

As a graduate entrant, whether you have done a Biosciences degree or a non-science degree, it is prudent for you to expand on how your previous qualifications have aided your decision to pursue dentistry. The statement should eclectically weave the key learning points, traits and characteristics you have acquired to put you in best stead for entering this career pathway.

As touched upon earlier, the statement really does provide the only evidence (prior to interviews) for the university to assess your insights, ambitions and suitability for the career. For graduates wishing to enter onto undergraduate course programmes (those where both under-graduate applicants and graduates apply), it is even more important that the statement is outstanding due to the increased competitive nature.

Below we have compiled advice and personal guidance from previously successful graduates. Although this is largely anecdotal information, it is highly useful and serves a prominent starting point.

KEY STRUCTURE

The personal statement of a graduate will largely follow the framework set out for an undergraduate, as detailed earlier in the chapter. One key differentiation would be how you have spent the additional time, in comparison to an undergraduate applicant, in undertaking academic and non-academic pursuits to gain the desire and attributes to enter a career in dentistry.

MOTIVATION FOR A CAREER IN DENTISTRY

As with an undergraduate statement, a graduate statement will also highlight career insight and motivation with work experience and other initiatives such as undertaking online courses, engaging with current dentists and reading relevant articles. Conversely though, as a graduate, you may wish to undertake further insight and research. Why? Well, as a graduate, you will naturally be undertaking more of an investment in time and finances. As such, you must conduct due diligence to ensure you make the correct decision.

Maximising Your Undergraduate Degree

The advantage being a graduate is the wealth of experience and relevance you can generate from your undergraduate degree.

For instance, if you plan to study dentistry, you should not view your current degree just as a 'space filler' or just a stepping-stone. Rather an academic supercharger to boost your application with highly relevant credible information.

Yes, many schools do wish for a minimum degree classification of an Upper Second Class Honours but this will only makes you eligible to apply. It certainly doesn't guarantee an offer.

More information on entry criteria for graduates can be found earlier in this chapter.

Our advice to those considering applying is to eloquently tailor your undergraduate degree endeavours to aid with your prospective dentistry studies. Maximising your undergraduate qualification is not simply limited to high attainment in your academic results. The judicious selection of course modules can also be pivotal in building traits or interests for a dentistry career. For example, a head and neck anatomy module that stimulated your interest in the oral cavity, dentition and function of mastication. Or perhaps a physiology module sparked a fascination with the buffering capacity of saliva and its role in mitigating common dental diseases. The key here really is to use your own academic learning and mould this to how you wish your career to unfold.

In addition to compulsory modular learning, there is much benefit in grasping opportunities related to research which may arise during your undergraduate studies.

A relatable example of this could be your involvement with a research project. These types of undertakings can be incredibly useful in multiple ways. Firstly, in terms of career decisions it can reinforce (or in some cases dissuade) your affinity to work more closely with people rather than independently within a laboratory. Secondly, it will help to develop your professional skills of working and learning independently. Thirdly, depending upon the level of intricacy, this may help to exhibit an eye for working with your hands and displaying dexterity. Finally, a sound understanding of how to undertake a research project and, arguably most importantly, how appraisal data will help with a career in dentistry. Evidence based dentistry is reliant upon utilising the best available data and therefore an appreciation of how to critique evidence is a valuable skill. In addition, this could later lead to your involvement in publications; endeavours which are useful for career options such as specialty training or research.

EVIDENCING INTERPERSONAL SKILLS, TEAMWORK & COMMUNICATION

Pursuing another degree is a truly notable achievement. That said, a dentistry degree is a vocational degree and aims to generate new, highly enthused, clinically skilled professionals with strong interpersonal and communication skills. As such, admissions teams will be seeking out those candidates whose statements emit strong flavours of these traits.

Graduates may wish to discuss salient characteristics that evidence these skills in their statement. When detailing valid attributes of leadership, teamwork, communication or problem solving, candidates are advised against listing these accounts. Instead, we encourage you to write with cogitation, linking how these actions can benefit a career in dentistry.

ALTRUISM

Whilst academic attainment and ability to communication are important, showing a genuine compassion to serve others is an overarching characteristic of a dentist. By conveying altruism in your statement, i.e. through a volunteering commitment or community, religious or charitable activity, you will be able to convey to the reader these valuable qualities.

INTERESTS OTHER THAN ACADEMIA

The statement should also reflect how you can exercise a healthy work-life balance. With dentistry being a stressful career, hobbies that facilitate stress relief are essential.

GRADUATE ENTRY PERSONAL STATEMENT

PERSONAL STATEMENT 1

Dentistry is a profession that I was inspired to study ever since I underwent a 6 week work experience placement at a local dental practice. It was evident that a dentist must have immense interpersonal skills required for communication, leadership and teamwork, which are vital to create an effective working environment. The process of alleviating patients of pain and distress after skilled treatment and reassurance along with knowing that I improved quality of patients' lives, would give me satisfaction. By not achieving the grades for dentistry whilst at college, I was regrettably unsuccessful. This directed me to study Biomedical Sciences with the knowledge that I can apply for dentistry after graduating. On reflection, this experience made me more dedicated and determined to achieve my goal of becoming a dentist. After 3 years at university, I know that I have gained the necessary study skills to be successful in dentistry. I have matured and gained confidence which are invaluable qualities when dealing with patients in clinics. Practical experiments improved my analytical and manual skills, reflected by a score of 86% in that module. I organised a post-graduate 8 week placement at Newcastle University to research the pathophysiology of salivary gland dysfunction in Sjogren's syndrome.

I feel that my enhanced biomedical knowledge, time management and organisational skills will serve as strong fundamentals when studying dentistry. I arranged work experience at two NHS dental practices for 6 weeks and 2 weeks respectively. During this time I observed a range of treatments from simple scaling to surgical tooth extractions and root canal treatment. I was also given an insight into the main differences between NHS and private dentistry. It was insightful to observe the empathetic nature of the dentist towards nervous patients. I witnessed this when the dentist treated a patient with Meniere's Syndrome and another that suffered a vasovagal attack. Knowledge from my degree was reinforced when a tooth extraction was refused in practice as the patient was being treated with alondronic acid. This emphasised the need for critical thinking and decision making when treating a patient. My dental laboratory placement highlighted how different dental establishments work alongside dentists to achieve collective success.

I understand that dentistry can be stressful yet rewarding, routine yet diverse and requires a great deal of problem solving. This reaffirms my aspiration to become a dentist as I believe I possess all the necessary attributes to become a competent, ethical dentist. Over summer, I voluntarily worked at a nursing home, nursery and an institute for autistic children. This allowed me to hone my interpersonal and empathetic skills as I learnt to interact with people of different ages and abilities. I always approach new challenges enthusiastically and with passion. At university, I was elected vice-president of the Afro-Caribbean society, allowing me to experience another culture and further improve my communication and teamwork skills. I also taught Urdu to children in classes within my local community, which demonstrates that I can communicate effectively to children between the ages of 6-10 years.

Part-time work at a football stadium as team leader exercised leadership and interpersonal skills by directly dealing with complaints from members of the public in a composed and professional manner.

I captained my local cricket team, which expressed my motivational, leadership and teamwork skills. I also helped to organise a charity cricket match this year, which raised £25,000. I enjoy playing the dhol and painting, which requires patience, manual dexterity and attention to detail.

I feel that the combination of my maturity, enhanced biomedical knowledge and dedication will serve as strong fundamentals to the challenging demands of becoming a dentist. I would feel privileged to be part of such a rewarding profession.

Used in 2012 – Offers from the University of Liverpool

STATEMENT EVALUATION

For graduate entry this personal statement is very well written. It begins by explaining why the individual wants to study dentistry and their initial interest in the subject. A great point to take away from this personal statement is how the student mentions not just their strengths but also explains their weaknesses. This gives them the opportunity to capitalise on their whole university experience as a great learning curve. This shows how they have developed as an individual and have learned from their previous mistakes. This is very important, especially in a career like dentistry, where you are expected to learn and adapt from your mistakes.

The main body of the statement relates to the key aspects that the student has taken away from their work experience and previous degree. They have shown their desire to study dentistry years later, which indicated dedication towards the course – an ideal attribute to have as a dental student.

The conclusion touches upon some personal achievements to show the reader that the individual is a socially caring and a well suited candidate for the course. This personal statement is the perfect example of the student indicating their personal development after not meeting the entry requirements the first time.

PERSONAL STATEMENT 2

My decision to pursue a career in dentistry arose whilst I was studying a dental anatomy module as part of my BSc in Biomedical Science. During this time, I participated in the dissection of a human cadaver head and neck. I marvelled at the intricate structures of the oral cavity and soon it became evident to me that it could be reflective of an individual's general health in a way I had not considered before. This sparked my curiosity into what a day in the life of a dentist entailed. I have since endeavoured to gain first-hand experiences to help me develop my knowledge of the profession and the responsibilities involved. I began by shadowing a dental team in a practice offering NHS dental care and another providing private dental care. In both settings I witnessed routine procedures, such as new patients and recall examinations, restorations and extractions. Assisting at the reception showed me the importance of the non-clinical, administrative aspects of dentistry and the organizational skills required to manage a dental practice. Although I recognised the labour-intensive nature of the work, I often saw the gratitude of the patient when the dentist had completed their treatment. I then sought opportunities to enrich my understanding of the pathways of specialised dentistry. Observing the formation of crowns and dentures by a dental technician gave me insight into restorative dentistry and how this can cross over with other specialties such as oral surgery and periodontics. Through discussions with dentists on my placements and reading dental literature, I have recognised the multi-faceted nature of Dentistry and the pace of its development. These experiences have helped me understand that effective communication between the dentist, patient and dental team is central to the provision of high-quality care. One example of where I have exhibited strong interpersonal skills is in my role as a customer service advisor. This has required communication with individuals of diverse backgrounds and managing challenging situations in a calm and compassionate manner, as well as adapting the way in which I communicate to fit the person I am speaking with. Furthermore, I have volunteered as a project leader for the Flourish project run by the University of Sheffield, where I ran weekly activity groups for adults with neurological disorders. I feel this experience enhanced my leadership skills alongside my ability to work effectively in a team. Manual dexterity is a skill that is fundamental for working within the confines of the human mouth, and a skill, which I have taken many opportunities to refine. The dissection of facial muscles and the extremely fine cranial nerves that I carried out in my BSc enabled me to exercise fine motor skills, as well as providing me with detailed anatomical knowledge of this area. The laboratory work I carried out during my MRes required meticulous hand-eye coordination on a daily basis, as my research relied upon pipetting thousands of control and patient DNA samples for further testing. My degrees have provided me with a firm knowledge of normal and disrupted physiological systems, which I believe would complement my study of dentistry. Aside from academic study, I have pursued many interests. Hosting a weekly university radio shows has allowed me to develop my public speaking skills and engage in debates surrounding current affairs. Understanding other cultures and traditions has been an interest I have explored through travel and travelling around different continents unaccompanied has aided my personal development. I believe that dentistry is the career for me as it combines my dedication to lifelong learning with practical aspects of problem solving and daily patient interaction. Whilst I recognise the high demands Dentistry carries, its evolving nature attracts me to the profession. With my determination and academic resilience, I feel I can thrive in this dynamic career.

Used In 2017- Offers from University of Liverpool

STATEMENT EVALUATION
This statement includes what the candidate has learned from their previous degree and how their knowledge would make them a more suited candidate for dentistry. Furthermore, the statement follows a logical structure where each paragraph follows on from the previous one. The paragraphs in this statement are clear and straight to the point. The candidate has written an enthusiastic introduction by highlighting their accomplishments through their previous degree, of which they should be proud.

PERSONAL STATEMENT 3
A healthy, beautiful smile is the best thing to wear. What would happen if routine dental care and cosmetic dentistry were not readily available

to the public? Apart from the inability of people to confidently bare a smile, there would be the inevitable consequences of ill health, pain and malnutrition. Since early secondary school I have developed a passion for both science and art, and I knew I wanted to pursue a career which would give me the capability to contribute positively to society. I pursued a Biomedical Sciences Degree, in which, I am on course for first class honours. This degree has been invaluable to me, in confirming the chosen career in which I am inspired to pursue. It has allowed me to grow as a person, gain a more detailed knowledge of the human body, and acquire transferable 'hands-on' techniques in the laboratory. Through my degree I became increasingly more aware of the demands of academic study, the necessity for self-directed learning and the importance of time management. I have been fortunate enough to obtain several weeks of work experience in four general dental practices providing both NHS and private care, plus a week in the oral and maxillofacial department of a hospital. It became very clear to me that dentistry is the discipline I wish to pursue. Observing the roles of a receptionist, nurse and hygienist in addition to a dentist, I saw how dentists have to not only lead their team, but also be integral members. Good communication and teamwork are vital. Patient anxiety, fears and apprehensions all need to be considered to be an effective practitioner. During my placements, I received small amounts of training in decontamination, and benefited tremendously from direct observation of restorative and cosmetic work. I observed check-ups and treatments ranging from extractions and implants to work with oncology patients. This further motivated me to relish the challenge that becoming a dentist will involve. A particularly memorable case I observed was with a nervous oncology patient who had a maxillectomy and required a bung to be fitted on their dentures to fill the space and allow effective speech and eating. The practitioner had the expertise to calm and reassure the patient while carrying out the treatment to make them feel more comfortable. It was enthusing when I was allowed to visit the prosthetics lab where these dentures were made and I was taught how to model a prosthetic nose. This, combined with when a dentist instructed me how to perform a root canal treatment on a model of a tooth, helped me gain an insight into the attention to detail required in dentistry. I am aware that as a dentist, I will be treating all ages of patients from a variety of backgrounds with different ailments. As such, the capability to empathise and relate is imperative. A placement at a child development centre in addition to volunteer work at The British Heart Foundation Shop and a residential home for people with dementia helped enhance my social skills and increase my confidence in dealing with a variety of people. Years of flute playing in front of audiences also helped to build up my confidence and taught me to perform under stress, as well as honing my manual dexterity skills. My love for using my hands to create things was evident to all and lead to me being awarded my school's Creative Arts Prize. I play hockey for Keele University and enjoy the teamwork involved, while the role of Prefect and Games Captain at sixth form developed my leadership skills. On my placements I was fascinated to see the reconstructive work oral and maxillofacial surgeons can do for road traffic accident patients. Good dental care can give someone more confidence in themselves, in their dentist and has a remarkably positive impact on their quality of life. I am an ambitious and enthusiastic individual, awaiting the opportunity to fulfil my potential in a career in dentistry.

Used in 2015- Offers from University of Birmingham

STATEMENT EVALUATION
This statement addresses how the candidate's undergraduate studies have prepared them for entry into dentistry. The applicant mentions skills which they have developed through their degree, which will aid them in studying dentistry. Work experience mentioned is equally as useful as it implies that the applicant still has the willingness to learn further.

PERSONAL STATEMENT 4
A dentist is required to have a number of roles, whether it's relieving pain from a periodontal abscess, giving someone the confidence to smile or promoting a healthier lifestyle. These are the reasons why I am drawn to dentistry. A key attraction is the ability of the dental

team to tailor its approach to each individual patient, considering their own perceptions and cultural influences. Over the course of four weeks at a general NHS dental practice, I observed many of the qualities I would like to emulate as a dentist in the future. Explaining a procedure to an anxious patient in a way that fully informs them but also allays their fears is a skill I hope to master and this inspired me to complete an Extended Project Qualification into what causes a fear of the dentist.

One procedure I saw was a difficult root canal treatment. I admired the dentist's careful attention to detail and dexterity. Furthermore, each appointment was an opportunity to sensitively and tactfully discuss lifestyle interventions which would not only improve oral hygiene but also the patient's overall wellbeing, such as stopping smoking.

Greeting patients at reception and organising their appointments reminded me that each member of the dental team has an important role and much organisation is required behind-the-scenes to keep a practice running smoothly. A week on an orthodontic and maxillofacial ward gave me the opportunity to see oral surgery being performed under general anaesthetic. A number of the cases I observed were due to oral cancers and this prompted me to read further into what causes them and how they can be treated.

From the dental drill to 3D-printed teeth, the field of dental materials has paved the way for advancements in clinical dentistry. My degree has helped me to understand how properties like biocompatibility and polymerisation shrinkage must be considered when designing materials such as composite fillings. A week at a dental laboratory meant that I could put this into practice, building a complete wax denture. Observing the use of a CEREC machine at a private practice, which was used to tailor-make a crown, highlighted to me how Material Science and Dentistry are able to complement each other. I have particularly enjoyed working on group projects, where I have found that clear delegation of tasks and a methodical approach allow for the best possible way to solve a problem-based learning task. I have recently embarked on my final year project, which will focus on materials that can facilitate tooth remineralisation through the release of fluoride, for example layered double hydroxides. A highly rewarding experience for me was on a Mencap Summer Camp, where I was responsible for looking after children day and night for a whole week. Whilst a daunting prospect at first, I found that by being flexible in my approach to each individual child's needs, I was able to engage them in activities such as arts and crafts. I was delighted to be invited back to volunteer on subsequent camps. As a Student Ambassador for my university, I have taken the opportunity to visit schools and promote university education to children who may never have considered it before. I am the Media Secretary for the Queen Mary Snowsports Society, where I'm responsible for updating our social media pages and creating videos to promote our club. I am particularly proud of creating a new logo and redesigning the club's website. I am also a member of an Enactus social enterprise team, which teaches the importance of dental care in youth centres. I enjoy playing football in a weekly league as a way to unwind. Making model aeroplanes in my spare time has allowed me to hone my manual dexterity skills. I feel that the experiences that I have gained from my past three years at university have left me better informed and even more driven to pursue a career in Dentistry.

Used in 2017- Offers from Bristol University

STATEMENT EVALUATION
The best personal statements have clear purposes and easily draw readers in, which is something that this statement does really well. The candidate is clear and they understand the demands of the course through their various experiences. The candidate highlights the need for good dentists and how if they become a dentist they will have a positive impact in the community.

PERSONAL STATEMENT 5
As a NHS Territory Manager working within the Royal Hospital for Neuro-disability, I learnt how refining the standard of care enhances

the psychosocial wellbeing of a patient. Reflecting back to my dental experience, I can now fully appreciate how prevention and treatment of serious oral diseases not only alleviates pain but also improves a patient's lifestyle, happiness and self-esteem. Working within the healthcare field for 3 years, my resolve to become a dentist has only strengthened as it combines the use of precise diagnosis, technical ability and patient education in salient areas such as dental hygiene. Working within the dynamic NHS environment I am responsible for providing services in specialist areas to educate clinicians on innovative technology, aiming to improve patient care. As a mediator between my company and the NHS, I have developed my communication skills; building and sustaining successful professional relationships. This responsibility has enabled me to not only work well under pressure but also taught me to adapt in a fast paced environment and multitask, to complete objectives efficiently. I believe that these attributes build a foundation for a successful dental career and are also necessary building blocks to succeed in today's NHS. During my 6-week placement, I was fortunate to witness the diversity of procedures dentistry offers, from medically compromised and complex patients in the Oral and Maxillofacial department to routine check-up and complex rehabilitation of patients post cancer in general dental practices. It was exciting to see dentists couple their knowledge and manual dexterity to decide on specialised procedures, using cutting edge technology. However, it was evident how the close relationship between the dentist and patient sometimes influences the course of treatment. Furthermore, I realised that communication and coordination are vital aspects within an efficient team. Learning from this experience I was able to implement these attributes in my career, allowing me to work effectively in a multidisciplinary team. Throughout my degree, my interest in the intricate mechanics of the dental field, led me to focus my dissertation on 'The Use of Local Anaesthetics within Dentistry and their future'. Always knowing I want to pursue dentistry, this experience elucidated the possible options of furthering the advancement of dental care through clinical research. In addition, my degree enabled me to think analytically while meticulous laboratory work enhanced my manual dexterity. My passion for science led me to tutor autistic students which appealed to my caring and patient nature. I thoroughly enjoyed learning how to effectively communicate with those who have learning difficulties in an empathic manner; helping a student raise his grade from an E to a B was a particularly satisfying and rewarding experience. Working within the Territorial Army, I advanced my leadership and teamwork skills whilst learning to persevere in extremely stressful situations. I am currently a Captain of Men's 2nd XI and Coach to the under-14 boys team at Slough Hockey Club. For this I completed a level-1 coaching and safeguarding course, which taught me the importance of respecting confidentiality whilst maintaining a nurturing relationship. Moreover, I have run the Windsor Half Marathon on behalf of the Alzheimer's Society and currently volunteer with SWAT, providing necessities for the homeless. These experiences allow me to de-stress and have taught me to both work well in a team and thrive as an individual to achieve desired goals. With a perpetual interest in dentistry, I have learnt from and continually built upon the key attributes required in becoming a respected dentist. I believe my years of experience and diligence within the NHS, to improve patient care, coupled with my myriad positive qualities are vital characteristics needed to succeed in the dental field.

‖ Used in 2016 – Offers from The University of Glasgow

STATEMENT EVALUATION

This statement portrays not only the applicant's academic ability but also their hobbies and things they enjoy doing in their spare time. This is equally important to mention as it demonstrates to the reader that the applicant is a well-rounded individual who can de-stress when things get tough. Another positive from this statement is the candidate is clear in their future goals. This implies that the candidate is motivated and will become a good dental student in the future.

PERSONAL STATEMENT 6

My ambition to work in dentistry began when visiting my cousin at his dental practice. I remember being in awe of his meticulous craft – his exceptional patient rapport, how he made people smile, both metaphorically and literally. Here I learnt how the dental profession could improve a person's quality of life and have a great impact on their well-being. Since then I have remained focused in pursuing a career in Dentistry. Past experience of working as a dental nurse and currently studying Dental Hygiene and Therapy, I have been able to closely understand dentistry and my interest is ever evolving. Oral hygiene is such an important part of a person's routine and I was taken aback by the lack of dental awareness in the general public. More than 45% of the UK's population suffers from gum disease, and I feel the way forward is patient education and increasing awareness. During my course, helping patient stabilise their periodontal health and maintain their oral hygiene has proved to be extremely rewarding. I have learnt through my clinical experience that periodontal health is the foundation for successful dental treatment as any restorative or prosthetic work can have a compromised prognosis. My clinical interactions with paediatric patients has opened my eyes to the high number requiring restorations and multiple extractions, as well as dental neglect in children. This has inspired me to study further to obtain a dental degree and working within community and special care dentistry. I have also been fortunate to observe first hand different specialities of dentistry including orthodontists, implantologists and endodontists. I have understood that dentistry is a multi-faceted career. To achieve excellent dental care, one must have excellent patient interrelations, effective teamwork and professionalism. My A-level courses reflect my passion and motivation for the dental profession, as each subject taught me essential skills in preparation for the challenges in further studies and life within dentistry. Studying Biology and Chemistry allowed me to take an analytical approach on tasks. I conducted a retrospective audit at a dental practice as part of work experience looking at 'Success rate of root canal treatment over 10 years'. This spanned over 4-weeks, for which I was awarded the Gold CREST Award. Results showed 84% – a 10-year success rate, which has increased my confidence in conservative dentistry. My EPQ project; 'Why NHS dental care is so costly when its plan was proposed to be cost free?' enabled me to look deeply into the NHS history and gauge a better understanding of our health care system. Outside academia, I completed a BTEC Level 2 in the Fire & Rescue Service and tutored young adults, which provided me with distinguished leadership and teamwork proficiencies. I have volunteered weekly at a local nursing home providing emotional support and conversing with the elderly. My manual dexterity is gained through my love of nail art and intricate henna patterns, requiring prolonged concentration and excellent hand-to-eye coordination. Along with maintaining respectable grades, and extra-curricular activities, I take an active part in running of a family newsagents business, which over the years has given me confidence in public speaking alongside improving my organisation, interpersonal and technical skills. The experience I have gained at university and employment makes me aware of the complexities, essential skills and demands of succeeding within a dental career but I feel that my transferable skills, commitment and first-hand experience will allow me to fulfil my ambition to excel further and become a valued member of this competitive and demanding profession.

Used for 2018- Offers from University of Central Lancashire

STATEMENT EVALUATION

This statement provides strong reasons as to why the applicant wants to study dentistry. The statement mentions relevant projects, work experience and skills that provide evidence as to why the candidate would be a successful dental student. The statement also touches upon what the candidate will also bring to the university itself through their skills and continuing development.

The statement also explains what the applicant's main influences have been and what their career aspirations and how the course will help you achieve them.

Competitive Landscape and Statistics

It is well known that entry to dental school is no easy feat. Available data published online by universities clearly evidences the competitive nature of this application process.

Anecdotally speaking, candidates often hasten to prepare themselves for the dental school interview, prior to fully mastering their dental personal statement, UCAT and BMAT revision and without actually securing a dental interview to begin with.

For those wishing to succeed, our advice is to optimise your application to secure an interview rather than worrying about an interview you have not yet received.

A google search of UK dental schools reveals the raw demand for such limited spaces. Here is a non-exhaustive list of some UK university dental schools and data related to their admission process. Certain data points have been obtained through Freedom of Information requests.

Belfast
2016
Approximate number of applicants: 160
Number interviewed: 123
Offers 77
Places: 45

Birmingham
2016
Approximate number of applicants: 439
Number interviewed: 218
Offers 148
Places: 76 (74 Home EU/ 2 overseas)

UCLAN

2020
Approximate number of applicants: 260
Number interviewed: 110 - 160
Places: 29

Leeds

Approximate number of applicants each year: 500
Places: 72

Queen Mary University Of London

2019
Approximate number of applicants: 700
Number interviewed: 300
Estimated Offers: 170
Places: 75 (67 Home, 8 Overseas)

Sheffield

2018
Approximate number of applicants: 861
Number interviewed: 360
Offers: 226
Places: 71 (up to 3 of these overseas)

Glasgow

2019
Approximate number of applicants: 446
Number interviewed: 205
Offers: 140
Places: 78

Liverpool

2018

Approximate number of applicants: 783

Number interviewed: 333

Offers: 155

Places: 72*

Manchester

2020

Approximate number of applicants: 1084

Places: 68

Manchester pre-dental (A204)

2017/18

Approximate number of applicants: 56

Number interviewed: 4

Offers: 4

Places: 68

Dundee Gateway to Dentistry

2018/19

Approximate number of applicants: 63

Number interviewed: 29

Offers: 12

Places: 68

Dundee

2016/17

Approximate number of applicants: 435

Number interviewed: 274

Offers: 122

Places: 57

---

2   There is no quota for international students. All applications are considered
together with no differentiation between home, EU and international students.

Plymouth (A206)

2017
Approximate number of applicants: 460
Number interviewed: 227
Offers: 76
Places: 59

Aberdeen

2019
Approximate number of applicants: 190
Number interviewed: 227
Offers: 26
Places: 59

UCAS Frequently Asked Questions

- Do I have to put any retake subjects that I intend to take in the future on my application?
  Any pending grades or subjects that you aim to take should be entered on your UCAS application, under the examinations and qualifications sections. You should select the grade as pending.
- How will I be notified if I have been accepted or rejected from my universities?
  You will be able to change the way that you are contacted by UCAS. This will include a text message, an email and even a letter. You will receive an email either from the university and or UCAS Track stating that there has been a change in your application.
- How can I change something in my application that I have realised is incorrect after sending it off?
  This depends on the type of change you want to make.
  You can change your address, phone number, and email address in UCAS Track.
  If you want to change your choices, this will depend on

where you are in the application process. For more information, see the UCAS 'Making changes' page.

- Am I allowed to get someone to write my personal statement for me?

  You should not get a third party to write your personal statement as this will be considered as plagiarism and cheating. Failure to follow these guidelines can result in the withdrawal of your application.

- If there are any changes to my application how do I inform UCAS or my universities?

  If there are any changes in your application you should contact UCAS. They will advise you further whether you should inform your chosen universities about the changes.

- If my GCSE grades are not the best can I still apply to Dentistry?

  Your GCES must meet the minimum entry requirements for your chosen university. This will make sure that your application is considered. For more information see Chapter 3: Study Dentistry.

- Can I change my university choices after I have sent off my application?

  You can swap a choice for a different one within 14 days of the date on your welcome email. You can only swap each choice once. However, for dentistry, we strongly advise that you are clear when making choices for university.

- What happens if I miss the UCAS deadline for Dentistry applications?

  If you have missed the UCAS application deadline for Dentistry you can still apply but it would be up to the university's discretion whether they consider your application further. We strongly advise that you start your application early to avoid this happening.

- Can I see what my referee has said in their statement about me and the predicted grades they haven't given me?

  You are allowed to see what your referee has put down for you. This is usually your teacher from your school or college. If you are a private candidate this can be a tutor. You can also find out about predicted grades from your referee.

- What is clearing and will I need to use it?
  Clearing is a service provided by UCAS which allows students who haven't received any offers for their course to choose a different pathway. Clearing is optional but will only be provided once you have received decisions from all of your chosen universities. If you do get an offer, you will not be entered in clearing, however if you do not meet the conditions of your offer then you will be able to access clearing on results day. You will also need to receive decisions from all your choices before you can make your firm and insurance choice.

CHAPTER 3

STUDYING DENTISTRY

INTRODUCTION

Studying Dentistry is a highly prestigious opportunity to embark on a career of fulfilment and reward, hence the entry process being so competitive.

With many universities to choose from, each with different teaching styles and entrance requirements, the process feels a little overwhelming.

Worry not, this chapter will take you through every aspect of the process to ensure you feel confident with your selection.

IN THIS CHAPTER WE WILL COVER:
- Universities offering dentistry
- Entry criteria for undergraduates
- International students
- Course fees and student loans
- Graduate entry dentistry
- Maximising your chances as a graduate
- Financing a postgraduate degree
- Life as a graduate dental student
- How to choose between each university
- 5th choice option
- Open day checklist

Which Universities Offer Dentistry?

Here is a list of UK Universities which offer entry to study dentistry.

DENTISTRY SCHOOLS
There are sixteen dental schools in the UK, out of which, two are graduate entry. There are two additional postgraduate entry dental institutes that only accept graduated dentists. Therefore, this resource focuses on individual students (undergraduate and postgraduate) wishing to study dentistry.

Undergraduate Schools

Belfast
Queen's University Belfast, Centre for Dental Education
Grosvenor Road
Belfast
Royal Victoria Hospital
Northern Ireland
BT12 6BP
Tel: 02890 976268
Email: dentistry@qub.ac.uk
Web: qub.ac.uk/schools/mdbs/

Birmingham
Birmingham Dental Hospital and School of Dentistry
5 Mill Pool Way
Birmingham
B5 7EG
Tel: 0121 466 5472
Email: dentadmissions@contacts.bham.ac.uk
Web: www.birmingham.ac.uk/schools/dentistry/

Bristol
University of Bristol, Bristol Dental Hospital
Lower Maudlin Street
Bristol
BS1 2LY
Tel: 0117 394 1649
Email: choosebristol-ug@bristol.ac.uk
Web: bristol.ac.uk/dental/

Cardiff
Wales College of Medicine, School of Dentistry
Heath Park
Cardiff
CF14 4XY
Tel: 029 2074 6917/2468
Email:dentugadmissions@cardiff.ac.uk
Web: cardiff.ac.uk/dentistry

Dundee
University of Dundee, Dundee Dental School
Park Place
Dundee, Scotland
DD1 4HN
Tel: 01382 381 600
Email: asrs-dentistry@dundee.ac.uk
Web: dentistry.dundee.ac.uk/

Glasgow
University of Glasgow, Glasgow Dental Hospital and School
378 Sauchiehall Street
Glasgow
G2 3JZ
Tel: 0141 211 9703
Email: med-sch-dental-ug@glasgow.ac.uk
Web: gla.ac.uk/schools/dental

Leeds

University of Leeds, School of Dentistry
Leeds
LS2 9JT
Tel: 0113 343 9922
Email: denadmissions@leeds.ac.uk
Web: medicinehealth.leeds.ac.uk/dentistry

Liverpool

University of Liverpool, School of Dentistry
Pembroke Place
Liverpool
L3 5PS
Tel: 0151 794 2000 (BDS admissions tutor: 0151 706 5298)
Email: dentenq@liverpool.ac.uk
Web: www.liverpool.ac.uk/dentistry/

London – King's College

King's College London, Faculty of Dentistry
Guy's Tower
Guy's Hospital
Great Maze Pond
London
SE1 1UL
Tel: 020 7848 7000
Web: kcl.ac.uk/dentistry

London – Queen Mary University of London

Barts and the London School of Medicine and Dentistry, Garrod Building
Turner Street
London
E1 2AD
Tel: 020 7882 2240 / 8478
Email: smdadmissions@qmul.ac.uk
Web: qmul.ac.uk/dentistry/

Manchester

University of Manchester, Faculty of Biology, Medicine and Health
Oxford Road
Manchester
M13 9PL
Tel: 0161 306 0211
Email: ug.dentistry@manchester.ac.uk
Web: bmh.manchester.ac.uk/study/dentistry/

Newcastle

Newcastle University, School of Dental Sciences
Framlington Place
Newcastle upon Tyne
NE2 4BW
Tel: 0191 208 8245
Web: ncl.ac.uk/dental

Plymouth

University of Plymouth, Peninsula Dental School
Portland Square
Drake Circus
Plymouth
PL4 8AA
Tel: 01752 437333
Email: meddent-admissions@plymouth.ac.uk
Web: plymouth.ac.uk/schools/peninsula-school-of-dentistry

Sheffield

University of Sheffield, School of Clinical Dentistry
19 Claremont Crescent
Sheffield
S10 2TA
Tel: 0114 215 9304/9306
Email: dental.genenquiries@sheffield.ac.uk
Web: sheffield.ac.uk/dentalschool

Graduate Entry Schools

Graduate entry schools formally accept individuals who have previously completed an undergraduate degree.

Kings College London also offers a fast track (4 year) dentistry programme for graduates.

Plymouth and Barts and the London School of Medicine and Dentistry also formally accept graduates only into their 5-year graduate entry Dentistry programme.

More information on which schools consider graduates can be found later in this chapter.

Aberdeen
University of Aberdeen, Institute of Dentistry
Polwarth Building
Foresterhill
Aberdeen
AB25 2ZD
Tel: 01224 551 901
Email: dentistry@abdn.ac.uk
Web: abdn.ac.uk/dental/

Preston (University of Central Lancashire)
University of Central Lancashire, School of Dentistry
Preston
Lancashire
PR1 2HE
Tel: 01772 892 400
Email: cenenquiries@uclan.ac.uk
Web: uclan.ac.uk/schools/dentistry/

POSTGRADUATE ONLY DENTAL INSTITUTES (YOU DO NOT NEED TO CONSIDER THESE SCHOOLS)

These schools only accept dentists who have already graduated and wish to pursue further post-graduate dental studies.

- University College London, Eastman Dental Institute
- University of Edinburgh, Edinburgh Dental Institute

Keep this contact information at hand when visiting universities for open days, when calling Schools for further information, and even for results day if you need to quickly contact the universities.

Entry Criteria for Undergraduates

Knowing exactly what entry requirements the dental schools ask for should be one of the first questions running through your mind when considering applying.

It is estimated that approximately 60% of applications submitted to dentistry schools are rejected prior to interview. As such, fully understanding the intricacies of the admission criteria for your prospective university is of paramount importance.

Here's what you should know at the very least for each of the four dental schools you wish to consider selecting on your UCAS:

- Minimum GCSE requirements (including subjects and grades)
- A-level subjects and grades you must attain
- Whether the University accepts alternative academic qualifications such as Scottish or Irish Higher's, International Baccalaureate, BTEC, Access to HE Diploma, Cambridge Pre-U or other equivalent
- Is re-taking academic examinations allowed?
- Whether you must sit the UCAT or the BMAT assessment
- If so, how are these assessments used?
- Is there a cut-off score for these assessments?

- If UCAT, will the SJT component be factored in?
- If you plan to enter via a widening access or participation scheme, have you contacted the University to determine what the adjusted grades will be?
- If you are a mature student wishing to enter via an access scheme, have you first checked that this is suitable?

To save you time we have scoured the internet and taken the liberty of contacting the dental schools directly to ensure you have this information to hand.

Due to the large volume of information we have gathered, we have added a link to a freely viewable spreadsheet document. This 'Standard Entry Table' has been constructed with all the available information collated. Whilst we have taken extra care to ensure that this table is populated with the correct information, we strongly urge you to verify any information with the official university websites.

This table is useful for both undergraduates and postgraduates, however, we have also created an exclusive postgraduate table.

Postgraduate applicants should view the standard entry table, too, as this contains minimum entry criteria for other academic qualifications such as the A-levels which certain dental schools may require.

'Standard Entry Table'
Scan the QR code here.

Graduate Entry Table
Scan the QR code here.

‖ International students

Getting into dental school is slightly different for individuals classified as 'international students'. Although the application process is the same – i.e. you will still require equivalent entry requirements, to sit the UCAT and/or BMAT, and undertake an interview – there are additional factors to consider.

WHO COUNTS AS AN INTERNATIONAL STUDENT?

You are classed as an international student if you are from a country outside of the European Economic Area. A list of these countries can be found via scanning this QR code.

For those applying from overseas, the yearly intake for the number of students is limited by government guidance and controlled through targets operated by the Office For Students.

WHAT ARE THE STATISTICS ON PLACES AVAILABLE?

The anticipated overseas dental intake for 2019/20 can be viewed in this table available from the Office For Students. For the 2019/20 intake, there were 43 anticipated overseas students for dentistry in the UK.

How fees differ for international students?

Each University has its own fee structure. Individuals should contact the official universities to determine the costs.

Due to the clinical nature of dentistry requiring equipment, tools and materials, dentistry is one of the more costly courses for students. As a rough guide, fees are likely to be above £35,000 for each year of study. Furthermore, universities may require deposits payable on confirming your offer, and tuition fees may be subject to annual increases.

Please bear in mind that course fees only cover tuition, not living costs (including study tools and equipment such as books, computers etc.) The decision to pursue dentistry should not be taken lightly as the total cost can quite easily surpass six-figures.

Universities usually divide fee status of the students into 'home' and 'overseas' categories. Home students are usually citizens and residents living in the European Economic Area countries for at least three consecutive years.

More on the criteria for home status can be found on the UK Council For International Student Affairs.

Usually, in order to be classified as a home student, you must fulfil the following criteria:
- Be a citizen (so be able to live in the UK/EU/EEA unrestricted by visas)
- Be an ordinarily resident in the EEA (you must currently live in the UK/EU/EEA and be living here for at least the last three years)
- The reason you have lived here (UK/EU/EEA) has not been for education (for example you cannot be on a student visa)

What are the entry requirements for non-UK applicants?

Each UK Dental School will have their own requirements for which non-UK academic qualifications they accept. We advise international students to first visit the official university website to seek this information. A list of these schools can be found in the 'useful resources' section of this book.

Where the exact information cannot be found, applicants should contact universities directly to discuss their individual circumstances.

HELP COMPARING INTERNATIONAL & UK QUALIFICATIONS
The UK National Recognition Information Centre (NARIC) provides comparison statements for those with international qualifications wishing to study in the UK. As such, it can be used by those applying to UK Universities.

FINANCIAL HELP
If you are a student from an EU country, we advise you to visit the Student Finance website and contact the team for advice concerning your individual circumstances.

For those who would not be classed as 'home students', overseas fees should apply.

The following organisations provide guidance and help regarding funding:

UK Council for International Student Affairs

British Council office

UCAS website

BURSARIES & SCHOLARSHIPS
Individual university websites have detailed information on funding and scholarships.

General scholarship information can be found by contacting the British Council office.

TIER 4 (GENERAL) STUDENT VISAS

A Tier 4 Visa is required for entry into the UK to study. You should apply for this after you have been offered a place on a course. More information about student visas can be found on the UK government website and the UK Council for International Student Affairs.

LANGUAGE REQUIREMENTS

For international and EU/EEA students, evidence of your proficiency in the English language is a requirement for entry into UK dental schools.

These are examples of some of the accepted criteria used to determine English proficiency:

- IGCSE English
- International English Language Testing Service (IELTS)
- Pearson Test of English (PTE) Academic
- Cambridge English: Advanced (CAE), or Cambridge English: Proficiency (CPE)
- International Baccalaureate diploma.

You should check with individual universities to determine which of the above are accepted as well as minimum acceptable scores as each school has its own requirements.

Course Fees & Student Loans

TUITION FEES

Tuition charges are the costs that universities charge to deliver academic content and teaching. For dental school this usually covers the following:

- Lectures, seminars, and tutorials
- Clinical training sessions
- Phantom head practice
- Dental materials and equipment

- Access to course-related facilities and equipment (e.g. dental laboratories, cadavers, communication training)
- Access to campus libraries and computer rooms
- Support services for students

Student's home region	Studying in England	Studying in Scotland	Studying in Wales	Studying in Northern Ireland
England	Up to £9,250	Up to £9,250	Up to £9,000	Up to £9,250
Scotland	Up to £9,250	No fee	Up to £9,000	Up to £9,250
Wales	Up to £9,250	Up to £9,250	Up to £9,000	Up to £9,250
Northern Ireland	Up to £9,250	Up to £9,250	Up to £9,000	Up to £4,395
EU	Up to £9,250	No fee	Up to £9,000	Up to £4,395
Other international	Variable	Variable	Variable	Variable

2020/2021 Tuition fees taken from (https://www.ucas.com/finance/undergraduate-tuition-fees-and-student-loans)

Student Loans

Student loans are intended to cover your tuition fees and living expenses while studying (maintenance loans).

- Tuition fee loans are paid directly to the university. This is paid back after completing the course and when your income exceeds a certain threshold.
- Maintenance loans cover your living costs, such as accommodation, food, books etc. The amount you will receive depends on several factors, including: household income; university location; length of study; and the location at which you live.
- Grants are non-repayable sums of money that you may be offered if you meet certain eligibility criteria.

More information on student loans, grants and how to apply for one can be found on the following resources:
UCAS
Student Finance

‖ Graduate Entry Dentistry

If you are considering a graduate entry pathway, there are several considerations you need to make when determining which route to take.

In the UK, there are many courses available, spanning 3, 4 or even 5 years. Some universities formally accept graduates into their undergraduate BDS pathway via a graduate only entry pathway. Others informally accept graduates onto their singular BDS teaching programme, along with undergraduates, typically those applying directly from college.

The key difference is that those university courses which formally accept graduates are exclusively for graduate entrants and they have a set number of guaranteed vacancies for graduates.

Schools which may accept graduates via an informal route accept both undergraduate applications and graduates for the same course cohort. As such, graduates compete for entry along with other undergraduates. Certain Schools may also open intake for graduates and undergraduates via two separate course codes for the same academic year, meaning graduates and undergraduates don't directly compete but end up in the same year group.

This may sound a little confusing so we'll explain this in more detail below.

WHAT ENTRY PATHWAYS ARE AVAILABLE?
Graduate entry pathways can be divided into:

FORMALLY ACCEPT GRADUATES FAST-TRACK (3YR)	FORMALLY ACCEPT GRADUATES FAST-TRACK (4YR)	ACCEPT GRADUATES (5YR)

FAST TRACK (3 YEAR)
https://www.kcl.ac.uk/study/undergraduate/courses/
dentistry-entry-programme-for-medical-graduates-bds

Kings College London (A204) is currently the only UK institute to offer a 3-year fast track dentistry degree programme. This is exclusive for Medical Graduates Only.

ENTRY CRITERIA:
Applicants must be qualified doctors (registered with the UK General Medical Council) and have completed Foundation Years 1 and 2, and wish to pursue a career in either oral and maxillofacial surgery or oral medicine/pathology. UCAT is not needed for entry.

Universities Offering Formal Fast Track (4 years)

ABERDEEN (A201)
https://www.abdn.ac.uk/dental/study/bds/index.php#panel438

ENTRY CRITERIA:
Applicants must hold a good honours degree (1st or 2:1) in a medical science or health related degree from a UK university. If you are in doubt about the acceptability of your degree, please contact the Dental Admissions Office directly for advice. Please include details on the courses and content of your degree. For BSc Oral Health Sciences

students, evidence of academic excellence in their programme of study will be required.

Applicants must be able to demonstrate that they have achieved marks that would be at least equivalent level to an upper second/ first class performance on their degree programme. This could include details of individual modules and the level of attainment achieved.

Please note: due to the large number of graduate applicants with 2:1 Honours degrees or better, an additional qualification such as an MSc will not improve the chances of acceptance for those with 2:2 Honours degrees.

UCLAN (A202)

https://www.uclan.ac.uk/courses/bds_dentistry_graduate_entry.php

https://www.uclan.ac.uk/courses/assets/Frequently_Asked_ Questions_2016_updated.pdf

ENTRY CRITERIA:
2:1 Degree in a Biomedical discipline, plus 3 A-Levels at grade C or above (at least 2 must be from Biology, Physics, Chemistry and Mathematics). General Studies is not counted towards A Level entry.

KCL (A202)

https://www.kcl.ac.uk/study/undergraduate/courses/ dentistry-graduate-professional-entry-bds

This is one of Kings College London's formal dentistry pathways for graduates. The other being the three-year programme for medics only.

ENTRY CRITERIA:
- A minimum 2:1 (upper second class honours) undergraduate degree (or international equivalent) in a Biosciences subject, or

- A 2:2 (lower second class honours) undergraduate degree with a postgraduate degree (with at least a Merit) in a Bio-sciences subject.

Graduate applicants do not normally have to satisfy the usual A-level or other entry requirements. You are not expected to have A*AA at A-level on the first attempt. The minimum entry requirement is grade B at A-level in Chemistry and Biology, plus an upper second class honours degree. Alternatively, a lower second class honours degree combined with a master's degree (with at least a merit) is acceptable. Graduates who have a sufficient quantity of Biology or Chemistry as part of their degree may not need the A-Level in this subject.

KCL also allows graduate entrants to apply for the 5-year undergraduate programme.

Listing both A202 and A205 should maximize the chance of studying at King's

Universities Accepting Graduates (5-year programme)

PLYMOUTH (A206)

https://www.plymouth.ac.uk/courses/undergraduate/
bds-dental-surgery

ENTRY CRITERIA:

If applying as a graduate you will be classed as a non-direct school leaver. Candidates are shortlisted for interview by GAMSAT score only. As such, previous academic profile, performance at school, college or on the first degree will not be considered.

The GAMSAT (Graduate Medical Admissions Test) is the only academic entry requirement for non-direct school leavers.

GAMSAT thresholds are calculated annually, once all applications are received and the scores are collated. However, as a guide, the thresholds used during the 2018 application cycle (for 2019 entry) are included below:

Dentistry GAMSAT Cut off
Section 1 - 50
Section 2 - 54
Section 3 - 52
Overall - 56

Graduates from the University of Plymouth BSc (Hons) Dental Therapy and Hygiene (DTH) who achieved a distinction are invited to apply to join Year 2 of the Bachelor of Dental Surgery (BDS) degree. This entry route is valid for two years post BSc completion. All applications must be submitted through UCAS between 1 September and 15 October. All eligible applicants will be subject to the standard selection interview for the BDS course and all offers will be conditional.

For DTH graduates who did not achieve a distinction, the current process remains in place, requiring you to sit the GAMSAT exam to apply to join Year 1 of the BDS course.

Find out more about the GAMSAT here.

https://www.plymouth.ac.uk/uploads/production/document/
path/4/4170/GAMSAT_booklet.pdf

BARTS AND THE LONDON (A200)

ENTRY CRITERIA:

Graduates are eligible to apply for Dentistry (A200). The minimum academic entry requirements are an upper second class honours (2:1) degree. Degrees are divided into three categories:

- Bioscience degrees which DO contain sufficient biology and chemistry – no further A or AS level requirements.
- Candidates with science degrees lacking biology or chemistry must have a minimum A or AS level grade C for biology and/or chemistry (depending on what is missing in your degree).
- Non-science degrees. Candidates must have a minimum A or AS level grade B in chemistry or biology, plus one other science also at grade B.
- Accepted science subjects are Biology, Chemistry, Physics, Maths, and Psychology. You may apply with achieved or predicted grades. It is acceptable for a graduate applicant to take their required AS/A levels in order to achieve a grade B during or after their degree.

LIVERPOOL (A200)

https://www.liverpool.ac.uk/media/livacuk/study/undergraduate/healthsciencesentrycriteria/A200-Entry-2021.pdf

ENTRY CRITERIA:

2:1 classification in any subject (at the discretion of the Admissions Tutor). Only the first full degree which the applicant was awarded is considered. Foundation degrees are not accepted.

Those with a degree that is not classified (MBChB etc.) should have achieved an overall grade of 70% or above. A minimum of 3 A-levels at grade ABB or above, including Chemistry and Biology. The 3rd subject may be from the Arts or Sciences. However, General Studies, Critical Thinking and Vocational/Applied A- levels are not accepted. A minimum of 7 GCSEs at grade B/grade 6 or above, including Maths, English Language and a Science subject. Vocational/Applied GCSEs are not accepted. The GCSE requirements should be in place at the time of application. Unable to consider pending grades at GCSE level.

KCL (A205)

https://www.kcl.ac.uk/study/undergraduate/courses/dentistry-bds

This is Kings College London's 5-year Undergraduate Degree Pro-gramme, which accepts undergraduate applications and entries from graduate students.

ENTRY CRITERIA:
The same criteria for A202 applies to A205. Information on this is detailed later in the chapter.

Graduate applicants who do not wish to be considered for A202 may apply directly to A205 and their application will be considered in the normal way. Graduate applicants can list both A202 and A205 on their UCAS form if they wish to maximize their chances of studying at King's.

DUNDEE (A200)

https://www.dundee.ac.uk/undergraduate/dentistry/how-to-apply

ENTRY CRITERIA:
A minimum of an upper second class (2:1) Honours degree preferably in a relevant life science subject.

This should be the first degree obtained.

BRISTOL (A206)

http://www.bristol.ac.uk/study/undergraduate/2021/dentistry/bds-dentistry/

ENTRY CRITERIA:
Graduates are required to obtain a 2:1 in their degree and BBB at A-level including Chemistry and one of Biology, Physics or Mathematics.

BIRMINGHAM (A200)

https://www.birmingham.ac.uk/undergraduate/courses/med/dental-surgery.aspx#EntryRequirementsTab

ENTRY CRITERIA:

Graduates must have achieved 2:1 in a health sciences related degree (or 65% average if unclassified degree), and a minimum of ABB at A Level to include Chemistry and Biology plus one other.

CARDIFF (A200)

https://www.cardiff.ac.uk/__data/assets/pdf_file/0004/642649/UG_Admissions_Policy_-_General_Information_UG_Programmes.pdf

ENTRY CRITERIA:

Minimum of Upper Second class Honours classification in the first degree that they have taken.

CARDIFF (A204)

This 6-year course (with a preliminary year) is for those who have attained AAA with either no science subject or a maximum of one science subject (from Biology, Chemistry or physics). For applicants taking Science A-levels, a pass in the practical elements is normally required. General studies and critical thinking is not acceptable.

Graduate applicants can apply for admission to either the 5-year (A200) or the 6-year (A204) Bachelor of Dental Surgery programmes, according to their previous academic experience in the sciences.

Applicants must have completed their degree or must be in the final year of their Current degree programme in order for their application to be considered.

Glasgow (A200)

https://www.gla.ac.uk/schools/dental/

Entry Criteria:
The Dental School considers applications from graduates who have a 2.1 Honours degree or equivalent (e.g. GPA of 3.0 or above) in a relevant subject, and must demonstrate the equivalence of Chemistry and Biology (Grade A, A Level/Higher) and Maths or Physics (Grade B, GCSE/Higher) obtained within the last 6 years. Please be aware that a graduate who has attained a 2.2 Honours degree will not be considered for entry, regardless of whether they have undertaken an additional qualification such as an MSc.

Graduate applicants who have obtained an MBChB and at least part one of the MCRS may be considered for entry to year 2 of the 5-year BDS programme. However, entry to year 2 is not guaranteed and is dependent on a space being available in year 2. If no places in year 2 are available, the candidate may be offered entry to year 1 and would be expected to complete the full 5-year degree.

Due to the nature of BDS, Glasgow do not offer an accelerated entry to graduates from any other subject area.

Newcastle (A206)

https://www.ncl.ac.uk/mediav8/study-with-us/general-documents/applications-amp-offers/admissions-policy-2019-entry.pdf

Entry Criteria:
Graduates are accepted onto the full 5-year course. A degree with a 2:1 or higher is required, and must include Biology and Chemistry as a significant percentage of the degree.

QUEENS BELFAST (A200)

https://www.qub.ac.uk/courses/undergraduate/pdf/howwechooseour-students/Filetoupload,927402,en.pdf

ENTRY CRITERIA:

Applications from graduates or those in the final year of their degree are considered and the full academic background is taken into account. The minimum A-level threshold (or equivalent in other qualifications) is either BBB at first attempt, i.e. prior to commencing degree studies for those with an Upper Second Class Honours degree, or BBC at the first attempt for those with a First Class Honours Degree or a PhD and an Upper Second Class Honours degree. Applicants must have an appropriate science background at GCSE and A-level or equivalent (see below) and at least a 2.1 Honours classification in their primary (first) degree, which can be from a wide range of different subjects. A-levels in Chemistry and Biology/Human Biology are required. In addition, GCSE Mathematics minimum grade C/4 is required, if not offered at AS-level or A-level. Graduate applicants who fulfil these criteria are then scored with their UCAT.

Graduate applicants from a non-science background but who fulfil the conditions in terms of grades achieved at the first attempt (i.e. in their original choice of A-level subjects) and degree performance will be considered if they undertake the appropriate Science quali-fications on completion of their degree.

MANCHESTER (A206)

https://www.manchester.ac.uk/study/undergraduate/courses/2021/00398/bds-dentistry-first-year-entry/application-and-selection/#course-profile

ENTRY CRITERIA:

Applications from graduates or those in their final year of study towards an undergraduate degree are welcome. You should have achieved or be predicted to achieve a minimum of an upper second (2:1) honours degree and should have achieved a minimum of BBB at A-level (32 in IB) in your first sitting.

Applicants with a relevant science degree are exempt from subject specification at A-Level, but the BBB academic standard must be met. Relevant subjects include most Biomedical and Life Sciences disciplines or other approved courses. Please visit the university's FAQ pages.

Applicants offering other degrees will need to hold at least two science subjects at A-level, including Biology and Chemistry.

Please note that ordinary or ungraded degrees are not accepted. If you have a non-relevant degree and don't have the requisite science A-levels you are eligible to apply for the university's foundation year. Alternatively, you may sit the missing A-level subject(s) and apply for the 5-year course.

LEEDS

ENTRY CRITERIA:
To apply as a graduate, a 2:1 or higher in a relevant science or health-care subject plus GCSE Maths at grade 4 or C is required.

Applications from those who have taken, or intend to take, A-Level re-sits can be accepted. Only one re-sit per subject (i.e. a total of two attempts) will be accepted. Applicants with more than one re-sit in the same subject will not be considered without an exceptionally strong case of mitigating circumstances.

SHEFFIELD (A200)

ENTRY CRITERIA:
Minimum of 6 grade As or Grade 7s at GCSE to include Maths, English Language and Science, plus a 2.1 in a core science degree, plus the UCAT test.

Sheffield do consider re-sit applicants and those applicants who reapply.

Can't find what you're looking for on the official university website?

If the qualifications you have attained are not detailed on the university or dental school website, you are advised to email the School with a detailed list of the qualifications you have taken including, where required, transcripts of study showing module results and year of study.

For ease, we have summarized the findings of all the criteria available online into these tables.

STANDARD ENTRY CRITERIA

This table gives information about every dental school in the UK and categorizes the entry requirements for undergraduates and post-graduates. Some of the academic requirements that must be met by the graduate entrant are available on here. Please note: we have aimed to ensure this information is factual and up to date, however with admissions process constantly changing, so we advise you to always use the official university website to verify any information printed here.

GRADUATE ENTRY CRITERIA

This table displays the universities which offer graduate entry and those which may accept graduates alongside undergraduates onto their existing BDS programmes.

Non-Standard Entry

Commencing a dentistry degree later in life can be hugely rewarding.

For those individuals who may have been out of education for some time and wish to enter as mature students, there are a number of valid pathways to entry. It is of utmost importance to first contact the universities directly as these applications are often unique and the universities may deal with them on a case-by-case basis.

For those mature students who may wish to consider an access course such as an Access to High Education Diploma, it is important to determine what is accepted. You should determine whether the Dentistry Diploma is recognised by the 'Quality Assurance Agency for Higher Education' (www.accesstohe.ac.uk), as many universities will want to ensure the education is quality assured. Often, these entry qualifications are considered acceptable for those applicants who were unable to continue their formal education at school or college post-16 (e.g. for personal reasons). It is not usually an acceptable qualification for applicants who have sat, but failed to attain, the needed grades at GCE A2 Level, degrees for entry initially. In all cases, contacting the prospective university is prudent to ensure that all your current and intended qualifications meet their entry requirements.

Maximising Your Chances As A Graduate

Benefits of Being a Graduate

Graduates with additional years of education and life experience have had a chance to develop and enhance their professional and personal characteristics, habits and skills. These skills acquired during university life are also developed in the network and environment around you.

If you are a graduate, the breadth of related skills, activities or experiences which you have picked up along the way may not be obvious to you.

Be sure to reflect on these skills and state them clearly in your statement in order to optimize your chances. Here's a list of skills, experiences and activities you could consider including:

DEGREE RELATED

- Undertaken dental related modules (i.e. Head & Neck Anatomy, Oral Physiology etc.)
- Partaking in academic research projects
- Involvement in publications and appraising research
- Undertaking practical skills laboratory experiments
- Performing cadaver dissections evidencing manual dexterity
- Data analysis and critical reasoning
- Involved with self-directed learning
- Worked with larger team to culminate results or achieve a larger goal
- Mentored younger students
- Involved with teaching
- Worked with individuals from differing backgrounds
- Attained a prize, award or accolade

NON-DEGREE RELATED

- Community, religious or charitable activity involvement
- Regular volunteering
- Part of a wider organization or team i.e. member of society at university, team sport or involved in event organization
- Travelled to different countries, integrating with difference backgrounds
- Charitable work abroad
- Partaking in hobbies related to problem solving, skill development, creativity, manual dexterity.
- Part-time work related to customer service, patient care or management
- General life skills and confidence
- Developing a better work-life balance

Financing a Postgraduate Degree:

There is a significant difference in the financial support you can receive depending upon whether you gain a place on the 4-year fast track dentistry program or on a traditional 5-year undergraduate program.

The 4-year program entitles you to student finance from Year 1, which includes a tuition fee loan and maintenance loan, plus a grant if you qualify.

In addition, you can claim an NHS bursary from the NHS Business Services Authority (NHSBSA) from your 2nd year of study, which partially contributes to your tuition fees and provides you with a monthly stipend for living expenses, including a means-tested component.

For students who have gained a place on the 4-year fast track program, because you don't receive the NHS Bursary until the 2nd year of the course, you will have to pay the portion of your tuition fees in Year 1, which is later paid by the NHS Bursary in years 2, 3 and 4. This means you should start to save well in advance of starting your course to avoid financial difficulties and stress during your studies.

For students who are graduates and have gained a place on a 5-year undergraduate program, there is very little in terms of financial support for most of the degree programme. Students have to self-fund the entire tuition fee for years 1- 4 and are not eligible for the NHS Bursary until the final year of study. In Year 5, students can receive the full tuition fee amount as part of their NHS bursary. Students can apply for the student finance maintenance loan for the duration of the course.

For students with childcare costs, support is available from NHSBSA if you are in receipt of funding from them. Alternatively, student finance may provide support.

When you are a student of dentistry, each university will offer financial advice and will have their own schemes for providing hardship funds for students who are struggling financially during the course and this will vary between different universities.

Life as a Graduate Dentistry Student

Entering university as a graduate to study dentistry can be highly rewarding. Here, we have interviewed two current dentistry graduate entrants to learn more about their journey to dental school. If you are a graduate entrant and have doubts about your prospects you might find these articles inspiring examples of entering dentistry at a late stage of your career.

Entering Dentistry After Biomedical Sciences

Brinder Singh Shergill is currently a graduate dentistry student in his fourth year at Glasgow Dental School. Brinder initially studied Bio-medical Sciences (Hons) at Royal Holloway, The University of London and attained 2:1. He then worked for four years in the NHS and private medical sector as a Territory Manager. He later developed a keen interest in dentistry and judiciously decided to embark upon his studies at a later stage.

Learn more about his journey on our website via scannig this code.

Entering Dentistry After Dental Hygiene and Therapy

Khushbu Morar BSc MSc is currently in her 1st year at UCLAN Dental School. Khushbu is an excellent example of how commitment, perseverance and a relentless work ethic can propel one to gain a place at Dental School. Khushbu left high school and 6th form and lacked the required entry criteria for Dentistry. So she re-sat some of her A-level modules while also completing an NVQ Level 3 in Dental Nursing to enhance her chances of gaining a place to study Dental Hygiene and Therapy at Cardiff University. But she didn't stop there!

Khushbu wanted to increase her scope of practice, so she applied for Dentistry in her final year. Unfortunately, once again she was unsuccessful with 4 straight rejections! Many may have been exhausted by now but Khushbu's determination enthused her to complete a Masters in Oral Biology in 2018-2019 and reapply. On her second application, she finally succeeded in gaining her, much deserved, place at UCLAN.

Hear about her exciting pathway here by scanning this code.

How to Choose Between Each University

With so many choices of dental schools, it can be difficult to know if the four universities you choose are the best match for you.

There may be lots of questions running through your mind: "Do I choose a lecture-based course or PBL?"; "Shall I live near home?"; "Should I choose a university that does not require the UCAT?" And many, many more.

We have put together the main factors which tend to influence decision-making when deciding which university to choose. This by no means is a definitive solution but should be adequate as a guide. Remember to use this in addition to your own personal views when contemplating your selection of four final choices.

LOCATION
When it comes to location, there are a few things you should consider. There are several factors that you can take into account to help make this decision. These include: distance from university to your home; the university's location; the cost of living; the campus and the accommodation available.

Visit universities on open days to help you make a decision. As well as touring the campus facilities, ask questions and spend time getting a feel for the city where you may have to spend 4 to 5 years.

It's worth visiting the university campus, the area local to where the dental school is located and the city of the university.

COURSE STRUCTURE

Each university has a different style of teaching. It's important to identify which style suits you best as you will be committing 4 to 5 years of study there. Currently, the 3 major teaching styles are EBL, PBL and lecture-based learning. We recommend that you research each teaching style using the university websites, and attending open days where you can partake in taster learning sessions. You could try attending a sample EBL lesson to experience how each teaching style differs to help you find the most suitable one for you.

The nature of the clinical exposure you will receive is another important factor to consider. The amount of time you spend at clinics with patients or on outreach programmes, electives and hospitals varies across the country. Speaking to students and reading about course structure on university websites is the best way to get an understanding of the pros and cons of the clinical aspects of the course.

OPPORTUNITIES AVAILABLE

Each university is unique in the different opportunities it offers, be it academic or social.

If you are more academically inclined, you may prefer universities that provide you the opportunity to join research societies or do an intercalated degree.

On the other hand, some universities may offer societies that you really like (dental or non-dental related), so speaking to students and reading about the student union is the perfect way to check out societies.

Success Rates

Contact individual universities and read through their websites to get an idea of your chances of successfully getting an interview, and how you might fare after interview. Whilst some universities accept about 65% of candidates after interviews, others accept only up to 35%. You can use this information to give yourself a few 'safe options' to increase your chances of obtaining an offer. We recommend having one safe option and then choosing three universities that you really love.

UCAT & BMAT

Your UCAT/BMAT, personal statement, GCSE grades and predicted grades will be used differently by each university. Contacting each university to find out how they use each of these different pieces of data in their selection procedure gives you a better idea of which university is more likely to grant you an interview.

For example, QMUL uses a 50:50 weighting on academic and UCAT whilst Bristol gives GCSE 15% weighting, A-Level predicted/achieved 15% weighting and Personal statement and UCAT 35% each. Once you have this information for your top choices, it may be easier to narrow down your choices.

Ranking

University league tables can be a useful guide to gauging a university based on objective measures. It's important, however, to only use this as a guide and think about the other factors already mentioned.

University ranking tables may use criteria such as: entry standards; student satisfaction; research quality; research intensity and graduate prospects.

For any league table, you should carefully appraise how the rank has been decided and importantly, base your decision on the aforementioned factors, too.

UNIVERSITY OPEN DAYS

University open days can really help you make an informed decision. They are a great way to meet current students, view the dental facilities, experience the campus and have a glimpse of the city.

We strongly recommended that you visit every university that you aim to apply for a place at. Find out the dates the open days as early as possible and use our 'Open Day Checklist' to objectively compare UK dental schools.

5th Choice Option

When you apply to study dentistry through UCAS, you are only allowed to use four of your five course choices for 'Dentistry' itself, leaving you with an unused fifth choice.

By having access to the information within this book, you are putting yourself in a good position for your application. However, despite anyone's best efforts, dentistry is still an extremely competitive course to get into, therefore it's important to have a Plan B and carefully consider an alternate route.

Students often worry about being put at a disadvantage for using the fifth choice for an alternate course. This is not the case. Universities encourage applicants to use this option and it by no means suggests that you lack the intent to study dentistry. Rather it allows you to plan for all possible outcomes.

Selecting a fifth choice is not mandatory, however, and we suggest you should only add a fifth choice if you truly wish to go down this route.

There are many factors that you should take into consideration when selecting your fifth choice. Here are some suggestions:

- Choose a degree you would still enjoy. This is equally as important as you may have to spend at least 3 years studying this chosen course so you need to make sure it will be something you will enjoy doing, at a location that suits you.
- Future finances. At the time of writing, most UK students are only able to get a Tuition Loan from Student Finance for a single undergraduate course, with the exception of gaining a place onto an Accelerated Graduate Entry Dentistry course, where you will continue to get tuition loans.
- The entry requirements for graduates who choose to apply for Accelerated Graduate Entry Dentistry courses vary greatly so you need to make sure that your fifth-choice option is suitable. For example, they may require you to have a Biomedical Sciences degree.
- Job prospects from your fifth-choice degree option. Should you be unable to obtain a place on a dentistry course applying as a graduate, or if you decide whilst undertaking your first undergraduate degree that dentistry is no longer for you, you should research what job opportunities might be available after you complete that degree.

The best way to check whether your fifth choice option will allow you to apply to dentistry courses in the future is to either: check the entry requirements regarding graduate entry on the website of the dental schools you are interested in, or contact the dental schools directly.

WHAT ABOUT MY PERSONAL STATEMENT?

Universities are acutely aware that those who wish to study dentistry are limited to only four choices so the fifth choice will be a non-dentistry option. For this reason, your carefully tailored personal statement specifically concerning your entry into dentistry will bear no relevance to that fifth-choice degree course. Fortunately, you won't be at any disadvantage as the course providers are fully aware that it will not be related with their course and that many applicants choose this route as a backup.

Open Day Checklist

Dentistry university open days are extremely useful for gaining a deeper insight into what life could be like as a dental student at university.

We have created a unique checklist featuring common criteria used by dentistry students when choosing between dental schools.

Print our checklist, take it to your open day and use it as a personal assessment tool for you to objectively rank each university. This will no doubt help you make a clear, straight forward decision. Good luck!

Dentistry University Open Day Checklist							
Dental School Selection Criteria							
University Name	Location	Course Structure	Entry Requirements	Success Rate	Opportunities	Ranking	My Overall Score
Belfast							
Birmingham							
Bristol							
Cardiff							
Dundee							
Glasgow							
Leeds							
Liverpool							

Dentistry University Open Day Checklist							
Dental School Selection Criteria							
University Name	Location	Course Structure	Entry Requirements	Success Rate	Opportunities	Ranking	My Overall Score
London – King's College							
London – Barts							
Manchester							
Newcastle							
Plymouth							
Sheffield							
Aberdeen							
Preston (University of Central Lancashire)							

CHAPTER 4

DENTAL WORK
EXPERIENCE

INTRODUCTION

This chapter features everything you need to know about work experience in dentistry. We'll cover the following:

- What constitutes work experience?
- Do I need to carry out work experience?
- Where, when and how to gain work experience?
- Template letter for email/ phone calls
- How to gain value from your experience
- Things to do if work experience is not feasible (COVID-19)

So, what constitutes 'work experience'?

Work experience covers any type of work you undertake before or during a chosen career path.

It can range from experience gained in a current role you formally hold (such as an existing job), or more commonly for those applying to dentistry, through shadowing or observation.

Due to the nature of dentistry, work experience is often limited to observations within the clinical setting that the dentist works. There are, however, certain hands-on activities that can be completed during work experience which we'll discuss shortly.

Do I need to obtain work experience?

Most importantly, work experience gives you first-hand insight into the daily life of a dentist with tasks including the clinical, managerial, administrative and leadership roles that a dentist has within the team.

Work experience gives you the opportunity to demonstrate your commitment to your chosen career pathway and helps you gain insight into the profession. In addition, this period of observation provides university applicants with evidence and experience to discuss and reflect upon in their personal statement and during their interviews.

Candidates should be aware that gaining work experience to satisfy entry requirements is essential but most important is your capacity to reflect on that experience. Therefore, it's important to use the experience to learn what you were not aware of, reflect how this has influenced your decision and how the skills and characteristics you observed relate to your personal attributes.

Observing also gives you knowledge of the different roles and responsibilities for each member of the dental team.

So we strongly advise you to speak to all members of the team and discuss their duties to determine how they play a part in the wider team. At an interview and in your personal statement, referencing that you have understood that dentists are part of a wider team shows insight and that you have researched the career properly in order to gain a thorough understanding.

As discussed in Chapter 1, a career as a dentist brings various challenges and benefits. The period of observation with a dentist can be used to ascertain the various aspects you may personally find difficult. It's important to use this time to be frank with yourself and realistically determine whether you can envisage yourself doing this type of work.

Where, When & How to Gain Work Experience

WORKING IN DIFFERENT SETTINGS

Gaining experience in a variety of settings is highly valuable as it proves that you have researched the career.

Remember, dentistry involves a wider team including (but is not limited to) dental nurses, laboratory technicians, therapists, hospital dentists and specialist dentists.

Each member of the dental team has a specific role in caring for a patients' dental needs. You should observe and take note of the qualities expressed by each member and the remit of each member's responsibilities.

An additional benefit from spending time with various team members also helps you develop an idea of the different career pathways in dentistry and how the entire team interconnects.

If practical, visiting and shadowing a registered GDC dental specialist can give you more clarity on the intricacies of dentistry, the complexities that may occur, and the advanced equipment and techniques used to treat these patients.

WHEN TO DO WORK EXPERIENCE

According to most universities, the personal statement should show evidence that applicants have researched their preferred professions and undertaken some work experience before applying. You should have at least a minimum of two weeks work experience under your belt in a varied range of dental settings. However, check the exact work experience requirements expected by your prospective dental schools on their websites.

In summary, having work experience before you write your personal statement and submit your UCAS application is critical.

For timelines and deadlines for UCAS application dates see Chapter 2 'The UCAS Application'.

You could also benefit from engaging in work experience shortly before any upcoming interviews as a 'refresher'. Use the additional opportunity to discuss any questions you may still have and talk to team members that you may have missed before. If you struggle to book an observation period, ask instead whether you can come in to visit the practice during a lunch break. Speaking to the dentist and wider team during this time will also prove to be very useful in contributing to your cumulative 'experience'.

How to Gain Work Experience

Unfortunately, despite there being a large number of dental practices in the UK, individuals still find it troublesome to gain exposure to clinical settings for observational purposes. Don't be disheartened if you get lots of rejections at first. There are several techniques you can use to enhance your chances of getting accepted.

Here is a list of people and resources that might help you find a place to get some work experience:
- Friends and family members that may work in dentistry
- Your personal / family dentist
- The dental laboratory that your dentist uses
- Your orthodontist
- A Google search for 'dentists near me'
- NHS 'find a dentist' https://www.nhs.uk/service-search/find-a-dentist

When contacting these individuals, it's very important to demonstrate a professional manner and have a clear explanation of who you are and why you are contacting them.

It's worth knowing that many keen students contact general dental practices only to be quickly dismissed by the receptionist. The key here is to quickly establish a rapport and obtain the details of the dental practice manager. Ultimately it is the manager (and the practice owner) that has the authority to grant you permission to observe. Although speaking to the practice owner is ideal, in most cases they will be busy, so the manager is usually the best person to contact.

WHAT DO I SAY?

For many practices the telephone is constantly ringing. The dental reception team's priority is dealing with patients at the desk so it's vital that you are clear and concise when contacting the practice. Ideally you will establish a rapport and obtain the practice manager's email address. Once you have this, we recommend that you note the name of the receptionist and send a well formulated follow up email request for work experience.

Here is a template you can use when contacting the person of authority at a dental practice, dental laboratory or hospital.

‖ Template letter for dental work experience

Subject: Dentistry Work Experience – Observation
Dear (Name of person of authority),
I spoke to your receptionist (name) today, who kindly forwarded me your details.
My name is (name).

I am currently studying in year (year) at (college/university) and wish to pursue dentistry as a career.

I am at the critical point of determining my career options ahead of my application to university. I am therefore using all the time I have to gather experience and knowledge in the field of dentistry to better my career decision and help strengthen my application for dental school.

As you may be aware, work experience for dentistry is becoming an essential criterion. I'd be most grateful if you could allow me the opportunity to undertake a period of observation at your practice

/ hospital/ dental laboratory, which would be a valuable learning experience.

Thank you in advance for considering my request. I am available to start immediately and look forward to hearing from you.

Here are my contact details.
Full Name:
Email:
Phone:
Yours sincerely,
(name)

How to Make the Most of Your Experience

Once you have secured a place to start observation, there are several things to consider to get the most value out of your experience.

As touched upon earlier in this chapter, it's essential to be able to reflect upon your period of work experience. It is the detailed appraisal of your time spent observing and learning that will be extracted at interview and from your personal statement. Here are some tips for making the most of your placement for future reference:

- Make a list of what you learnt. These will form fantastic discussion points for your interview and can be used to expand your personal statement
- Observe and record the key personal characteristics of the dentist and the wider team and link them to your own skills and traits
- Note any challenges you witnessed and how the team overcame them, focusing on the attributes demonstrated
- Have a basic understanding of the types of procedures seen and some of the specific equipment used. This will impress the interviewers
- Aim to observe a broad variety of clinicians, including other members of the team if possible. Take note of their roles and responsibilities

- If possible, aim to gain experience in a wide range of settings such as a general dental practice (NHS & private), hospital, community, dental labs etc.
- Talk to all team members, especially to the dental nurse (this is the dentist's closest team colleague)
- Visit and observe at a dental laboratory (if possible, follow up on a case that you may have observed in the clinic). The lab may allow you to undertake a hands-on exercise such as making wax carvings or helping polish dentures.

In summary, aim to acquire a wide range of experience and to do so early on. Use the tips above to gain the most value from the time you spent on your placement. The knowledge and detailed reflection from this will help structure a well-rounded personal statement and give you ample points to discuss during interviews.

What to do if work experience is not feasible?

As we write this book, the world is facing a global pandemic – COVID-19

The current buzzword is "unprecedented", and it is easy to see why. School is out the window, the work experience you spent weeks organizing may be cancelled, and it might be seeming like your chances of getting into dental school are slipping away.

If your work experience has been cancelled then much of the previous information within this chapter may not be directly relevant to you. However, despite work experience being cancelled, there are many ways for you to gain insight into the career. Use this downtime to your advantage and boost your application in other ways. These include:

VOLUNTEERING
In the current climate, it's unlikely that dental practices will be opening their doors for observation anytime soon. However, this

does not preclude you from gaining some of the benefits that work experience provides.

One of the main learning points from work experience is recognition of the salient traits, characteristics and interpersonal skills exercised by the clinician. Fortunately, you don't need to be in a dental setting to gain this. There are other settings in which you will be able to gain this credible experience. Look around in your local area and see how you can help in these times.

Are local care homes looking for voluntary help?
Are food banks or soup kitchens looking an extra pair of hands?

You might even be able to set up a local initiative providing support for the elderly and vulnerable. All of these things will demonstrate that you are a proactive, compassionate individual and willing to help – and all require excellent communication skills.

Seek Insight by Reaching out to Current Dentists & Dental Students

Even if you are not able to directly observe dentists you can still learn a lot from them. Get in contact and ask questions about what it's like being a dentist – the pros and cons, what a normal day or week would look like.

Also use this opportunity to learn from their experiences. Perhaps what would they have done differently, or what in their journey made them successful?

You can find many influential dental students and dentists online. For instance on Instagram, YouTube and Facebook, politely reaching out to these individuals can give you further insight and inspiration.

Undertake Online Dentistry Courses

The internet is a wonderful resource, where you can gain further exposure to what a career in dentistry may provide you with.

Although you may not be able to gain direct physical access to observing a clinician, there are hundreds, if not thousands of resources online to help you learn more about the profession. Lots of universities run free online courses, which give you a foundation of knowledge to discuss at interviews.

Free resources that you may wish to access include:

- Discover Dentistry – The University of Sheffield
  https://www.futurelearn.com/courses/discover-dentistry

Introduction to Dental Medicine – The University of Pennsylvania
https://www.coursera.org/learn/dental-medicine-penn

- I Want To Be A Dentist- The ' Dentistry Experience'
  https://www.iwanttobeadentist.com/work-experience-dentistry

We have developed a free online course 'The Dentistry Experience Course'. This course is a short modular programme designed for those wishing to learn more about dentistry. This course is not intended to replace traditional work experience. However, it aims to provide more information about the career and relevant topics surrounding it. Scan this code to learn more.

TAKE UP A NEW HOBBY

Now is a great time to brush up on your manual dexterity. Although you will not be required to possess exceptional dexterity, showing evidence that you are eager to build these skills is beneficial. There are many activities you may wish to take up, including (but not limited to): knitting; painting; playing musical instruments; woodwork; sewing; crochet; origami; model-making; cross-stitch; ceramics... The list is endless. Our advice is to pick something you enjoy, find a few YouTube videos, and practice!

When you discuss your adopted skill in your personal statement, reflect on it and show that you have worked hard at it and seen an improvement.

Conduct Your Own Mini Research Project

Many students will undertake an extended project qualification, but if you haven't, you can still tackle a project under your own initiative. It doesn't have to be a huge dissertation. Instead, you could research a topic and present it when back at school.

It will only be as complicated as you make it. Pick a simple topic that you are interested in and will be able to confidently discuss at the interview.

You could debate a controversial topic such as water fluoridation, or explain the link between oral health and whole-body conditions. Not only will this reinforce your enthusiasm, but presentations and public speaking are key communication skills that are good discussion points in your personal statement and interviews.

The key is to capitalize on the time you have. Don't feel that a lack of dental work experience equates to a poor application. After all, in these 'unprecedented times', many applicants will be in the same boat. As detailed in the chapter, there are numerous methods to substantiate your application and allow you to gain further career insight and detail into a career in dentistry.

CHAPTER 5

THE SELECTION
PROCESS

INTRODUCTION

This chapter will cover everything you need to know from the assessment tests required by the universities, to the typical interview scenarios and questions that you should prepare yourself for.

There are four parts to this chapter. If you are just preparing for your assessments then focus on part 1 for now. If you have received an interview then you should skip to part 2 and 4. Part 3 is dedicated for international applicants.

We have also included a full practice mock interview with answers to help you prepare and ace your dental interviews.

Below are the following contents of this chapter.

- Part 1: Pre-interview – Assessment Tests
  - What is the BMAT and how is it used
  - Dental Schools Requiring BMAT
  - Topic Breakdown
  - Essential Revision Tools
  - What is the UCAT and How it's Used
  - Timeline
  - Topic Breakdown
  - Dental Schools Requiring UCAT
  - Revision Ethic
  - Materials for Success

- Part 2: The Interview – Formats & Techniques
  - Interview formats
  - MMI Interviews Versus Traditional Panel Interviews
  - Common Interview Questions & Scenarios
  - Manual Dexterity Tests
  - Interview Do's & Don'ts
  - Expectations & How to Conduct Yourself
  - Station Specific Questions & Advice
  - 100 Interview Questions
  - Key Terminology

- Part 3: International Applicants & Interviews
  - Selecting a University
  - UCAS & Funding
  - Example Interview Questions
  - Preparing for International Applicants Interview (Skype or in person)

- Part 4: The Mock Interview
  - Simulated Mock Interview
  - Answers & Analysis

PART 1

Pre-interview - Assessment tests

A lot of candidates tend to worry about how they will perform in the interview, but overlook the fact that they have to attain it first. Part of your application to dental school will require you to sit an admissions test. For UK dental and medical schools, there are two admissions tests that you could do; the Biomedical Admissions Test (BMAT) or the University Clinical Aptitude Test (UCAT). Different universities will require different entrance exams. Each test is different in structure and format; testing different qualities that a medical professional may need in their career.

What is the BMAT and how is it used?

The BMAT will be a very familiar format of exam as it is very similar to other exams you may have sat in the past such as GCSEs and A-levels. It's a standard 3-part paper exam with each section individually timed. The first two sections are multiple choice, whereby one answer is correct and the rest are wrong. The final section is different as it is an essay that you have to write. The only piece of equipment you will be allowed is a pencil; this is a non-calculator exam.

BMAT Section	Questions	Duration
Section 1 - Aptitude and Skills	32	60 mins
Section 2 - Scientific Skills	27	30 mins
Section 3 - Essay	1 (From a choice of 3)	30 mins

2020 Timeline

For the BMAT, there are usually two main sittings: one is in September and the other is late October/early November.

Due to COVID-19, the September test date has been cancelled, however the November test date remains. Further 2020 BMAT updates can be found via this link.

Registration for the November sitting is around September. Once you have completed your test, you will receive a Metritests login where you can sign in to the BMAT site and access your exam results, usually a month after you sat the exam.

Below is the latest 2020 timeline at the time of publication:

Date	Event
1st September 2020	BMAT – November registration opens Centres can register candidates from this date
30th September 2020	Last date to request modified question papers
1st October 2020 (5pm BST)	Standard fee BMAT – November registration closes
15th October 2020 (6pm BST)	Late fee BMAT – November registration closes Last date to request Access Arrangements Last date to request reimbursement of BMAT - November fees
4th November 2020	BMAT – November test date
27th November 2020	BMAT – November results released
4th December 2020	Last date for BMAT – November Results Enquiries

SCORING

Sections 1 and 2 are scored on a scale from 1.0 to 9.0. The average score achieved is around 5.0. Better candidates get results of 6.0 and a few exceptional candidates will get a score of 7.0 or higher. Section 3 has a slightly different scoring method; you have a number value from 1 to 5, and a letter score from A to G. For example: 4B, 3C, 5D etc. The number score reflects the quality of your answer's content and the letter represents the grammar, spelling and structure of your answer. Two examiners will look at your essay and each give a score to make sure the final grade is accurate. If there is a significant disparity, a third examiner will be brought in to check the essay and give the final grade.

Which dental schools require BMAT?

The only dental school which requires BMAT is Leeds Dental School. As a prospective dental applicant, it may seem to be a considerable amount of effort just for one school. However, there are many reasons for the BMAT for Leeds being a very good option.

- The different style of entrance exam may better suit you than the UCAT. If your scientific knowledge is coherent and you have confidence in your essay writing and analytical abilities, it may be well worth you attempting the BMAT as you may naturally get a better score.
- Leeds can provide you another chance at applying for dental school if your UCAT score is unfavourable towards the other dental schools that you are applying to. Having an extra chance at applying to dental school could potentially save you another year of waiting before applying again. Remember, you can only take the entrance exams once per admission cycle!
- Leeds is a great and diverse city. The university has a very inclusive and broad range of societies, where you can find any group to fit into. The dental community is very close-knit and whatever help or support you may want at your time in Leeds, you can find it there!

Topic breakdown

SECTION 1 - APTITUDE AND SKILLS

The first section relates to the different skills you may need working as any medical professional. There are two main skills which section 1 tests for: problem solving (reasoning using mathematical skills); and critical thinking (reasoning using written language). Many of the problems that you'll face in your career can't be learned simply from a text book and therefore having a problem solving mindset is very useful. Critical thinking is important as you may be asked to put forward an argument or draw a conclusion, requiring you to explain things or interpret information/data.

The types of questions are in various formats, including charts, graphs and tables of data from which you'll be asked to extrapolate information in a multitude of ways. You'll be asked to calculate certain things, interpret some portions of the data or be given a scenario for which you need to calculate specific results.

For some of the written questions, you may be given a text or article in which you could be asked to identify a flaw or any assumptions that may have been made within the text itself (if it's presenting an argument). Sometimes you can be given a series of statements on the text itself and be asked which ones of those statements are true or false.

Here are some key tips to help you in section 1:

- **Make sure you read the question first** and then go through the context of the question to look for the answer. Time is very limited for entrance exams so any method which helps you save time on a question will be useful. In this case, identifying key parts of the question and parsing through the given context to find the answer is much more efficient than just reading all the information given and then answering the questions.
- **Practice doing lots of calculations** in your head or quickly writing them down to solve. You should practice percentage calculations, speed-time calculations or converting units as these are the key calculations that can come up in section 1. Reducing the time it will take for you to do these calculations will allow you extra time on questions later on which may require some more thinking or working out.
- **Read the question carefully,** or if you need to, read the question more than once. It may contain key words which can affect the answer you select. You may miss them if you go too quickly. Examiners tend to use one word in either the context or the question, which can dramatically change the meaning of what is being said or asked, and can lead students into making easily rectifiable mistakes.
- **Testing out all the given answers** might be easier than figuring out the methodology behind the question. If you are

struggling to identify how you are supposed to respond to a question, go through each of the answers and see what fits. This can be a major time-saving measure to prevent you losing time if you are prone to panicking.

Section 2 - Scientific Skills

The second section requires you to apply your in-depth understanding of the fundamental science and maths to difficult questions. The fundamental sciences include biology, chemistry and physics. This section is only 30 minutes long, so completing 27 questions within this short time can be quite challenging. The questions are also not that straight forward. The level of science is around that of GCSEs / AS levels, which can lead you to think that this section is really easy however the questions are styled to make answering them much more difficult. The number of questions for each topic is listed in the table below:

Topic	Number of Questions
Biology	7
Chemistry	7
Maths	7
Physics	6

The types of questions you can expect varies wildly. For some questions you may be asked to interpret a diagram, chart or pieces of data and be asked to draw a certain conclusion or outcome. Sometimes you can be given questions where you need to recall certain scientific concepts and be asked to implement them to either a written example or as a diagram. You could also be asked to use some visuospatial skills to identify how 3D shapes can be manipulated to be shown from a specific angle. For some maths questions, you can be asked to do multi-step calculations or do statistical/ probability based questions.

Here are some key tips to help you when practicing for Section 2:
- **Do not neglect physics!** The order of difficulty for questions, from highest to lowest, tends to follow this pattern:

Biology; Chemistry; Maths; Physics. Physics questions tend to be easier objectively because applicants are less likely to have taken Physics as a subject, and examiners know this. Physics questions comprise about 25% of all the questions in Section 2, which is a significant portion of marks that you could risk losing if you don't brush up. Try going back through GCSE specifications for Physics and familiarise yourself with the fundamentals.

- **Be confident with your science subjects** that you are taking. This can help you in two ways Firstly it will help you consolidate all the learning you would have done up to this point and highlight areas that you need to focus on. Secondly, Section 2 questions can involve AS level questions from time to time so having a deeper knowledge of your sciences can alleviate any hurdles that examiners may try to throw at you in the exam.
- **Practice past papers!** Section 2 questions may seem a little unorthodox in the way they are structured or the way they may ask you to solve something, which can lead you to be taken by surprise in the exam. Reading all the previous questions that students have undertaken will allow you to see how the exam board implements the science you already know in a different manner for these questions. Getting used to the questions is good for any section but especially handy for this one.

SECTION 3 - ESSAY

This is the last section of the BMAT. It takes half an hour. The reasoning behind this section is to help identify which candidates can build a cohesive and well-structured logical argument, accounting for multiple viewpoints. In this section you will be given the choice of 3 questions/statements. The statements will include one which is scientific, one philosophical statement and a medical statement. Each of the statements will have questions underneath that the examiner will want you to address in your essay. Below are the questions used in the 2019 examinations to give you a clearer idea of what the essay titles can be:

The most important consideration when answering this question is that you will have one answer sheet to write your essay. The answer sheet has some space at the top for admin details such as your name and candidate number and space below to write your essay. That means the space for your essay is less than a single A4 side. THIS IS THE ONLY SPACE YOU HAVE! Any mistakes or space you use for scribbles or notes will mean less space for your essay. You are not allowed to ask for any extra paper. You need to make sure that your essay fits in the given space properly!

People are often motivated to deny the existence of problems if they disagree with the solutions to those problems. Explain what you think is meant by the statement. Present a counter-argument. To what extent do you agree with the statement?

'*In science, there are no universal truths, just views of the world that have yet to be shown to be false.' (Brian Cox and Jeff Forshaw)* Explain what you think is meant by the statement. Argue that scientists need to accept some things as "truths" to advance their understanding. To what extent do you agree with the statement?

Teamwork is more important for surgical innovation than the skills of an individual surgeon. Explain the reasoning behind this statement. Argue that the skills of individual surgeons are more important for surgical innovation or progress. To what extent do you agree with the statement?

Here are some tips for Section 3:

- **Take the time to plan!** 30 minutes really isn't a long time so it would seem very counterintuitive to spend what limited time you have on planning but trust me, it's worth it. Examiners don't care how long the essay is, so long it has the necessary parts needed to answer the statement and that the overall piece is well structured. You are being examined on the quality of the argument, not the length; so spending 5-10 minutes planning what you will write so that it's clear and coherent will be a massive advantage. Due to the limited space you have to write this section, it is worth planning on the back of the answer sheet so you have the full amount of space to write what you need.

- **Don't fuss over the question.** Just choose a topic you think you can build the best piece of writing around. Some people may say you should choose the question which seems the most difficult to answer, which is usually the philosophy question, but actually, the examiners don't care. They just look for a quality argument, not which topic you have chosen. Your choice of topic doesn't give you any extra marks or credit so just choose what you feel comfortable with.

Essential revision tools?

When practicing for the BMAT, there are some essential materials that you need to help you get used to the exam and get the highest possible score:

- **Official past papers** are available on the BMAT website from previous years up to 2003. However the ones that are related to the current specification only go back to 2008. When revising, review the older papers first before moving on to the papers before 2008.
- **Sitting down with others or undertaking tutoring**, whether one-on-one or in a small group, going through past questions or learning techniques can give you a massive edge. Other people may be able to help you out by pointing out what information you are missing to answer a question or what you could do differently for certain questions.
- **Books with BMAT question banks** or online question banks are a vital resource when becoming accustomed to the different styles of questions present in the BMAT. Practicing questions is the best way possible to improve your chances at the BMAT.

What is the UCAT?

This exam is quite different from other exams you may have done in the past. For 2020, UCAT may be taken on a computer in a test centre, usually the same place that you would do a driving theory test. Or candidates may choose to sit the test at home using the online proctoring service by Pearson Vue (UCAT Online).

UCAT have also developed a guide for both the test centre and the UCAT Online, offering advice on what to expect and what to consider when making your selection of test venues. It has been specified that those taking the assessment in either venue will be given access to an erasable white board and pen for calculation and notes. Further information can be found at https://www.ucat.ac.uk/ucat.

The UCAT consists of 5 different parts. Each part allows one minute for reading instructions followed by the specific timings for each section. If you have any special education needs, you may be applicable for the UCATSEN, which is the UCAT with extended timings for each section, specifically 25% more time per section. Below is a table with all the timings for each section as well as the number of questions for both the UCAT and the UCATSEN.

UCAT Section	Questions	UCAT Timings	UCATSEN Timings
Verbal Reasoning	44	1 minute instruction section 21 minutes test time	1 minute 15 second instruction section 26 minutes 15 seconds test time
Decision Making	29	1 minute instruction section 31 minutes test time	1 minute 15 second instruction section 38 minutes 45 seconds test time
Quantitative Reasoning	36	1 minute instruction section 24 minutes test time	1 minute 15 second instruction section 30 minutes

UCAT Section	Questions	UCAT Timings	UCATSEN Timings
Abstract Reasoning	55	1 minute instruction section 13 minutes test time	1 minute 15 second instruction section 16 minutes 15 seconds test time
Situation Judgement	69	1 minute instruction section 26 minutes test time	1 minute 15 second instruction section 32 minutes 30 seconds test time
Total	233	5 minute instruction section 115 minutes test time	6 minute 15 second instruction section 143 minutes 45 seconds test time

‖ 2020 Timeline

Due to COVID-19, the traditional testing dates have been changed. Below is the 2020 timeline:

Date	Event
1st July 2020 (9am)	Registration opens Booking opens Bursary Scheme opens Access Arrangements / UCATSEN applications open
3rd August 2020	Testing begins
17 September 2020 (Midday)	Registration closes Web booking closes Access Arrangements / UCATSEN application deadline
30th September 2020 (Midday)	Final booking deadline (for registered candidates)
1st October 2020	Last testing date Bursary application deadline (4pm)
15th October 2020	UCAS application deadline
Early November 2020	Results delivered to universities

SCORING

The first four sections are scored the same; the raw marks are converted into a bell curve giving you a score from 300 to 900. Most candidates will score around the 600 mark with better candidates scoring around 700 or higher. The situational judgement section is slightly different. Instead of a score, you are placed into a band between 1 and 4, with band 1 being the highest. The majority of people end up in band 2, with a fewer number attaining band 1.

Topic Breakdown

VERBAL REASONING

This section contains 11 passages of around 300 to 400 words each. For each of the passages, you will be asked 4 different questions on them. You can be asked either true / false questions or questions with free text answers (each option will be a statement of part of a statement). Every question has only one correct answer. This section tends to be most difficult for candidates in the historically. The scores from previous years all have the Verbal Reasoning section as its lowest scoring section.

The verbal reasoning section highlights important skills that are required as a medical professional. When working in any medical environment, you will have to read vast tons of information and be able to appropriately extrapolate information and be able to interpret it correctly. This can be seen working in a professional setting but also from an academic standpoint; scanning through research papers and scientific posters. The skills being tested in this section are also important in the doctor-patient relationship when communicating with patients; obtaining information about their problems and conveying medical information to them in a way that's easy for the patient to understand.

There are 4 main types of questions that you may find within this section:
- **True/False/Can't tell**. You will be given a statement based on a passage which has one of three options. All the questions have only one correct option. The statement may be

from information which can be found directly in the passage as well as indirectly – logically deduced from pieces of information from the text.

- **Incomplete Statement.** This is self-explanatory. You will be given part of a statement and the answers are possible endings to that statement. You have to choose the correct ending.
- **According to / Deduced from the passage**. For these types of questions, you have to use logic and correctly interpret which of the 4 statements given is correct. The information to solve these questions usually won't be directly visible in the passage but can be put together from information in multiple parts of the text.
- **Exceptions.** You can treat each of the answers as mini true/false questions, where all but one of the statements will be false. You can systematically go through each statement; checking whether it is true from the given context and concordant with the passage

Here are some tips for verbal reasoning:

- **Improve your reading speed!** One of the most challenging parts of this section is the time pressure. It's the main reason that students find this the most difficult section due to the length of the passages. There are several tactics you can use to scan through the passages more quickly. The first thing is to practice your comprehension. Read articles and as fast as you can and see how much of the relevant information you can take in from it. Another thing you can do is practice doing online speed reading challenges. They are akin to the verbal reasoning section, where they give you a passage to read as fast as you can and ask you a series of questions on it. They will give you a score at the end and you can try it multiple times to improve your score.
- **Read the questions first!** This can highlight key words that you can identify within the passage to give you more context to help you answer the question. This will dramatically reduce the time needed to spend reading.

- **Don't get bogged down with one question!** It is easy to get carried away when dealing with one question and you might find that you are spending too much time on it. If you think you have spent too much time on a question and are still struggling with it, take a calculated guess and move on. It will be much more important to allocate enough time for the questions later on so you can answer them properly. It will be better to have tried all the questions and potentially getting some wrong than having spent too much time on a question, leaving you with a block of unanswered questions at the end which will automatically be counted as incorrect.
- **Practice your timings.** This links in with not being bogged down with just one question but if you can find a general pace for each of the questions which works for you, allocating enough time to appropriately answer each question confidently, this will help alleviate the time pressure that you will face in this section.
- **Use a Strategy**. There is a main strategy that you can use to solve verbal reasoning questions. Using and adapting this basic strategy to your personal needs will help you become quicker at answering these questions, and ultimately become more efficient:

1. Don't actually read the passage. Read the question and note any key words and terms.
2. Scan through the passage and locate those key terms.
3. Make sure to read before and after the key terms to ensure you get the context around where the key term is being used.
4. Repeat all instances of the key terms.
5. Finally choose the answer based on what you have read.

DECISION MAKING
In this section, you are asked questions based on given information or data. This data can be in the form of text, charts, tables diagrams

or graphs. Questions can either have their own data or multiple questions can be asked about the same dataset.

These questions are analogous with the information you will receive as a medical professional and you will need to act with logic and reason when making a decision. When taking care of a patient, it can be viewed as a puzzle which requires logical steps, back up with evidence, to solve.

Here are the main types of questions:
- **Logical deductions.** In these questions you are given statements where you need to come to a conclusion using logical deduction.
- **Syllogisms.** These are a type of logical puzzle that can be presented where logical deductions are used to come to a conclusion. An example of this is: "All Humans are Mammals, all mammals have a heart, therefore all humans have a heart".
- **Probabilities.** Although this seems like it will fall under quantitative reasoning, you could be asked probability questions.
- **Diagrammatic.** This is where you can be given different shapes as well as charts and graphs and be asked to interpret them.
- **Assumption Recognition.** This is where you are given a text which has an argument presented and within it there will be an assumption made. You will need to identify that assumption. Potentially, you could be asked how the assumption affects the argument.
- **Data analysis and interpretation.** These questions can give you different forms of graphs and tables which you will need to read and work out certain conclusions or complete certain calculations to get to the answers.

Here are some tips for decision making:
- **Eliminate irrelevant data.** Within the given information, the question may only require you to focus on certain parts. For

example, you could be given a table with multiple column headings but the question may only require you to focus on the data in only one of the columns. Ignoring the other data allows you to focus on what's required to solve the question; reducing the time spent.

- **Practice logical reasoning.** You can find logical reasoning puzzles and quizzes on various different websites which you should try out. Even though they may not be directly related to the UCAT, practicing the skill will help.
- **Revise probabilities.** The mathematics behind this section is inextricably linked. If you practice GCSE level probability, it will give you an edge when answering questions. Skills to practice include venn diagram interpretations and tree diagrams.
- **Sketch Diagrams and Notes.** This links with probability but also can be linked with logical deduction puzzles and syllogisms. Drawing diagrams to help visualise the logic behind questions or showing probabilities writtenout will reduce the number of things you need to keep track of in your head and focus solely on calculating your answer. This also reduces the time taken for questions to be completed.

QUANTITATIVE REASONING

Understanding numbers may not seem that important when working as a medical professional but in fact the opposite is true. Numbers are used everywhere in a medical professional's career; from measuring the ranges of normal levels of chemicals to calculating dosages of certain drugs. It also bears a significant weight on the academic side of medicine as for that you need to analyse and interpret numerical and statistical data.

As a general rule of thumb, a GCSE level maths foundation will give you the necessary tools to solve these questions.

Generally, all the questions will involve you doing a calculation or a series of calculations to get to an answer. To help you with these calculations, there is a very simple on-screen calculator that you have access to. When practicing UCAT questions, use our online calculator, included in our UCAT mock test (which is exactly like the official UCAT one) ito help you familiarise yourself with the on screen calculator.

Here are the main type of questions:

- **Interpreting Statistics and Graphs.** Questions can give you data in the form of charts and graphs where you can be asked questions about the data or using the data. Questions can also ask you to apply the data given to a specific scenario and calculate certain things.
- **Interpreting Verbal Data.** Mathematical questions can be written as a block of text where you have to identify the calculations that need to be done. It is important to highlight any numbers or key mathematical terms when going through the text.

Here are some tips for quantitative reasoning:

- **Eliminate irrelevant data.** This is similar to the reasoning behind the tip mentioned in decision making. If you focus on only the data you need to solve the question and nothing else, you will solve it much faster.
- **Use standard form when possible.** This is the method of writing out numbers as a small 1 to 10 multiplied by a magnitude of 10. Writing out large numbers in standard form will allow you to do larger calculations in your head and avoid using the on-screen calculator. The on-screen calculator should only be used as a last resort if you can't calculate the answer on paper or in your head. Alongside standard form, you should practice the Index Laws as they are very important in standard form.
- **Use the answers to solve the question instead of calculating.** Questions may arise where it may actually be faster to test out the given answers and see which ones fit.

- **Convert Correctly!** Questions can include multiple types of units or different magnitudes of units, which can throw you off choosing the correct answer.
- **Don't round early.** Even though it may make the maths easier, any rounding that you do earlier can lead you to compound that small error, leading you towards an incorrect answer when all the calculations are done. When calculating, only round at the very end of the question!

ABSTRACT REASONING

This is a very strange section at first glance. It just seems like a random bunch of shapes and colours which have no resemblance to anything related to medicine but it actually practices something vital that medical professionals use. When you have to start diagnosing someone, all the symptoms and signs aren't just given to you. You need to look for them by analysing and identifying signs and patterns. This is exactly the premise for the abstract reasoning section.

This is the most time pressured section, as you have 55 questions to complete within just 13 minutes. The reasoning behind this extreme time pressure is that multiple questions are based on one pattern pair. Instead of averaging time based on each question, you need to pace your time for each pattern pair, i.e. spend more time trying to analyse the patterns to identify the rules linking them and then you'll only need a very short amount of time answering the actual questions.

Here are the types of abstract reasoning questions:
- **Pattern Set A/B/Neither.** Here you will get two sets, each with 6 patterns. The 6 patterns will have a common rule between then. The two sets will have similar but distinctly different rules. The question will give you a pattern where you will be asked which set it falls into. It can fall into either set A or B, or it may not fit into either set. The rules can vary but there are a few characteristics which you can look for when trying to identify the pattern.

- **Completing Pattern Series.** You will be given 3 patterns; each pattern is the next stage of the pattern before. You will have to choose one of 4 patterns that will be the next stage. The patterns can be changing due to one rule of a small set of different rules and changes.
- **Pattern Set Belonging.** This is similar to the Set A/B/Neither questions but instead of being given a pattern and be asked which set the pattern belongs to, you'll be given 4 different patterns of which 1 will fit into a set.
- **Pattern Relation.** This is similar to the completing pattern series. You will be given a pattern and a set of rules for changing the pattern. You are then shown a pattern and will be asked what the pattern will turn into by using the same set of rules as with the previous pattern. The answers will be different patterns, of which one will be correct.

Below is a list of the different things you should take into consideration when identifying patterns in pattern sets:
- Positions and direction of objects
- Colours of objects
- Intersection of objects
- Number and type of angles
- Symmetry of objects and individual patterns
- Number of objects
- Type and Size of Objects

SITUATIONAL JUDGEMENT
The ethos behind this section is self-explanatory. You will be using your judgement in your everyday university life as well as in your career. Each situation you encounter will be unique, so understanding the ethical and social rules that professionals need to follow is essential.

The time pressure for this section in practice is actually fairly low despite the 69 questions. The difficulty arises when deliberating which of the options is the most appropriate choice.

Here are the type of questions you can see:

- **Appropriateness.** You will be given a passage which outlines a scenario, either as a dental student or as if you were a professional. You will then be given a series of possible statements and be asked about the appropriateness of that action.
- **Importance.** You are given a scenario and questions will be a series of actions relating to that scenario. You will be asked how important something is from "Most important" to "Not important at all".
- **Most and Least.** The last few questions in this section will be of this style. You will be given a scenario and 3 different courses of action for that situation. You then will have to rank the actions from least to most important. You will need to get both of the options correct to attain the mark.

Scoring in the SJT is slightly different to the rest of the UCAT. Instead of there being a single correct answer, there are partially correct answers which count as half a correct answer. These exist as situational judgment questions and they can be subjective, so it can be argued that certain answers have a significant amount of merit but not enough to be the full correct answer.

Here are some tips for this section:

- Read the General Medical Council's "Good Medical Practice"
- Read the General Dental Council's "Standards and Guidance"
- Understand three key values: Integrity, Teamwork and Common Sense

Reading and understanding these texts can help you get a better understanding of the ethical foundation required for situational judgement questions. They contain the different morals and ethics that real world medical professionals use.

Which dental schools require UCAT?

Individual dental schools use the UCAT slightly differently. When you get your UCAT score, you should think tactfully about the places you are applying to; making sure you are taking full advantage of your UCAT score. The earlier that you get your UCAT done, the better idea you'll have about where you would want to apply. Below is a list the dental schools which use the UCAT and how each of these institutions use them.

- **Aberdeen** - Candidates' UCAT scores are considered in selection for interview but they aren't the sole indicator for selection. They are considered along actual and predicted academic achievements in deciding who gets an interview. Aberdeen takes an average of the numerical scores of the first 4 sections. SJT is not scored but may be used when giving out offers. There is no minimum cut-off score. As a rule of thumb, academics count for 60% and UCAT 40%.
- **Birmingham** - They don't accept the bottom decile of scores from the UCAT as well as people with a band 4 in the SJT.
- **Bristol** - All parts of the UCAT count towards a candidate's performance when being selected for an interview. Applications are scored and ranked based on their academic record, according to their achieved or predicted results with the following weightings: GCSE 15%, A-Level 15%, Personal Statement 35%, UCAT 35%.
- **Cardiff** - It is required for entry into Cardiff but no extra detail is given on how it is used.
- **Dundee** - You are required to sit the UCAT in the year of application for entry into Dundee, however, there are exceptions if your country has faults in its testing service.
- **Glasgow** - The UCAT forms an extremely important part of the BDS entry requirements. If your score is deemed too low then you will not be selected for an interview, regardless of your qualifications. The 2019 cut-off score was 2470.
- **Kings College** - King's does not have a threshold UCAT score in any particular year, but all candidates are still

required to take the UCAT examination for this course. The overall UCAT score averaged across the four subtests is given more consideration than the individual subtest scores. The Situational Judgement Test (SJT) is also taken into account when shortlisting.

- **Liverpool** - There is no cut-off score for Liverpool, however, it is highly unlikely that you will be accepted if you have band 4 in the SJT.
- **Newcastle** - They do use a minimum threshold scoring system. The threshold is based on all applicants' scores as well as those specific scores of people who applied to Newcastle. The threshold changes year on year.
- **Plymouth** - You will be required to meet a minimum over-all target score which is set and reviewed annually by the Admissions Advisory Panel. The threshold score applied to determine candidate selection for interview can alter each year and is influenced by overall candidate performance in the UCAT and the number and quality of applications received. There is no cut-off banding for the SJT. They only look at the overall score, not individual sections.
- **Queen Mary** - You will not be offered an interview if your score fell in the lower third of all scores. If you are above this threshold, the UCAT counts for 50% of applicant selection for interview.
- **Belfast** - For UK and EU candidates UCAT will be scored using the overall results from four papers. Candidates can obtain up to a maximum of 6 additional points depending on banding. Banding of UCAT Scores Points Awarded:
  - 1200 – 1899 = 0
  - 1900 – 2099 = 1
  - 2100 – 2299 = 2
  - 2300 – 2499 = 3
  - 2500 – 2699 = 4
  - 2700 – 2899 = 5
  - 2900 – 3600 = 6

- **Sheffield** - The score required needs to be above the mean score of all UCAT applicants. Those who have a band 4 will not be considered for interview.
- **Manchester** - There is no overall threshold for UCAT scores. Band 4 SJT will not be accepted. Band 3 will be accepted, however, those with Band 2 and 1 will be given priority.

Revision Ethic

There are a lot of reasons to start early for revision for both the BMAT and the UCAT. Higher scores will maximise your chances of getting into a dental school. Regardless of how the schools use the score, a higher score will always improve your chances of getting in. Universities don't have any excuse for lower scores (except for exceptional circumstances) as the entrance exam is separate from your learning at school or college. Finally the biggest thing to consider is that there is only one sitting of the entrance exam per admission cycle, so if you get a higher score, it will improve the likelihood that you won't have to wait another year to enter into university.

Generally, when it comes to revising, there are some key features you should keep in mind for the most effective outcome that overall culminates in a good revision ethic or revising hygiene:

First and foremost, structure your revision. Take the time to set out all the sections and types of questions that you may come across in the exam or past papers/questions that you have access to. At first, this may seem like something which will hardly have an impact on your revision but on any given day, you will already know what you'll be doing and you will have an idea about what materials you'll need for the day.

Linking to structure, make sure that you plan to take breaks and exercise. There is no use revising solidly for long time if you end up getting burnt out and not retaining information. That's just a waste of time!

Taking breaks allows your brain to have a soft reset and get ready to take in more information. Three hours of well-structured and efficient revision is much better than 6 hours of inefficient revision. Exercise is generally important to your health and surprising can make a massive difference to your overall confidence and ability to take in information. I'd try to get in around 40 minutes of exercise a day to see a positive impact on revision.

The last major part of a good revision ethic is making sure you are in a different environment. Dedicating another space away from your room will naturally put you in a different mindset for revising and will motivate you to try out questions or attempt a paper. This could be in your local library, sitting on the grass in a park or even just another space in your house which isn't somewhere you spend most of your time. It's really good to separate your home and your work!

PART 2

The Interview

The interview forms one of the most important aspects of the entire application to dental school. It is used by dental schools to see which candidates are the best suited for the course and it's one of the ways for the university to filter out students who will potentially receive an offer to study the course. Due to the competitive nature of dentistry, getting an interview in itself is a huge achievement. It goes to show that the university is impressed by your academics and UCAS application.

The interview should be seen as an opportunity to showcase your abilities to the interviewers. Remember, this will be the first time they meet you, so it's important to make a good impression.

Universities will often contact students by email, (which is provided on their UCAS form), or even through the post about their interview. The email will contain confidential and critical data on how the interview day will run as well as the date and time of the interview.

Most universities allow for minimum notice of two weeks from the invitation to the interview day. You should use this time to prepare to the best of your abilities. Revisit your personal statement during this time as the university may ask you questions based on what you have written in your statement.

Universities will use either a 'Multiple Mini Interview' (MMI) or a 'Traditional Panel Interview'. The type and format of your interview will be included in the invitation from the university. We have listed below each university and their current interview format as of the 2021 application cycle.

All the information compiled below has been obtained from the official university websites.

‖ Interview Formats

University of Dundee
- MMI
- 10 interview stations in total
- 7 minutes in each station
- Some of the stations are one-to-one, and some will be interactive

Queen Mary, University of London
- Panel interview
- Interviewers can include tutors/dentists/doctors/students

University of Manchester
- MMI
- 7 interview stations in total
- 7 minutes in each station with a 2-minute gap between stations

Plymouth University
- MMI
- 7 interview stations in total
- Approximately 50 minutes in total

University of Aberdeen
- MMI
- 7 minutes in each station
- Approximately 90 minutes in total

Queen's University of Belfast
- MMI
- 9 interview stations in total
- Approximately 60 minutes in total

University of Birmingham
- MMI
- 10-12 interview stations in total
- Approximately 1 hour in total

University of Glasgow
- MMI
- 7 stations in total
- 6 minutes at each station, plus 1 minute reading time
- Approximately 45 minutes in total

University of Liverpool
- MMI
- 10 stations

University of Leeds
- MMI

King's College London
- MMI
- 7 stations in total
- 5 minutes per station

University of Cardiff
- MMI
- 10 stations in total

University of Bristol
- MMI
- Approximately 90 minutes in total

University of Central Lancashire
- MMI
- Approximately lasting 70 minutes
- Plus 2 manual tasks
  - The first will be 5 minutes. Candidates are given advance notice of the particular type of task so they can practice beforehand.
  - The second will be 20 minutes long – an unknown task

University of Sheffield
- Panel interview
- Panel will comprise of 2 members of staff and a final year dental student
- Up to 15 minutes long
- Interpersonal skills test testing communication, empathy and compassion

University of Newcastle
- Panel interview
- 2 interviewers
- Approximately 20 minutes in total

Multiple Mini Interviews Versus Traditional Panel Interviews

MMI

The Multiple Mini Interview (MMI) comprises formal interviews consisting of different 'stations'. Candidates are presented with different scenarios with a different interviewer at each station. The mix of scenarios is designed to test different qualities such as: communication; critical thinking skills; and ability to make ethical decisions.

The interview time at each station is usually ten minutes or less. As you only have a short time at each station, you have to quickly respond with an answer to the scenario or question presented. The interviewers are looking for candidates that demonstrate having the right attitude and qualities to become a successful dentist as well as having correct academic abilities.

Each candidate is assigned to a station to begin with and candidates rotate around the timed stations in a circuit. No station has a greater value than another. The same standardised questions are asked for each candidate. Each station is marked independently and scores for individual candidates are collected at the end. Your performance in one station will not affect the scores in any other. The scores are used to rank candidates, which ultimately determines who receives offers. The interviewers base the scores off the performance in the station, as well as the applicant's suitability to a career in dentistry; determined by his or her ability to make correct decisions and justify their explanations during the scenarios, as well as the ability to keep calm.

The team of interviewers often comprises members of the Dental Faculty, dental students and even actors. There may also be a 'role play' station in which a candidate is placed in a scenario with an actor and asked to break bad news, discuss a problem, or take part in an ethical scenario.

What skills does the MMI assess?

Each dental school assesses a variety of factors during the interview. However, there are certain skills which the interviewers generally look out for:

1. **Communication**

Dentists must be good communicators. You will have to talk to a lot of patients from all walks of life. Some of them may not be as understanding as others when things go wrong so it's important for candidates to display a high level of communication throughout the interview, for example, by effectively explaining your answers to the interviewers within the time limit. Be concise with your responses and make sure you actually address the question being asked. Interviewers will be assessing your verbal and non-verbal communication, too. Eye contact, hand gestures, smiling and maintaining a good posture are all vital body language to convey when speaking to your interviewer.

2. **Critical Thinking Skills**

The scenarios given to you on the day will be unseen and unexpected. The interviewers will want to see if you can come up with a solution to the problems presented. There is no right or wrong answer. Most important is your ability to back up your answer with an explanation that justifies your reasoning.

Having critical thinking skills allows you to evaluate the scenarios in a holistic manner rather than a narrow view. It's better to consider different outcomes than give a single, limited answer.

3. **Commitment Towards Dentistry**

Dentistry is a career in which you will face many challenges. The interviewers want to assess whether you have the ability to overcome these challenges and meet the demands of dental school. You will need to demonstrate that you are physically and mentally prepared to commit to the career, and that you have undertaken work experience and additional reading to provide you with a good insight and understanding of what dentistry entails.

4. Professionalism

As a dental student you must always conduct yourself profession-ally – not only in university or in clinics but also outside of work. Interviewers will want to see whether candidates are aware of these requirements. Dentists have to treat all patients equally and must abide by the GDC principles, as well as be ethical in their approach and make the right decisions. Candidates must display a professional approach at every station and maintain this throughout the day.

5. Reflection

It is important that candidates reflect on their performance in the stations. The interviewers will want to see that a candidate has the ability to reflect on the strengths and weaknesses in their answer, and how they could be improved. In dental school, it is crucial that students reflect on their work, as the result may not always be what they expected. However, it is important to learn from past mistakes and how this has all allowed them to improve.

Reflection is a quality which you will have to exercise in most stations. CARL is an acronym for a framework you can memorise to help you reflect. Start with C for 'context'. This requires you to comment on the context of a specific situation. A is for the 'Action' you took to deal with a situation. R is for 'Results' – discussing the outcomes of the action which you referred to. Then L for 'Learning' – what lessons did you take from the entire experience?

TRADITIONAL PANEL INTERVIEWS

The Panel interviews have gradually been phased out at most universi-ties over the years and replaced with MMIs. Only Queen Mary's, Sheffield and Newcastle universities still make assessments with panel inter-views, which usually consist of 1 to 3 interviewers made up of dentists, admissions tutors and occasionally even a student of the dental school.

The interviews usually last about 20 - 40 minutes. These interviews are question-focused rather than task based. You must have a strong understanding of the dental school you are applying to. The interviewers will ask you a number of questions about your application, experiences and general understanding of dentistry as a career, as well as its role within society.

Generally, more in-depth questions on the Personal Statement are asked, so it is critical that everything you write in the statement is true so you don't get caught out in the interview.

Preparation is key for panel interviews as you only have one chance to impress. However they can be less formal than MMIs as the interviewers usually treat it more like a conversation, which is much less intimidating.

Try and practice your answers so they come across as naturally as possible. Try getting friends and family to ask you potential questions so you become used to speaking in front of other people. However, don't make your responses overly rehearsed. Candidates that respond with spontaneous, yet well-thought-out answers to questions are much more likely to perform better in traditional interviews than candidates who present rehearsed, robotic-sounding answers. You should use this opportunity to let your personality and genuine suitability for dentistry shine through.

Common questions and scenarios to expect

Question: Why do you want to be a dentist?
Comment: This is an obvious but vital question that you will be expected to answer. It is also the question to which candidates most frequently reply with coached and practised answers!
The key is to make the answer personal. Don't learn a generic answer. Try and start the answer off with your initial motivation and interest in dentistry. This may have been when you visited the dentist, or during any personal dental treatment you had. Identify specific experiences that have influenced your decision to study dentistry.
Research the required skills and qualities a dentist requires, so that you can mention and expand on these in your answer. Also try and

keep up to date with current affairs related to the dental profession. You can talk about how dentistry combines science and practical skills but try and expand on this by mentioning how this personally relates to you.

The interviewer can then also expand on these statements. Another way to improve your answer is to mention how your passion was reinforced by your work experience. Keep a log of any work experience so you can reflect on this, which also gives the interviewer a nice way to ask you more questions so you can expand on the answer.

Question: Why do you want to apply to X Dental School?
Comment: The dental schools will want to know why you want to apply to their particular dental school, so research here is key. You can mention ideas about the course, university life and the location of the city in which a dental school is situated. We recommend that you start off by mentioning that you went to their open day, but make sure you expand on this. Mention the university atmosphere, facilities and anything that might possibly have stood out for you. The interviews will want to see that you have an insight into areas other than academia, including the societies, city and social aspects. Additionally, you should have a strong knowledge of the way the course for the dental school you are applying for is taught. This information can be found by visiting the university's website and reading the prospectus. All dental schools teach their students in different ways, so it is important you bring this element into your final answer. Considering the opportunities and societies available at the university is also a way to show that you are well-researched and keen to get involved with the activities on offer by the university.

Question: Can you tell me about your work experience?
Comment: The easiest way to prepare for this question is to ensure that you take notes when you do your work experience. The interviewer will be looking to make sure you know what the job of a dentist entails. Try and mention qualities and skills that the dentist

would have used while seeing patients such as communication, empathy, compassion and teamwork skills. Make sure you know the GDC principles and try and make a note of how the dentist is putting these principles into practice. Provide examples of things you saw during work experience. Again, make sure you expand on your answer.

Question: What personal qualities should a good healthcare professional have – And when and where have you had to exhibit these qualities to date?

Comment: You should mention qualities such as empathy, compassion, integrity and honesty. A healthcare professional should have a desire to work with people and a commitment to a life of service, as well as have the ability to lead and cooperate. Be sure to provide a relevant example of the qualities you list. It's your opportunity to draw on your experiences and reflect how they may have taught you skills needed by a healthcare professional.

Further qualities to mention include the dedication to continuous learning, flexibility, the ability to communicate effectively and sensitively, plus critical judgement to solve problems.

‖ Manual Dexterity Tests

Manual dexterity is the skill of using your hands to carry out a task skilfully and to a high level of proficiency, which is incredibly important in dentistry as you will be working in a small, tight space in the mouth. You need to be able to navigate with ease while using the appropriate tool for the task. You need to be very precise (often to the nearest mm) and skilled enough to demonstrate optimal communication and empathy while working. You will also need to work gently, as you will not just be working with teeth but will be working on a person!

There are two types of stations that can come up at an interview on manual dexterity:

1. Explaining the importance of dexterity and how you have previously demonstrated it.
   You should expect this type of question at a panel interview.

2. Completing a task practically to show your ability on the day. This type of question is more likely to come up at an MMI.

Some good examples of manual dexterity include the following (this is by no means an exhaustive list):
- Baking
- Origami
- Painting or Henna
- Threading (eyebrows)
- Playing musical instruments
- Magic (sleight of hand)
- Sewing
- Crochet

Manual Dexterity Scenario Examples

Scenario: Make small knots approximately 3cm apart along a piece of string.

> Tip: Staying calm in this situation is most important to keep your hands steady. This exercise isn't solely about how many knots you can do. Good candidates will carry on with friendly conversation, perhaps about the weather (nothing political or opinionated), and form good quality work that is not rushed.

Scenario: Build tower blocks of 3 Lego bricks each. Make as many towers as you can but you must keep your eyes closed throughout.

> Tip: Move all the Lego pieces to one side. Feel the Lego bricks carefully to make sure you are connecting

the correct sides that slot together. Work quickly but try to make conversation at the same time.

Scenario: You are given an A4 piece of paper that has been divided into small squares. Use the scissors provided to cut the squares. Try to be as neat as possible. You will be marked on how many individual squares you separate.

> Tip: A steady hand helps here. The question guides you to be neat, so try following the lines. It may be easier to cut along one whole line/rectangle and then split the squares up. Keep track of time because you want to produce as many individual squares as possible.

Scenario: Use the pliers (two mini pairs given) to bend a piece of wire into 3 continuous loops.

> Tip: Do not bend the wire with your fingers, even if it seems like the easier option. You can practice using the pliers without the wire first to get a feel for them. Hold the wire steady in one hand with the pliers and bend the wire with the other pliers.

Scenario: Talk about one hobby that you do, which demonstrates manual dexterity.

> Tip: Reflect on your hobbies (which should be planned before) and examples. Focus on why you enjoy it and try and make the answer personal. Try to mention how the skills you gained from this hobby relate to dentistry.

Tips for Practical Stations

Communication

A key skill for dentists is carrying out dental treatment whilst building a rapport with their patients. Examiners will want to see whether you can demonstrate good manual dexterity whilst holding a conversation. Engage in conversation but ensure the subject isn't controversial – speak about the interviewer's career, the task, or something related. Your interviewer will be impressed if you can do both. If you feel like you cannot communicate and do a good job, then speak less (but don't stay silent).

Follow instructions

Read the instructions carefully and follow them to the T. Even if the end result is not perfect, you'll get a higher score for following the correct method, especially if the task is very technical. You won't necessarily be judged on the end result. The approach you take is more important.

Stay calm

As mentioned above, your approach is the most important thing. If the result is not brilliant but the approach is, you will still score well. Don't get stressed (or at least try not to show signs of stress), as they want to see you can remain calm, even in a tough situation. If you find it challenging, it is guaranteed other applicants will as well. Remember this!

‖ Interview Do's and Don'ts

Don't panic. Although easier said than done, try to stay calm. If you cannot answer a question, take a deep breath and compose yourself. If time permits, you can also ask the interviewers to start your answer or station again. The interviewers won't expect you to answer all their questions straight away, so take your time to gather your thoughts and come up with a balanced answer. It can sometimes be useful to prepare a list of cues or key points that you would like to remember to say or do during the interview. Prepare this the night before, maybe on your phone so you can read it on the go the next day as a refresher.

Don't dwell on stations and answers. In a similar line to above, try to not dwell on how you answered your questions or performed at a station. This can negatively affect how you perform for the rest of the interview. The MMI is not based on one station, so even if you perform badly in one station it will not necessarily affect your overall score, as you will have lots of other opportunities to prove yourself. Similarly, with panel interviews, your performance is assessed based on how well you answered all the questions as a whole. The interviewers will understand that you might not answer every question perfectly and will take this into account.

Don't use slang and words such as "yeah", "erm", "you know, "dunno", "like", "stuff". They make your answer seem informal and indicates to the interviewer that you are beginning to lose your train of thought. Using these words is completely natural when you are under pressure but to avoid using them, take time to think of your sentence and what you wish to get across. It is okay to take a break and have a think, rather than saying things that don't make sense.

Don't turn up late to your interview. First impressions always count so make sure that you are smartly dressed in a professional manner and that you turn up on time. Being late, regardless of the reason, displays a lack of commitment and can easily get you rejected. If in the unfortunate case that you are late for the interview, be sure to call the university immediately to explain the reason. They will often be more understanding if you make them aware beforehand.

Expectation and how to conduct yourself

The interview is one of the most demanding parts of a dentistry application. This is the chance to prove yourself to admissions tutors by demonstrating your passion, ability and skills, so it's important to prepare thoroughly to perform to your best abilities.

Interview days are generally very long. You will most likely be at the university for the whole day. Make sure you arrive at the interview in good time, having considered travel time. This may mean that you have to stay overnight nearby the day before your interview so be sure to check this beforehand and plan accordingly. Find out if the university requires you to take any form of identification such as your passport or driving licence.

When arriving at the interview, depending on the university, you may be split into separate smaller groups. Some universities may give you another tour of the dental school.

For panel interviews, you will usually have to wait in a room with other candidates until it is your turn to be called. Try to stay calm during this waiting time. You can brush over some questions and answers but ensure that you do not over prepare and get too stressed. Feel free to talk to other interviewees, which may help you feel more relaxed, but don't feel pressured to talk either if this exacerbates your nerves.

The wait for MMI interviews is not usually as long as for panel interviews because you have lots of stations to get through and a group of applicants can be interviewed at the same time.

There's usually a small break between each station so use this time to gather your thoughts and to stay calm. Try and use the brief intervals to prepare for the next station. Don't dwell on the previous station as doing so could negatively affect your performance going forward.

Always remember to stay professional and polite throughout the interviews. Try and reflect on the interview afterwards, as this can be a good learning experience if you have any more upcoming interviews.

First impressions. As a dentist you are a medical professional and members of the public will hold you to a high standard. You will be meeting patients every day, and people will judge you from the moment they see you. First impressions count! At the interviews, the dental schools will also be taking these factors into account, so it is important that you present yourself in the best way possible.

Appearance. Dress smartly just as you would for any interview. Make yourself look as presentable as possible. Males should wear a shirt and tie, smart trousers and polished shoes. Females can wear skirts or trousers with a smart blouse or shirt and smart, polished shoes. Avoid high heels and make sure all your clothing is nicely ironed. If you want to wear makeup, try and make sure it's not too garish. Also make sure any colognes or perfumes worn are not overpowering or too distracting for the interviewers. Make sure your hair is neat and your nails are clean. Most importantly, make sure you are comfortable in whatever you are wearing, as interview days are usually long.

Posture. Be sure not to slouch! Try not to fidget and wriggle too much during the interviews, as this can be distracting for the interviewers and make you come across as unprepared. It may be helpful to place your hands on your laps when you are sitting down. Try and keep your back straight also. It will be helpful to ask your friends and family to assess your body language during practice interviews.

Eye, facial and hand movements. Try and maintain eye contact with the interviewers and keep them all engaged. Try and smile at the interviewer, and if there is more than one, make sure to smile and look at each of them every now and again. This will confirm to the examiners your engagement and portrays self-confidence. Feel free to use your hands to emphasise your points. Just don't go overboard with exaggerated hand waving. React appropriately to the information that the interviewers give you, whether this is by laughing and smiling, or conveying sadness and empathy. Do not be upset if the interviewers do not reciprocate your smiles, this does not mean that your interview is going badly. It is their job to remain as impartial as possible.

Practice. Ask friends and family to practice mock interviews with you. Use the opportunity to practice remaining calm under pressure.

Getting immediate feedback will help you improve your interview techniques. You can also familiarise yourself with the format you will be faced with, as well as experiencing different communication styles.

Don't have answers prepared to the extent where you sound like a robot. Have some brief bullet points prepared as cues to remember, so that what you say is natural.

PERSONAL STATEMENT

Your personal statement is a representation of you, detailing the attributes that make you the perfect candidate for dental school. Not all dental schools ask about your personal statement specifically, but will ask around the topic, so it is good to be aware of where you can apply it. The key to practising for personal statement questions is to know your personal statement inside out. Be sure to continuously review it and keep on top of what you have mentioned, especially if you have discussed research. However, remember not to overly rehearse your answers, as it's important for your personality to come through.

ANALYSING YOUR PERSONAL STATEMENT

Step 1 – Work out what your main talking points are. Examples include work experience, volunteering, hobbies, research/reading and roles of responsibility.

Step 2 – Break up these into further categories. Example questions include:
- Why did you do it?
- Did you enjoy it?
- What did you learn?
- Did you have any challenges?
- Would you carry it on in the future?

Step 3 – Reflect. This will help answer the questions you came up with in Step 2.

Step 4 – Peer review. Ask someone to read your personal statement and analyse it with you.

COMMON PERSONAL STATEMENT QUESTIONS

I've read your personal statement and you said/did/read/play/are...?
What did you learn from your work experience?
What are your weaknesses?
What are you most proud of?
Tell me a bit more about the research/reading you have done? Can you teach me a bit more about it?

These are all types of questions you may be asked but it's important to note that they will be specific to your personal statement. They will also often be asked in a conversational format, rather than as specific questions. If they are asked as a general question, you should use these more specific questions as pointers to break down and structure your answer. A key point to note is to try and understand why they are asking these questions. The interviewer is usually trying to find out more about you and see what sets you apart from other candidates. These questions are also trying to gauge your communication and professionalism.

ANSWERING THE QUESTIONS

Be professional. Professionalism isn't just about your appearance, but how you present yourself. You don't need to use big fancy words but you need to be clear and formal, allowing the interviewer to see that you are competent and respectable.

Be engaged. This includes having good body language, making and maintaining eye contact, having confidence, maintaining the flow of the interview and avoiding one-word answers.

Be interested. Try to actively listen to ensure you actually answer the question. If you do not know the answer, then show that you want to find out, specifically with regards to questions surrounding research you may have included in your personal statement.

Be yourself. Show your personality and achievements. Try and be genuine while talking about personal experiences that are unique to you.

THINGS TO AVOID SAYING & DOING

Do not lie. The whole point is to show yourself off so don't put yourself at risk of being caught in a lie and coming across as fake.

Do not over practice. This is very important and is a big thing the interviewers notice; it can make the interview quite boring and monotonous. Remember that they are trying to find out about you, not your ability to regurgitate information.

Do not look bored. This could come across as rude and unprofessional. Remember that they are trying to gauge your potential for being a dentist.

Do not use generic answers. Try to be unique. Everyone's experiences, journeys and achievements are very different. These questions/stations are often specific to you, so make sure to share your personal experiences.

Station specific questions and advice

MOTIVATION TO STUDY DENTISTRY

Example questions:
Why do you want to be a dentist?
Why do you want to be a dentist over another healthcare profession?
What strengths do you have that will help you in a dental career?
What qualities do you have that will help you in dentistry?
What have you done to prepare yourself for a career in dentistry?
What qualities do you think a dentist should have?
What are the negative aspects of dentistry?
What would make students drop out of the dentistry degree?
How do you cope with stress?
How do you relax?

Before answering any questions relating to your motivation to study dentistry, reiterating the main reasons to choose this career is worthwhile.

1. Patient factors: management of dental disease; alleviating dental pain; improving confidence, function and aesthetics; and working with people.
2. Technical aspects: Dentistry is a very hands on profession that combines the finer technical aspects of surgery with a communication centric approach.
3. Admiration of a certain mentor: This can include a family member, someone who works in the profession, or teachers.
4. Wide range of career opportunities, including: general dental practice; specialities; working abroad; and maxillofacial surgery.
5. Employability and job security: consistently high graduate prospects and employability ratings.
6. Team management and leadership: Dentists need good management skills and teamwork.
7. Business Opportunities: Self-employed and practice purchasing.
8. Lifestyle choices: High-paying jobs and more sociable working hours.

It is important to note that some of these answers will not be looked at favourably in interviews, despite being genuine reasons for wanting to pursue a career in dentistry. An answer relating to job security and lifestyle choices, particularly regarding pay, will make the interviewer question your true intentions for pursuing this career.

Dentistry is undoubtedly a difficult career, so speaking about these factors can undermine the challenges faced, no matter how attractive they may seem. Instead, focus on demonstrating a genuine passion for what is involved in your day-to-day work to show your genuine intentions.

Why choose dentistry over other health care professions?

MEDICINE VS DENTISTRY

Similarities include a strong basis in science, intimate knowledge of physiology, patient interaction and problem solving. Differences include: working hours; registration; contact with patients during training; building relationships; and varied career and skills. You also work with your hands a lot in dentistry (manual dexterity).

CONTINUITY OF CARE

Unlike in a GP setting, patients will seek treatment on a regular basis, meaning you can build up long-term relationships with both your patients and their family members. As a dentist you conduct both the treatment, planning and diagnosis, meaning you are fully involved at each stage of the way.

Examples of other dental care professionals include dental nursing, hygiene, therapy and dental technicians. The GDC have produced a document called the 'Scope of Practice', detailing what different dental professionals are allowed to carry out. Have a read through this document and try to think why dentistry appeals to you more than these careers.

AWARENESS OF NEGATIVE ASPECTS OF DENTISTRY AND DENTAL SCHOOL

Educational expenses: High tuition and maintenance fees.

Lengthy educational programme: Five-year programme with optional additional intercalated year. Postgraduate: 4-year accelerated programmes available.

Difficult course: As well as having a lot of contact hours, and being very content heavy, you must also be able to work independently.

Competitive environment: High competition for student places.

Phrases to Avoid in Interviews When Answering Motivation Questions

"When I was younger, I had orthodontic treatment."

This is a very cliché answer which the interviewers have had countless times. Try to come up with something more unique. If you put this in your answer, make sure you expand on it and make it personal; perhaps by detailing the specific things your dentist did to make you fall in love with the career.

"I want to be a dentist because they earn a lot of money."

There are easier jobs than dentistry where you can earn lots of money. Money should never be a sole motivator.

"I am good at science and a high-achieving student so I thought this would be a good option."

You will need more than good science knowledge to do dentistry. Interviewers are looking for well-rounded individuals with good communication skills, among other qualities.

"My parents are dentists, so I knew a lot about what they did, and I wanted to do it too."

The interviewers want to know about your motivation, and not assume that you were pushed into the career due to your parents.

"I didn't know what I wanted to study and didn't know what else to apply for."

This shows a lack of passion and motivation and will obviously not come across well.

"I wanted to study medicine but couldn't get in."

It is important to realise early on that dentistry is just as hard as medicine. You will be in dental school for 5 years and will be a medical professional when you graduate.

> "I am scared of blood – medicine has too much blood and surgery compared to dentistry."

The mouth can bleed a lot! You will also undertake oral surgery as a dentist.

> "There is less risk and responsibility as a dentist compared to doctors."

Once again dentists are medical professionals. As you are treating the public you will be held to standards equally as high as high as a medic.

Use the above points to help structure your answer but remember your reason for studying dentistry can only come from you. Use examples of events that have happened to you during work experience to make your answer more personable. The right motivation is needed when choosing a career as a healthcare professional, and is of the highest importance for successful completion of studies.

WORK EXPERIENCE

As work experience is a requirement of the application process, you are very likely to be asked questions about it in the interview. Some examples of questions you can expect are:

- What are the key things you learnt from your work experience?
- What can you tell us about your work experience?
- What did you see during your work experience?
- What aspect of your work experience would you recommend to a friend thinking about applying for dentistry, and why?
- Did anything surprise or shock you during your work experience placement?

- Was there anything which the dentist did that impressed you during work experience?
- Can you tell me the key things you learned from your work experience, in caring or other settings?
- In your work experience, what skills have you learnt that you can apply to Dentistry?
- In your work experience was there anything the dentist struggled with?
- Did you do any work experience non-dentistry related, and how could the skills from this experience relate to dentistry?

As you can see, all these questions are very similar but phrased in different ways. The key to answering these questions is making sure you reflect during your work experience. Take a notebook and write down anything that interests you. Make notes of the skills the dentist uses during patient interactions, especially those relating to communication and empathy.

Research and memorise the 9 GDC principles so that you can see how the dentist is implementing these throughout the day. Make sure you also mention how you arranged the work experience.

If anything shocks you, write that down also and ask the dentist questions. This means when it comes to answering your questions, you will have information to go off and you can phrase the answer in a way that is personal to you. The interviewer is looking at how you can reflect on experiences, as this is something that you will be doing throughout your dental career.

General answer: "I arranged my work experience by sending out emails to my local dental practices and was lucky enough for one of the practices to reply to me.

During my work experience, what stood out to me was the many skills the dentist used when dealing with patients. I noticed that the dentist always had positive body language; smiling at the patient and making sure they were sitting down without their mask when talking to the patient to ensure they had eye contact.

The dentist also had optimum communication skills. One patient was very anxious about getting a restoration. To relax the patient and make them more comfortable, the dentist made sure the patient understood the procedure and told the patient to put their hand up if they wanted to stop the treatment. I thought that this showed good communication skills because it showed that the dentist was addressing the patient's needs first.

Another thing I noted is how much dentistry is a team job, from the dentist, nurse to the practice manager. I particularly noticed the positive relationship the dentist and dental nurse had, as they were always checking in on each other and the dental nurse was very supportive. This emphasised to me the importance of good teamwork skills."

PROFESSIONALISM

Professionalism in dentistry is a moral contract between the profession and society that is underpinned by a set of values, behaviours and relationships. The GDC is the main regulatory board for this. In order to work as a dental professional, you need to be registered with the GDC. Serious or persistent failure to follow the guidance set out by them could see you removed from the GDC register and not be able to work as a dental professional.

As a dental student, you must adhere to the GDC guidance on student professionalism and principles of behaviour in order to become a registered dental professional.

Student professionalism is the way you respond to the standards required of you, and how you take responsibility for meeting them. Even if you do not need a standard on a particular occasion, your recognition of the issue and ability to respond in the right way also demonstrates professionalism.

FITNESS TO PRACTICE

As a student, you are expected to meet certain student 'fitness to practice' requirements during your training. Training providers are responsible for determining the fitness to practice of individual students. If a student demonstrates unprofessionalism, their university can question their fitness to practice. This is serious, as it can have an impact on registering with GDC and becoming a dentist. This is a last resort!

The GDC has 9 set standards that all dentists are expected to meet whilst practising. These standards should be reflected in the way dentists treat their patients. They ensure that the public's confidence in the dental profession remains high.

1. Putting patients' best interest first – reflects the importance of a patient-centred approach.
2. Communicating effectively with patients – an essential skill when planning treatments and handling patient's concerns.
3. Obtain valid consent – ensure you have the patient's permission to perform any procedure.
4. Maintain and protect patients' information – keeping patients' details confidential protects them and maintains their trust in the professions.
5. Have a clear and effective complaints procedure – if something is to go wrong, patients' complaints should be dealt with promptly and respectfully.
6. Work with colleagues in a way that is in patients' best interest – different members of the dental team have different roles which must be carried out appropriately.
7. Maintain, develop and work within your professional knowledge and skills – dental care professionals have to undergo continued professional development (CPD) to keep their skills up to date.
8. Raise concerns if patients are at risk – every member of the dental team should feel comfortable about raising concerns if the situation is deemed to be appropriate.

9. Make sure our professional behaviours maintain confidence in us and the dental profession – patients need to know that they are receiving a high standard of care and that they are going to be well looked after.

Using these 9 guidelines as the backbone to your reasoning and judgement in an interview is a useful way to go about tackling professionalism scenarios.

Below are some questions to help you prepare using the above guidelines. Try answering these questions and then check the ideal responses to see which points you could have taken into consideration when answering.

1. You're in the clinic at lunchtime. You notice a senior colleague has just had their food, not washed their hands and touched some sterilised equipment. What would you do?

2. You just finished an exam at dental school. After the exam you hear some of your fellow classmates discuss how they had the exam paper 3 days ago. What will you do?

3. It is a busy day at the clinic. One of the nurses is off sick and you notice that the other dentist working is displaying signs of frustration as patients are having to wait longer. How will you approach this situation?

4. A patient walks into the clinic at 2:40pm. Their original appointment for a routine check-up was at 2:25pm. The receptionist informs you that the patient has arrived, however, your next appointment is in 5 minutes and seeing the late patient will mean that the clinic will run behind schedule. Which factors do you need to consider before making your judgement?

5. You are observing a dentist whilst on a placement. A patient starts to ask the dentist some questions regarding their X-ray that they had taken a few days ago. You notice that the dentist is struggling to answer these questions and is constantly using their phone for guidance. What should you do?

6. An elderly patient walks into the clinic and other patients move away from their seats. They start complaining that the elderly patient smells and should not be allowed in the clinic. As the dentist in charge, what will you do?

7. When observing a dentist you notice that they are hesitant to get close to a patient as they have halitosis. They are wary and are not getting the full view of the mouth during the examination. What steps will you take?

8. Your dental school has strict guidelines that students must be in the correct uniform during their clinical practice and must have their hair tied back with no jewellery. However, one of your close friends decided that they will go to clinics wearing clothes they feel comfortable with because they have dinner after clinics and they want to look their best. What advice would you give your friend?

9. Just before you begin a root canal on a patient, they tell you that the receptionist mumbled a racist remark under their breath when they walked past. What will you do in this moment?

10. A first year dental student has come to your practice to observe for the day. At lunch you notice the student disclosing some personal information on the phone about one of the patients who came in the morning. What is your approach to this situation?

Points to Consider:

1. In this situation it's important to take into consideration that the equipment in a clinic must always be kept sterilised to maintain the safety of all patients and staff members. The colleague touching the equipment without washing their hands is in breach of quality control regulations. Regardless of the colleague being senior, their actions can harm patients and should be brought to their attention, and the equipment should be re-sterilised to keep everyone safe before the next patient is seen.

2. Honesty is key in the dental profession. Dentists are entrusted with the health of their patients. Cheating in a dental school exam shows that the students are not fit to practice such a career, as knowledge of everything that is learned in dental school is required once the students go onto practice. The students will need to be confronted and asked why they would decide to cheat, whether they struggled with the content or due to personal reasons. Members of staff will also need to be informed so that they are aware of this situation and can prevent it from affecting students that have worked hard for the same exam. Preventative measures could be put into place to stop this happening again.

3. It's important to talk to the dentist in this situation. Their frustration may not only be due to the nurse being absent, it may also be due to personal reasons. If the dentist is not calm they may cause harm to the patients, so to avoid this happening it may be an option to allow them to go home. Patients who are waiting should be informed that there is a bit of a delay in the clinic. For the future, if a nurse is absent it may be useful to alert patients with appointments that day, reducing pressure on the dentists and rest of the team.

4. It will be useful to consider the exact nature of the next appointment. If the following appointment is of urgency, then it may be useful to speak to the patient and explain that they have missed their appointment and their routine check-up may need to be rescheduled. You can also check to see whether there are any appointments available to accommodate the patient later in the day.

5. The dentist not being able to communicate effectively with the patient could be due to any number of reasons. Perhaps they aren't able to stay up-to-date with their work, or there could be personal reasons making it difficult for the dentist to concentrate.

6. The dentist may find it useful to talk to someone so that we can determine the precise issue. They may need extra support, in which case the practice manager could be told

to help keep in touch with their staff members. The dentist may need more training to keep their skills up to date through CPD courses.

7. Every patient has the right to be treated fairly, regardless of their age, religion, race and ethnicity. The dentist should act in a professional, composed manner in this situation. The elderly patient should be offered support as the comments made can hurt their feelings and affect them mentally. The dentist should explain to the patients who are complaining that it is not right to remove the elderly patient from the clinic, and that their appointment should go ahead as usual. The patient should not be treated any differently.

8. It will be important to raise any concerns with the dentist, as not having a complete view can put the patient at risk. The dentist has a duty to treat each patient equally. It will be important to discuss this with the dentist as their behaviour would be classed as inappropriate. Being a dentist means behaving in a professional manner and therefore the dentist will need to be reminded of their duties.

9. The uniform has been set out by the dental school. Your friend will need to be reminded that they have to dress professionally as the rules are set out for a reason. Patients need to have confidence in the dentist treating them. Turning up without the correct attire will put patients off. They will not be allowed to enter the clinics due to safety reasons as wearing the correct footwear and no jewellery is important, as the latter can cause disruption to the treatment.

10. In this case it is important that the patient feels comfortable before any treatment has begun. Being transparent with the patient and seeing whether they prefer to discuss the issue before or after their treatment is useful. As a part of a team it is important that the dentist does not jump to conclusions and has trust in team members. The patient may be hurt and offended by the situation, and asking the receptionist to clarify the situation will be helpful. The complaints procedure should be explained to the patient, as this is within their rights.

11. The student does not have the patient's consent to share their information and is therefore breaching their confidentiality. It is the dentist's responsibility to maintain and protect patient information. The student should be confronted and made aware that what they have done is unacceptable. Equally important in this case would be to inform the student's university so that this can be prevented from happening again. For any future students who come into the practice to observe it may be useful to remind them of their duties to protect patients' information.

DENTAL LAW & ETHICS

Ethics forms the foundation upon which the profession of dentistry is based. There are many ethical and legal guidelines that dentists have to follow. Ethics is the set of values, moral principles, and standards that need to be followed. Here is a brief overview, which will allow you to gain a deeper understanding of your ethical responsibilities as a dentist.

As a dentist, you must:
- Read and comply with the GDC's standards
- Always act in your patients' best interests
- Comply with the GDC's requirements for CPD
- Work within your knowledge and competence; do not attempt treatments you have not been trained for, and always refer a patient if necessary
- Always obtain the patient's valid informed consent to the treatment proposed
- Maintain the confidentiality of information which you hold about your patients.

Below are the four ethical pillars which you need to be aware of:

BENEFICENCE

Dentists should always act in the patient's best interest, doing the greater good whilst balancing risks and benefits.

Non-Maleficence

Dentists should do no harm to the patient and should protect all patients from harm.

Autonomy

Respecting an individual's dignity and ability to make decisions with regards to their own health.

Justice

In relation to fairness and equality, you should not treat patients differently on any basis other than that which is clinically proven.

In addition, remember to refer to the duty of candour. This is a legal responsibility for every healthcare professional to be completely honest with their patients/family when something goes wrong. Keep the patient fully informed about the long- and short-term effects of what has happened. This isn't limited to patients but also extends to your colleagues and team members. You will need to have a good awareness of all the points mentioned and try to include them within your answers.

It is vital to refer back to the GDC principles when answering questions relating to ethics. Remember there is no right or wrong answer. The interviewers want to see that you have weighed both sides of the argument before reaching a conclusion. Always try and identify the problem and provide a solution that can be used to solve the issue.

Try not to simply give a one-sided answer or over simplify your response, as it shows that you have not thought about both sides of the argument. Go through the scenario logically and confirm the exact problem. Try to make your answer as concise as possible and go straight to the points you wish to make. Do not rush your answer and be sure to think before giving your response. Be sure to end your answer with a balanced conclusion referring back to some of the main points you mentioned during your explanation.

Here are 10 ethical dilemmas with responses for you to contemplate.

1. You have only one lung donor available to give out but two patients are waiting. One patient is a 26 year-old pregnant female, and the other patient is a 40 year-old regular smoker. Who would you give the organ donor to?
2. Should benefits be removed from society as it is unfair for those who work to pay for other people's needs?
3. Do you think teeth whitening should be allowed on the NHS?
4. A patient comes into the practice complaining of a toothache. You wish to do an X-ray to establish the exact problem and make an informed decision. However, the patient refuses to have the X-ray done as they believe it will be harmful for them. What do you do?
5. Do you think the implementation of a sugar tax would impact all members of society equally?
6. Do you think euthanasia should be legal for everyone should they wish to undertake the procedure?
7. Should organ donation be made compulsory?
8. Should all dental services be free of charge for everyone?
9. Alcohol and smoking should be permanently banned as it causes more harm than good. Discuss this.
10. An obese patient comes into the practice. They are clearly too overweight to sit on the clinic chair. If they do sit on the chair you know that it will not support their weight. What should you do?

Points to Consider:

1. The main issue with this scenario is that there is only one organ donor available. Both patients deserve to be treated but your duty as the doctor is to look out for your patients' best interests. As one of the patients is a regular smoker, they are less suited to have the lung transplant now. This is not to say that their treatment should be neglected. The

patient needs to be given advice and guidance on the effects of smoking so they can gradually start to quit. This makes the 24 year-old female currently more suited as she is a non-smoker and in this case is more suited to receive the donated lung.

2. Benefits are derived from taxpayers' income to help people in society to survive financially. One argument for the continuation of benefits is that it will help aid families/individuals who are in genuine need of financial aid. As a society we should help those in need. Nevertheless, it can be seen as unfair on those people who work hard only to get taxed and pay for someone else's needs. People may also misuse the funds they receive from the benefits, which is a supporting point as to why benefits should be stopped.

3. A point to consider would be whether teeth whitening counts as an essential treatment for patients. One argument for teeth whitening to be on the NHS is that having discoloured teeth can really impact an individual's confidence. This suggests that it is a crucial treatment which should be covered by the NHS. However, one point to consider is that many people use teeth whitening for cosmetic purposes and teeth whitening is not an essential treatment in the sense that someone will not be in pain or suffer physically if they do not receive it. Also, including teeth whitening under the NHS will strain the health service financially.

4. Following the GDC principle, you have to do what is best for the patient. In this case, the patient is worried about the potential harm that an X-ray could cause. You as the dentist will need to calmly explain the positives of having the X-ray done, as well as exploring their preconceptions. The benefits for the patient include you being able to make an accurate diagnosis and devise an appropriate treatment plan that will hopefully alleviate the pain. Showing the positives to the patient and explaining the whole X-ray process to them will allow them to trust you and the process.

5. In the UK there is currently a Soft Drinks Industry Levy in place, which places a small tax on drinks containing a specific level of sugar content. Sugar taxes have been implemented previously in countries such as Mexico and have proven to be very effective at bringing down tooth decay rates across the nation. However, not every area will be impacted in the same way. The nature of implementing a tax by the same standard across the country means that the price increments, which act as a deterrent to purchasing 'sugary foods/drinks', would not affect all members of society in the same way. As studies have shown that the standard of oral health is poorer in lower socioeconomic backgrounds, they will be more impacted as a whole by changes brought about by a sugar tax compared to those from more affluent backgrounds. Therefore, a sugar tax would support better oral health standards for members of society who may place less focus on their oral hygiene and lead to a good outcome for the NHS by preventing decay-related diseases.

6. There are two ways of looking at this argument. Legalising euthanasia would mean that people are choosing to die. This would mean that any temporary hardships they are facing in life would be concluded with euthanizing themselves. This would cause a detrimental effect on family members and friends. However, a point to consider is that people who have poor quality of life or are diagnosed with a terminal illness in which death is inevitable should have the option to end their suffering through euthanasia. People should have the right to choose to live or die as it is their life and should not be dictated by laws.

7. A positive outcome of organ donation becoming compulsory would be that there will not be any shortage of organs for those undergoing treatment. After a person has passed away they will not need their organs, and they should be donated to help someone in need, thus saving lives. However, people may not want to donate organs as they would want to preserve the deceased and let them be after they

have passed away. Organ donation should be a choice as ultimately it should be an individual decision.

8. Free dental care would result in more people visiting their dentist more frequently. They would therefore be more likely to take care of their oral health with the dentist educating them. However, with free treatment available, people may also begin to take their oral health for granted. Private practices would lose out on business and funding would be a clear issue if dental care were free. As most dental materials are expensive there would need to be a stable funding programme for free dental treatment, which would put a financial strain on the NHS. On the other hand, financial constraints are a barrier to dental treatment, so making dental treatment free would give people from lower socioeconomic backgrounds more of an incentive to receive dental treatment. This idea is in line with the ethical pillar of justice; every person should have the same access to healthcare regardless of their wealth or background.

9. There are two ways to evaluate this statement. If alcohol and smoking were permanently banned, this would cause a decrease in liver problems, tobacco related issues, lung dysfunction, and drinking and driving cases to name a few. This would promote a much healthier lifestyle for many people, as these products would not be readily available. Another way of looking at this argument would be that not everyone who smokes or drinks alcohol is necessarily an addict, so banning these would be an extreme measure. Also, those who are addicts would suffer great withdrawal symptoms if they are trying to quit, so banning alcohol and smoking would only further affect their health.

10. As a dentist it is your duty to make sure a patient is treated with respect and dignity. This situation must be tackled in an appropriate manner. It may be useful to get the patient to fill out a form disclosing details such as their height and weight. This way you will not be making assumptions about their exact weight, and can categorically decide whether

or not the patient is heavier than the weight that the chair is designed to hold. Once the results are back you can then begin to discuss the problem with the patient in a polite manner, being completely honest. As a solution you can also refer the patient to a dental hospital where they will be able to accommodate the patient further with bariatric dental chairs. The patient may also feel discriminated against if it is decided that they cannot have their treatment in the dental chair, so it's vital to communicate the reasoning behind your choices clearly if you choose to refer them to a dental hospital. They should know that you are acting in their best interests, in line with the first GDC principle.

TEAMWORK & LEADERSHIP

Working in a dental practice is not a one-man job. The dentist is required to work within a multi-disciplinary team of dental nurses, dental technicians, hygienists and therapists, receptionists and so on. All of whom must communicate effectively. The interviewers will look out for candidates that demonstrate leadership qualities but also those who work well with others to complete the work at hand. This can be assessed during group tasks or even through general questions at both MMI's and Panel interviews.

Working in a team would mean that you are completing your role to the best of your ability whilst also making sure that your peers are getting along well. If you do come across difficulties whilst working in a team, it's important to tackle the issue and diffuse the situation. This also means respecting others, making contributions, meeting deadlines, monitoring progress, and listening to what others have to say.

The 'STAR' interview response technique will help to tackle questions about group tasks.

SITUATION

To give information about the context regarding where and when this project took place.

TASK

What was the group's aim?

Provide information about the particular project and explain the challenge that needed to be overcome.

ACTION

Describe the actions that were taken to complete the project or solve the particular problem.

RESULT

Finally, explain the result of the actions taken. Emphasise what your team accomplished or what you learned. Explain how each person's role was pivotal.

WHAT LEADERSHIP QUALITIES DO YOU NEED TO SHOW AND WHY?

CONFIDENCE

A dentist needs to show confidence as they need to communicate with a range of patients and reassure them that the dentist is competent.

PROBLEM SOLVING SKILLS

Most likely there will be a problem which needs to be overcome. As a dentist you will be expected to think quickly and provide a solution to the issue. Diagnosing conditions when given vague symptomatic descriptions requires an element of problem solving.

RESILIENCE

There will be times where you feel like giving up, especially when workload is increased at dental school. You need to show that you can cope with the pressure by not giving up during difficult tasks and giving it your best. Part of being resilient includes self-evaluation. You can only bounce back from a situation by stepping back and evaluating your actions to see how you can improve when encountering the same task or scenario in future.

Vision & Delegation

As a dentist you will need to lead a team of dental nurses and delegate tasks equally. You will need to know what you wish to achieve by the end, and have a clear vision of the steps you have to take to get there.

Communication

As a dentist you must have strong communication skills so you can interact and work well with your dental team, and you must explain treatments and processes to your patient. You should be able to tailor your approach depending on who you are communicating with as you will come across individuals of all ages and backgrounds. Pivotal to this is your ability to obtain valid consent from your patients as well as providing them with a sense of comfort and confidence in you as a professional.

Top Tips for Group Tasks

Be confident and speak up if you have an idea. You will be observed so be sure to make yourself heard in the group but do so without undermining any of your other team members. Try to sound positive and contribute to the discussion. Be respectful to other team members. It's okay to disagree with ideas but don't discourage others from speaking. Make the effort to include everyone and be a good listener when others are talking. Try your best and remain calm and composed if presenting at the end. If the opportunity arises, be sure to suggest what further improvements could be made to the way the group approached the task, this will show that you are a critical thinker. However avoid critiquing your peers, as you need to have trust in their abilities. Here are some ways you can motivate your team:

- Share the organisational vision with each member
- Create and maintain a team spirit
- Give each person opportunities to grow
- Give as much support as you can
- Make sure there is a good working environment
- Make people feel appreciated

Examples of teamwork and leadership experience:

- Playing in a team sport
- Duke of Edinburgh Award
- NCS awards
- Delivering a presentation
- Volunteering with a team
- Jobs involving other staff members
- Head boy/ Head girl / prefects/ mentors
- Clubs
- Raising awareness through charity projects
- Event organising

Below are 5 example questions or requests relating to teamwork and leadership skills:

1. Can you give an example of how you have displayed leadership skills?
2. Have you worked in a team, if so, when and what did you achieve?
3. Discuss in your group whether you think Brexit should happen or not
4. You are in your 4th year at dental school. You have a presentation to deliver with 3 other students. However, you feel as if an unfair amount of work has been put on you, and the other students are not concerned about the presentation at all. What will you do?
5. You are the captain for a local football team. Recently the team has lost 4 games in a row and the players are feeling demotivated. What steps will you take as the captain of the team?

Points to Consider:

1. This could be in the form of being a captain of a team whilst playing sports. A good example would be to include a time where you solved a problem or organised an event. Try not

to sound over confident when answering this question and make sure to mention what issues you faced and how you overcame them.

2. Once again, this could be answered with any time where you have communicated and worked with other people to achieve a common goal. Common examples include creating a presentation in school, playing sports for a local club, contributing to a fundraising event to raise money. This answer should be personal to you rather than a generic response.

3. Be aware of current hot topics such as Brexit, the NHS, and advancements within dentistry. They may come in handy in discussions. Try to explain your points within the time limit and hear what others have to say as well.

4. It's important to make yourself heard within the group. Avoid making assumptions, as the rest of the group may not be aware of how you are feeling. Be sure to address how you feel and what the team can do to support you, which in this case means distributing the workload and communicating well with each other.

5. As the captain of the team, it's important to keep the players motivated by suggesting what improvements can be made for the next match. Evaluating the matches with the team can be useful to address weaknesses within their match performance. You would also want to provide a solution to helping them win the game, for example by making sure everyone is training, leading by example and putting in extra hours. As players are demotivated it will be good to offer them support and tell them that they can reach out to you if they are feeling down. You need to encourage them and remind them about the positives in the game.

DATA ANALYSIS

This section of the interview assesses your ability to interpret data. If this comes up, you will usually have a few minutes to look at a graph or statistics. Use this time to identify a trend and make a note of points which you wish to address about the information that's presented.

This station is very common in MMIs as interviewers want to see whether you are able to reach conclusions based on data.

To tackle a graph, you need to start off by explaining what the graph is actually about. Remember to mention what type of graph is in front of you. Refer to the title of the graph and then state what the axis shows. This will allow you to consider the information as a whole before going into detail. Then mention the trends that you are able to see alongside any anomalies within the data. The interviewer is likely to ask you follow up questions regarding the data. For example: on a graph showing the number of smokers against the year, a follow up question may be, why do you think the number of people smoking decreases as the years increase. You will need to consider external factors such as age restrictions and more awareness campaigns.

For questions involving statistics it is crucial to read the question carefully and make sure you understand exactly what the question is asking you to do. It will also be useful to brush up on some common conversions and formulas, which we have included below. These will help in case you need to do some additional calculations.

CONVERSIONS & FORMULAS
- 1,000 grams = 1 kilogram
- 1 mile = 1.6 kilometres
- 1,000 millilitres = 1 litre
- 100 centimetres = 1 metre
- 1 centimetre = 10 millimetres
- 1 millimetre = 0.001 metres
- Percentage increase = (new value - old value) / 100
- Speed = distance / time

COMMUNICATION & ROLE PLAY
As a dentist you will be communicating with your patients every day; explaining complex procedures. You will also work as a team with your nurse, the lab, your peers, and your professors. Communication is key to building trust with your patients. It removes fear of the

unknown. Effective communication allows you to build a rapport with the patient. When you keep the patient comfortable through effective communication they have a better understanding of the procedure and will be happier to disclose information. We need to communicate ideas in a way that the patient understands (is at the correct level for the patient), allowing them to make an informed decision and give their consent.

Effective communication means getting your ideas across to the other person in a way that they will understand. In other words, you are presenting your ideas in a way that is best understood by the receiver. Effective communication also means the person that you are communicating needs to be a good listener to absorb and understand the knowledge.

There are many ways of assessing communication at your interview – firstly though your general tone. If you are not confident when answering questions you will have difficulty getting across your ideas. Communication can be in the form of a role play station, describing a picture, critiquing a video, describing a process and giving personal examples of good communication. The basic principles of how to tackle these situations remain the same.

During role play stations with an actor, you will be marked from the moment the timer starts. Firstly, make sure that your body language is correct. Keep an open posture and make eye contact. Be an effective listener and pay attention to issues that the actor raises in the conversation. When breaking bad news during a role play station there are a few things to keep in mind. The scenario may not always be dental or medical related. It can simply be an everyday situation. The interviewers want to see whether you are able to stay composed and show empathy. To begin breaking bad news it is important to follow the structure below:

SPIKES
Setting up and starting. Mentally be prepared to break the bad news and make sure there is privacy. You can replicate this in an

interview setting by asking the actor to take a seat before you begin the conversation.

Perception. Try and find the actor's perspective of the situation. How much do they know so far? Remember that the actor will pretend to be hearing the news for the first time.

Invitation. This means asking the actor how much they wish to know about the situation. Make sure to give the actor the opportunity to ask any questions should they wish to do so.

Knowledge. This requires you to pass on information to the actor. Warn the actor that you have some bad news. Try to do this using simple language and be direct to the point without raising anxiety. Keep a subtle tone and try to empathise with the actor.

Empathy. Address the actor's emotions with empathetic responses. Let the actor know you are here for them and take this moment to listen to the actor too. Try to show empathy through your body language too. Listening is key. Allow the actor to voice their feelings then try to comfort them as best as possible.

Summary. Reiterate the actor's wishes. Suggest how you can help them with a solution to the problem and let them know you are there for them.

When describing a picture, be sure to be clear in your description. Start off by explaining the bigger picture before you go into the finer details of the image. This is an important task because you use a similar technique when analysing X-rays, and explaining the findings to the patient. You first take a look at the whole picture, before looking at specific teeth and going in depth. Patients also cannot see a lot of the work and treatment you do in their mouth, so again it is important to be able to communicate and explain this.

For video critiquing stations, communication is a key facet of patient interaction, particularly if the patient is nervous around the dentist (a very common occurrence). Think about both verbal communication (tone of voice, pace, use of easy to understand language) and non-verbal communication (eye contact, posture, facial expression, receptiveness to the patient).

Even if you thought the whole thing was very good or very bad, always try to give constructive criticism; pointing out both positives and negatives. It shows that you can extract and distinguish between both sides of a situation – a key trait in effective reflection.

Be sure to take your time with tasks revolving around explaining a process. Use simple language and be clear with what you would like the actor to do. Stay composed during the explanation. Start off by repeating what you intend to do and the aim of the explanation. Then let the actor know that if they are unsure, they can ask you questions along the way. Make sure to encourage the actor when they do something right, and adapt your method if they don't understand what you want them to do.

For questions asking about your own experiences with communication you can personalize your answer. A good example is to mention your work experience, such as witnessing how the dentist was able to communicate with their team. Some personal examples may include:
- Communicating with elderly patients in care homes (volunteering)
- Delivering a presentation
- Interacting with customers through various jobs

Have a go at the following scenarios:

1. Explain how as a dentist you would deal with a patient who has dementia.
2. You have received blood test results of a patient. You have to break news to them that they have blood cancer.

3. Your friend asks you to pick up his post from his apartment. You notify him that he has a letter from his current job in the mail. He then asks you to read the letter and you realise that the letter is regarding his termination. How will you tell this to your friend?

4. You are asked to look after your friend's dog for the weekend. You take the dog for a walk but it runs away and now you can't find it. What will you do?

5. A patient comes into your clinic to have a tooth removed. Once you have finished the treatment you realise you extracted the wrong tooth.

6. Describe how to tie shoelaces.

7. Explain how to tie a tie.

8. Describe this image to another person without stating what the actual picture is:

9. Describe the following image without stating what the actual picture is:

10. A patient comes to your clinic with an appointment. However, the patient is deaf and unable to understand you. How will you communicate with them?

Use the tips given to practice with these questions. Remember that each station will be timed so it is important you are able to include everything you wish to mention before the time runs out.

‖ 100 Interview Questions

Have a look through the interview questions below to practice answering them.

1. Why do you wish to study dentistry?
2. What motivates you?

3. What did you learn from your work experience?
4. What would you say is your greatest weakness?
5. Why do you want to study at this university?
6. What can you bring to this university?
7. Why not pursue medicine or other healthcare professions instead of dentistry?
8. What is your greatest strength?
9. How do you cope with stress?
10. Have you read any articles about dentistry recently?
11. Can you tell us about some modern advancements in dentistry lately?
12. What challenges do you think a dental student faces?
13. If you didn't get into dentistry what would you do?
14. Can you tell us how you stay organised?
15. What do you do apart from academic studies?
16. What do you currently find most interesting in your life?
17. What are you looking forward to most about starting dentistry?
18. Why is manual dexterity important in dentistry?
19. Can you describe a time where you displayed good leadership skills?
20. Why not become a dental hygienist instead of a dentist?
21. Give examples of good manual dexterity that you have displayed?
22. What can you tell me about the NHS banding system?
23. Tell me about a time where you experienced a setback and how did you overcome this?
24. How do you deal with criticism?
25. How will you balance workload in dental school?
26. What does the GDC do and why do we need it?
27. Do you think the NHS should become privatised?
28. Why is dentistry more important than ever?
29. What advice would you give yourself 5 years ago?
30. How do you cope with frustration?
31. What are the advantages of evidence based learning?
32. Do you prefer evidence based learning or problem based learning?

THE SELECTION PROCESS

229 WWW.IWANTTOBEADENTIST.COM

33. If you had a patient who was really anxious how would you calm them down?
34. How do you help out in your local community?
35. Do you feel you possess the qualities of a good dentist?
36. Who inspires you?
37. Why should we select you compared to other applicants?
38. Where do you see yourself in the next 10 years?
39. What are your long term goals?
40. What are the disadvantages of using amalgam?
41. What problems do most dentists face today?
42. What did you like least about your work experience?
43. What are you least looking forward to in dentistry?
44. If there was one thing you could change about dentistry what would it be?
45. Who are the members in a dental team?
46. Would you rather be a leader or a follower?
47. What is your best quality?
48. What is your greatest fear about becoming a dentist?
49. What would you do if your friend decides to copy your essay at dental school?
50. You finish an essay which is due tomorrow. You have spent ages working on it but just as you are about to save your work your computer switches off and all your work is lost. What will you do?
51. Your friends go out without inviting you to go with them. What would you do?
52. Your friend asks to use your gym membership. She has been going through financial problems and asks to borrow your entry card. The gym membership is only for paying residents. What would you do?
53. You are having a drink with your friends and you notice one of them going outside. From the window you can see that they are extremely angry on the phone with someone. They come inside and tell you they're going home. What would you do?
54. You overhear one of your friends saying that they have pictures of the upcoming exam. What do you do?

55. Your friend calls you in the morning just before your lecture starts and asks you to sign them in as they cannot make it today due to a family emergency. What will you do in this situation?
56. Why do you think multitasking is important in dentistry?
57. Should people who smoke have to pay extra for their dental treatment as they are causing harm themselves?
58. You are observing a dentist. They smell of alcohol when they walk past you. What will you do?
59. A 13-year old patient comes in for an appointment. Just before you begin their treatment you notice they have bruises on their neck. The mother is present in the same room. What will you do?
60. Your friend starts a social media page asking people for donations as they are financially unstable. However you know that this isn't the case at all. What steps will you take?
61. A dental student you know shares an image online of a patient as a joke. Do you think this was appropriate to do?
62. Do you think all dental treatment should be completely free of charge?
63. What is fluoride?
64. Why do you think dentistry is known as a lifelong learning career?
65. Have you researched the university course?
66. Who is the most important member of the dental team?
67. What book have you recently read and enjoyed?
68. Who is one person you would love to have coffee with?
69. Is there a particular field of dentistry you are interested in?
70. What do you do in your spare time?
71. If you could improve one thing in your application what would it be?
72. Can you name some instruments the dentist used while at your work experience?
73. How do you think social media can be used to increase oral hygiene awareness?
74. Are there any societies that you wish to join?

75. What research have you done relating to dentistry?
76. What is one thing you look least forward to about university life?
77. How have you developed independence?
78. How do you think someone can improve their confidence?
79. One of your friends does not stay in contact anymore and doesn't attend their lectures. You see them on campus one day, what would you say?
80. Do you think teams need leaders?
81. When do you think a dentist may break confidentiality?
82. What is the difference between sympathy and empathy?
83. What is enamel?
84. Why do you think dentistry is a 5-year course?
85. How would you treat a patient that is disabled?
86. What are the risks associated with X-rays?
87. Why does a dentist require a dental nurse?
88. What advice would you give to a patient to look after their oral health?
89. What do you think prevents people from looking after their oral health?
90. How can dentists increase awareness about maintaining good oral hygiene?
91. What do you think are some of the factors which limit people from visiting the dentist regularly?
92. What do you think is the future of dentistry?
93. What is tooth decay?
94. What is gingivitis?
95. Name some differences between NHS and Private dentistry?
96. What are some issues the NHS is currently facing?
97. You are a final year dental student. Your senior dentist is extremely rude and has a go at you at every opportunity. What will you do?
98. Do you think signing petitions makes a difference?
99. You accidentally break your friend's glasses by stepping on them. Those were her only pair. How will you approach her?
100. Do you think you will be a successful dentist and why?

Below are some final tips with a summary of the points made in the interview section.

- Know your personal statement inside-out.
- Panel interviews will always have questions based on your statement.

Be ready to expand on any topic written in your personal statement. An interviewer may also share the same interest, or may be an expert in the field of dentistry you mentioned. When talking about these topics make sure you include the skills you have gained from it that will serve you in dentistry.

Know the university details, area and curriculum inside-out. This is available on pretty much every dental school website. Look into recreational/out-of-uni activities in the area too. The interviewers want to know that you genuinely want to be at that particular school, not that you just entered it randomly on your UCAS form.

Communication is key. Your answers are important but the way you deliver them is equally important. Verbally; speak in a clear, articulate and polite manner. Non-verbally; have receptive body-language (no arm-folding), sit up straight (no slouching) and make eye contact with your interviewers.

Some interviewers may be deliberately curt or distracting when you give your answers; they may avoid eye contact, seem disinterested and interrupt you. This is purposely done to see how you handle things supposedly not going to plan. Don't worry about it, continue to address every interviewer in the same enthusiastic, polite manner. Don't let them put you off!

Be ready to think on your feet, especially in MMI interviews, where you may be presented with scenarios that are completely out there and have nothing to do with dentistry. They're meant to see how well you can improvise and how calm you remain under pressure. For example, you might get asked to explain to someone how to tie a pair of shoelaces without using your hands to communicate (Try it. It's harder than it sounds!). Stay composed, make a miniature plan in your head and don't come across as frazzled, even if you are internally!

Practice manual dexterity. Try and practice things that involve fiddly, precise and fine movements. In MMI interviews they could ask you to demonstrate your skill, for example by giving you instructions on origami. Most musical instruments, sewing, sitting in front of a mirror and doing dot-to-dots whilst staring exclusively at the mirror are all good things to try.

Make yourself memorable for the interviewers! Think about your talents. Is there anything you can use to create something? It could be a song you published on SoundCloud, or an Instagram page showing off your baking skills. Show off your personality.

Don't memorise meticulous answers as you'll sound too robotic in your responses. You are better off having some general points in your head that you want to talk about and going off those in your answers. Of course, you should practice answering interview questions, but answering questions in a more natural way makes for better conversation and leads the interviewer to ask follow up questions.

Last but not least; smile and relax. This seems obvious but it's easy to forget to smile while caught up in it all! Enjoy yourself and show the interviewers that you've been looking forward to this interview for months! Enthusiasm can make all the difference!

Key Terminology

Being familiar with some key terminology is crucial for your interview. Below we have included a few of the terms you should know before heading into your interviewers as it's likely you could be asked about these and may even see them in a question.

- Plaque – a soft, sticky film that builds up on your teeth and contains millions of bacteria. The bacteria in plaque cause tooth decay and gum disease if they are not removed regularly through brushing and flossing.
- Enamel – the hard, outer surface layer of your teeth that serves to protect against tooth decay. Enamel is the strongest substance in the body, even stronger than bone.
- Fluoride – is a naturally occurring mineral found in water (varying amounts depending on where you live). It can help prevent tooth decay, which is why it's added to many brands of toothpaste and, in some areas, to the water supply through a process called fluoridation.
- Root canal treatment is a dental procedure used to treat infection within the tooth nerve. Root canal treatment is usually not painful and can save a tooth that might otherwise have to be removed completely.
- Tooth decay, also known as dental caries, is damage to a tooth that can happen when decay-causing bacteria in your mouth make acids that attack the tooth's surface (enamel). This can lead to small holes in teeth called cavities.
- Halitosis is the term for chronic bad breath.
- Amalgam fillings are a common type of filling used in dentistry. Also known as a 'silver filling', an amalgam filling is used to fill cavities caused by tooth decay.
- Resin Composite fillings mimics the appearance of natural teeth, these fillings blend right in. They are also known as 'white fillings' or 'tooth-coloured fillings'.
- Gingivitis is a common, mild form of gum disease (periodontal disease) which causes irritation, redness and swelling (inflammation) of your gingiva – the part of your gum around the base of your teeth.
- Oral cancer is the appearance of cancers of the mouth and the back of the throat.
- NHS Price Bands. There are 3 bands, each with a different price determining the cost of the dental treatment.

- Manual dexterity is the ability to use your hands in a skilful, coordinated way to grasp and manipulate objects and demonstrate small, precise movements.
- Topical anaesthetic is a local anaesthetic that is used to numb the surface of a body part.
- Duty of candour is a legal duty to be open and honest with patients or their families when something goes wrong that appears to have caused or could lead to significant harm in the future.
- Mental capacity is the ability to use and understand information to make decisions, and communicate any decisions made. A person lacks mental capacity if their mind is impaired or disturbed in some way, which means they're unable to make a decision at that time.
- Dental specialties are specific branches of dentistry. Thirteen dental specialties are practiced in the UK: Dental and Maxillofacial Radiology; Dental Public Health; Endodontics; Oral and Maxillofacial Pathology; Oral Medicine; Oral Microbiology; Oral Surgery; Orthodontics; Paediatric Dentistry; Periodontology; Prosthodontics; Restorative dentistry; and Special Care Dentistry.
- GDC principles are 9 principles set out by the General Dental Council, which dentists must be aware of. Make sure that you read the GDC guidelines in 'Standards for the Dental Team'.

PART 3

IN THIS SECTION WE WILL COVER THE FOLLOWING:
This chapter will cover the dental school application process for an international student. This process differs moderately from home students. We will cover the application process on UCAS, English proficiency exams, alongside fees, funding and preparation for your interview.

Selecting a University

Usually the application process for international students is similar to home students but with a few additional things to consider. Schools in the UK often follow the A-level or International Baccalaureate curriculums. Any other non-UK qualifications accepted by universities are usually listed on the university website. If not, contacting the dental school directly can help you resolve any queries. Researching required qualifications is important to ensure that whatever high school qualifications you have will be recognised by the UK dental school you are applying to, and that you meet their basic entry requirements.

Whilst it is of course important to choose a university based on its academic merit, when weighing up the 'pros and cons' for each option, taking note of travel options to the nearest airport, or the number of layovers needed to get back home is very useful. The easiest, fastest and most cost efficient travel routes can often prove to be a real plus if you are planning to travel back and forth a few times a year over some or all of your term holidays.

Leaving home for university can be daunting, let alone heading off to a different country. There are many factors to consider when deciding which city and university is the best fit for you. These may often include making sure that the town or city of your university has not only the right feel of a place where you think you can live for a number of years, but also has the sporting, cultural and other facilities that you believe you will need. If possible, pay a visit to the university and get to know the surrounding environment to see if it offers everything that you are looking for.

UCAS & Funding

Once you have an idea of where you would like to study dentistry, further course research can be done through the UCAS website.

This website is where international and home students are required to submit their university choices and applications. Step-by-step guides can be found in several languages on the UCAS website to help you with the application process.

UK universities often have two categories of fee status: Home Student fees and International Student fees. International fees can differ between degrees (especially when comparing clinical and non-clinical qualifications). They may also differ between universities located in England, Scotland, Wales and Northern Ireland. Probably the most important factor to keep in mind as an international student is that the fees will usually be substantially higher than for students with Home Student fee status.

Home students are required to be a British national and resident in the UK for a minimum of 3 consecutive years. Following the country's exit from the European Union (EU) in 2021, the home fees criteria is set to change. EU students commencing their academic studies in 2020-2021 will be granted home status. However, after August 2021, that is no longer possible.

If you have grown up as an expat abroad, you may not be entitled to home fees status if you are moving to the UK with the sole purpose of education, even if you hold a British passport. Thus you will likely be classified as an international student.

International fees, as mentioned, can vary between dental schools. Exact costs can be found on the university websites. It's important to confirm whether you can cover the fees as well as living and travel expenses, before accepting your place at your dental school, as you will not be eligible for student finance in the same way as home students. If you need some form of financial support, it is possible to check with your university to see if you are eligible for any scholarships and/or bursaries.

Example Interview Questions & Points to Consider in Your Answers

The interview process for an international candidate can vary slightly in the questions they might be asked. As there are limited international spaces in each dental school, it's important to prepare for these so you stand out. Here are some examples:

WHERE DID YOU DO YOUR DENTAL WORK EXPERIENCE?

This question is not specifically for international students but it is a chance to stand out from the other international applicants. Dentistry abroad can be run differently with different policies and etiquette. This kind of exposure teaches you valuable communication skills, and emphasises putting the patients' wishes first.

WHAT TYPE OF SCHOOL DID YOU ATTEND?

Attending an international school abroad often provides students with a broad cultural awareness. Having a good knowledge, understanding and respect for other cultures is a very helpful trait for any dentist. In dentistry we do not choose our patients, so being able to communicate with them knowledgeably and respectfully is important.

DO YOU SPEAK MULTIPLE LANGUAGES? HOW WOULD YOU HANDLE A NON-ENGLISH SPEAKING PATIENT?

In dental school, or throughout your professional career, you will treat patients who do not speak English. Often a translator attends with these patients, or alternatively a translator is used over the phone. This can be daunting to a patient who may have the same fears as any other English-speaking patient but cannot communicate those fears to their dentist in English. Even being able to speak a few words in their mother tongue when treating the patient can put the patient at ease. This can be a strong point to help you stand out in the interview.

WHY THE UK AND THIS DENTAL SCHOOL?

Dental school interviewers often like to ask why you are interested in their school specifically. They may also ask you to elaborate further and ask why you would like to move to the UK. It is important you have a couple of reasons behind your choice to move that shed a positive light on the university and the city in which it is located. Find some facts that interest you about the locations of your chosen universities. Having genuine excitement for this big move shows the interviewers how passionate you are. After all, you should also like the city you will be living in for the next 5 years!

DO YOU THINK YOU WILL CONTINUE YOUR DENTAL CAREER IN THE UK OR MOVE BACK HOME, AND WHY?

This can be a personal matter for each international student. Whatever your intentions, be well prepared with your answers for this question. If your intention is to return to your home country, then be prepared to be able to speak about issues in healthcare and dentistry there and why you believe that studying at a UK university will help you with dealing with those issues once you return. Equally, if you choose to stay in the UK, be ready to be able to discuss the same issues in relation to working in the UK.

Finally, ask the interviewers questions! You are making the move to this new country, so it is important you get all the information you need before you make your final decision to accept offers. Whether that be about the universities cultural diversity, or a specific dental school related question, asking these questions demonstrates your enthusiasm and passion while providing you with any other information you may need.

HOW INTERNATIONAL STUDENTS CAN PREPARE FOR INTERVIEWS & LIFE AS AN OVERSEAS STUDENT

If English is not your first language, practicing common interview questions ahead of time may help any nerves you experience on the day of your interview. Ensure you do not over rehearse any answers however, as this can make you sound scripted. Additionally familiarising yourself with the NHS in the UK would be beneficial for your interview. Ensure that you have a basic understanding on the differences between private and NHS dentistry, and how NHS dentists are funded in comparison to general practitioners.

Following your interview, if you are offered a place at your chosen university it will likely be in the form of a conditional offer, which often includes your required grades from your school or university (if you are applying for graduate entry). Additionally, the university can ask international students to provide proof of English proficiency (this is also needed from EU students). Most universities require you to take the academic version of the International English Language Testing System (IELTS). Dental schools will ask for a minimum score for entry into the degree. You can apply to take the IELTS exam online at test centres worldwide. On the website you can usually find example questions so you know what to expect before test day.

International students studying in the UK require a Tier 4 student visa. You can apply for this via the UK government website or the UK visas and immigration website. It is also important to note, that if you plan to have a part-time job with a Tier 4 visa, the hours can be limited. If you miss a registered day of university, the dental school may request a valid reason for this to ensure you are not in breach of your Tier 4 visa requirements.

Finally, once you gain a place at your chosen university, they soon contact you to arrange your accommodation. International students often get priority at universities with limited accommodation. Options can include, catering or self-catering. Universities often ask you what degree you will be starting so they can pair flatmates studying similar degrees, which can help to ease you into university life.

Preparing for International Applicants Interview (Skype or in person)

If the university would like to consider you as a candidate for their course, you will be invited to an interview. Of course if you are living abroad and unable to travel to your interview, there is often the option of having an online video interview on Skype for example. Alternatively, some universities may travel to certain cities abroad to host a period of interview days.

The university will provide you with a date and time for your Skype interview and they will require your Skype details in order to contact you. There are a number of things you should consider before your interview date:

- Choose a quiet room in your house in which to have your Skype interview. Ensure your family members are aware of your interview date and time to avoid any unnecessary distractions or disturbances.
- Tidy your surroundings. Interviewers do not want to see unmade beds in the background. Ideally chose a neutral backdrop to sit in front of such as a plain wall.
- Dress smartly and attend your Skype interview as you would a face-to-face interview. Ideal interview attire is often a suit or alternatively smart office wear. As you are not there in person, a professional appearance is even more important.
- Familiarise yourself with Skype before the day (or whichever alternative video conferencing software they are using).
- During the interview, ensure the camera angle has you in view, make sure you look into the camera and not at yourself in the bottom corner during the interview. Interviewers are likely to pick up on lots of eye movements, which can make you appear unfocussed.
- Posture is important!
- Remain calm if any technical difficulties arise.

- Speak clearly and use vocabulary and expression to show how enthusiastic you are about gaining a place at their university. As you are not there in person, interviewers are unlikely to pick up on as much body language.

Alternatively, if you decide to travel to have your interview in person, try and arrive at your destination with enough time to get settled and rest. This also gives you the opportunity to explore the city you might be living in and get a feel for your surroundings. As you will be unfamiliar with the city/country, make sure you know where you are going for your interview, and how you will get there. It goes without saying; leave in plenty of time!

When you arrive at the dental school you will probably be given a tour, which is sometimes conducted by a fellow international student. This is an opportunity to ask questions and gain some additional information from them before your allocated interview time.

Finally, above all, even though it is natural to be nervous, interviewers are looking for candidates who can conduct themselves well in an interview. So as hard as it might seem, try to stay calm and collected.

PART 4

‖Simulated MMI Mock Interview

The following mock should be used for preparation purposes only and does not represent the exact dental school interview of any university.

INSTRUCTIONS:
You are advised to take part in this interview under timed conditions with someone asking you the questions.

The following interview contains 10 stations with a 1-minute break between each station. The time spent at each station should be 8 minutes. The total interview time for this mock is 90 minutes (1 hour and 30 minutes).

Candidates are advised to prepare before attempting the questions and then refer to the answers and explanations section to see how their answers can be improved. It may also be useful for the interviewer to record the answers given so the candidate is able to listen back to their responses.

STATION 1: PERSONAL STATEMENT
Q1) What was the highlight of your work experience?

Q2) What qualities did the dentist display when you observed them?

Q3) Can you give us an example where you solved a problem?

Q4) What has been your greatest achievement?

STATION 2: ETHICS
Q5) Do you think it is right to deny NHS treatment for obese patients and patients who smoke?

Q6) Amy, a 17 year-old student, is your patient. She had an appointment with you and shortly afterwards you received a friend request on Facebook from her. Should you accept the friend request?

STATION 3: MANUAL DEXTERITY
Q7) On a blank paper draw a circle using a pencil. The circle must have a diameter of approximately 15cm and must be drawn in one go. You must not use a ruler. You must only submit 1 final circle to be marked.

Q8) Suggest what improvements you could make if you did this task again?

Station 4: Professionalism

Q9) You have just finished a long day at the practice. Before you head off home you notice the dental nurse reading confidential information about a patient you saw today. Upon asking you find out that the patient was the nurse's neighbour. What will you do?

Q10) One of your close friends in dental schools opens up to you about selling drugs to fund their degree. Who are the key stakeholders in this situation?

Station 5: Role Play

Q11) You have seen signs of oral cancer while a routine check-up for a patient. Although you are certain from what you have observed, you still want to double check by doing further tests. Break this news to the patient and tell them.

Station 6: Leadership

Q12) Give an example where you have displayed qualities of a good leader and what you achieved.

Q13) Why is leadership important in dentistry?

Station 7: Social Awareness

Q14) How has social media affected dentistry?

Q15) How is dentistry evolving as a career?

Q16) Which latest technology is being used in dentistry?

Station 8: Critical Thinking

Q17) What more can be done to raise oral health awareness?

Q18) The NHS is struggling financially. What are your ideas on how we can help out the NHS?

STATION 9: KNOWLEDGE

Q19) What is Plaque?

Q20) Why is smoking bad for teeth?

Q21) What extra research have you done about dentistry and what did you find out?

STATION 10: COMMUNICATION

Q22) Explain the following information:

A table showing the number of patients requesting teeth whitening in the capital of England.

Year	Number of patients requesting teeth whitening
2009	888,943
2015	1,892,750
2019	3,001,220

Q23) Suggest the trend shown in the table and why this may have occurred.

Answers & Explanations

STATION 1: PERSONAL STATEMENT

Q1) Answer: During my work experience I saw the dentist using a rubber dam. This fascinated me as I was able to witness a perfect display of manual dexterity. This was especially interesting as the dentist had to work in a limited space whilst paying close attention to every detail. Analysis: Try to mention something unique. A good point is to mention what you saw the dentist doing. Find something interesting from your experience to mention in your personal statement as you are more likely to remember it when being asked about it.

Q2) Answer: The dentist displayed many qualities. One which stuck with me was the level of professionalism. The dentist would always ask his patients whether they are comfortable with me observing. This made me research further into the GDC principles.

Analysis: This answer links back to what the candidate actually found when observing the dentist. The answer then informs the interviewer that the student went out of their way to research further, showing their ambition for the course.

Q3) Answer: In my secondary school I was the head girl. One of my responsibilities was to ensure no students faced any difficulties on their way to school. I realised that some students were consistently turning up late. After speaking to the students, I discovered that it was because they were facing financial difficulties, meaning they were unable to catch the bus. As a result I set up a meeting with the school governing body to create a bursary scheme for students who struggle financially.

Analysis: Since the time is limited in the MMI stations you want to mention as many positive points as you can. Each interviewer is different so don't worry about repeating similar points at different stations. This answer included a personal achievement as well as tackling the actual question.

Q4) Answer: My greatest achievement was when I won the debate mate programme and took part in regional competitions. This allowed me to develop critical thinking skills as well as representing my school. I was especially proud of myself because I invested a lot of time practicing with my teammates after school.

Analysis: This answer links back to dentistry through the use of critical thinking skills and commitment with after school training. This shows that the candidate is willing to commit the same way if they got the offer.

STATION 2: ETHICS

Q5) Answer: There are two sides to this question. On one hand, people who smoke, knowing that it is bad, should not get treatment under the NHS, as they are willingly damaging their health. Similarly, obese people who refuse to exercise and continue to consume unhealthy foods are also knowingly damaging their health. On the other hand, not everyone who smokes or is obese can control their behaviours. They may be trying their best to quit and stay healthy, so it will be unfair to deny them treatment under the NHS.

Analysis: This response mentions both arguments for and against without rushing into a one-sided response. It shows that the candidate has thought their answer through and backed their points up.

Q6) Answer: As a dental professional you should not accept the friend request from the patient due to privacy reasons, because you would want to maintain professional boundaries with your patient. Accepting the friend request on social media can blur professional boundaries between your professional and personal life. Amy may also be vulnerable and may consider taking the rejection to heart so it will be important to explain this to her.

Analysis: This response takes into consideration the actions that the dentist will take as well as their impact on the patient. This shows that the answer is well thought through and the candidate has considered the matter as a whole.

Station 3: Manual dexterity

Q7) Answer: The circle should be evenly rounded and have a diameter as close to 15cm as possible. Try to focus on doing it correctly with only a few attempts as quality is better than quantity. Use an educated guess and realistic estimates for the diameter. Make sure to use your time wisely.

Analysis: The main purpose of this task is to see your level of manual dexterity, so make sure to give it your best go following the structure given in the answer.

Q8) Answer: If I were given this task again I would have taken more time drawing the circle to do it more accurately in fewer attempts.

Analysis: The interviewers do not expect you to have perfect manual dexterity, as this is something you will develop on the course. However, they are looking for you to be able to reflect and criticize your own work so you can make improvements. This answer does just that, and suggests some useful points they have learned from attempting the task.

STATION 4: PROFESSIONALISM

Q9) Answer: The dental nurse should be aware of the requirements and standards of the GDC. The dental nurse has breached patient confidentiality so it's important that they are confronted about the situation. To stop this happening again with any other patient, a solution could be to ensure that patient files are secured. Regardless of whether the nurse knew the patient, they have no right to read sensitive information which the patient may not wish to disclose. The patient will also need to be informed of the situation and should be told about the complaints procedure should they wish to make a complaint. The dental nurse would also need to be reported for their actions and further action should be taken to ensure the same incident doesn't happen again.

Analysis: This answer refers to the GDC principle, which shows that the candidate has background knowledge. The main issue is identified by the candidate and a solution is also mentioned to prevent this from happening again.

Q10) Answer: One of the key stakeholders in this situation is myself, as my friend has told me about this illegal activity, and if I chose to stay quiet knowing what they are doing then it makes me an accomplice. Another stakeholder is my friends, as they are selling the drugs; an activity which they know is illegal and can get them removed from the dental school. Another key stakeholder is the dental school, because if my friend has been selling drugs to other dental students it can affect their health and needs to be stopped. Selling drugs means that the student has been dishonest to their dental school values and their dental career.

Analysis: The answer correctly identifies the main stakeholders and considers the people affected by the actions of their friends. It is important to mention who the stakeholders are and also explain why. That is what makes this answer stand out.

STATION 5: ROLE PLAY

Q11) Answer: You want to begin using the SPIKES technique. Firstly by indicating to the patient that you have something important to tell them. Then setting the tone by asking them to take a seat. It is important to get straight to the point and give the patient some time for their emotions to surface. You need to show that you care and you are there for them. Addressing what's next for the patient is equally important. In this case letting the patent know that you will wait for the results to come and that you are here for ongoing support for them.

Analysis: The SPIKES technique is a perfect way to ensure that you have covered everything during the role play session. This will allow you to take control of the situation and be there for your patient.

STATION 6: LEADERSHIP

Q12) Answer: I was the head boy in my secondary school. I led a group of prefects and delivered assemblies about bullying and general wellbeing. I had to give up my own time to prepare for meetings with the prefects. One achievement of mine as the head boy was to change the school uniform into something much more comfortable and that saved time for the students when putting it on in the mornings. This led to me and my team of prefects organising a vote in an assembly and delivering a report to our head teacher, which resulted in the uniform being changed.

Analysis: The answer covers all the points mentioned in the question. Leadership roles can also be as a sports team captain or in organising a charitable event. The answer should show how you were able to reach a goal that you set and the steps you took to achieve it.

Q13) Answer: Leadership is important in dentistry because as the dentist you are expected to distribute work and lead your team members each day. Strong leadership within dentistry is necessary to protect the profession's ability to provide care for others and to allow the profession to maintain its autonomy. Fulfilling these leadership responsibilities requires a number of skills such as communication, independent learning, and vision casting.

Analysis: The answer refers to autonomy. Using specialist terminology when making your points in the interview will always show the interviewer that you have made the effort to research the career and that you are well informed.

STATION 7: SOCIAL AWARENESS

Q14) Answer: social media has had both a negative and positive impact on dentistry. Apps such as Facebook, Instagram and Twitter are used by dentists all over the world to help them increase their outreach as well as connect with patients. This acts as a positive aspect of social media because the platform can be used to spread information on how patients can take care of their own oral health. However, social media can also have a negative impact as false information regarding oral health can be spread. Also, unrealistic expectations can be set by influencers with perfect smiles, which can affect users' mental wellbeing.

Analysis: This argument evaluates both the negatives and positive aspects of social media in dentistry. The points given were backed up by a relevant example. Further examples could be included in the answer such as breaches of patient confidentiality on social media. Good answers would have referred to the impact of social media on a larger scale.

Q15) Answer: I have read a book called 'The Smile Stealers', which shows the history of dentistry. This book fascinated me as I was able to see the misconceptions people had around the career such as barbers in 700BC carrying out tooth extractions using bow drills to extract rotten teeth. I feel as though dentistry is evolving in a much more professional light. The GDC was formed in 1956 and since then dentists have always strived to maintain the high standards of the profession. In the future, I believe oral health will be promoted even further and people will become more aware than they are today about their oral health through social media. I think more dentists will start to emerge in less developing countries where oral health is neglected.

Analysis: The answer is well thought out and it's evident that the candidate is well informed from their research and aware of current social issues. Informing the interviewer about something that not every interviewee will mention during the interview will definitely surprise them and make you memorable. This answer perfectly displays how extra research can elevate the level of response that a candidate gives.

Q16) Answer: After talking to the dentists where I completed two weeks of work experience, I subscribed to '123 Dentist' to keep up with the latest advancements in dentistry. I have read an article about laser dentistry. This is also known as no-drill dentistry. This new method of dental care involves using a powerful but safe laser, which means there's little or no pain and so less of a need for anaesthesia. In addition, because typical comfort and pain-relieving techniques aren't needed as much, laser dentistry is more time-efficient, which means patients can have several procedures scheduled for the same visit. The main disadvantage of laser dentistry is that dentists who offer it have to purchase the latest, most expensive technology and be trained to use it. Because of these expenses, laser dentistry will cost more than most other options for the same treatment.

Analysis: As well as talking about the latest technology being used in dentistry, the answer tells the interviewer how the student found the information. It is really useful to give the interviewer some background on how you found out the information. A positive point about this answer is that it discusses the latest technology with the interviewer plus it's a chance to evaluate the advantages and disadvantages of having that new technology in dentistry.

STATION 8: CRITICAL THINKING

Q17) Answer: To help raise oral health awareness dentists can start to promote good hygiene by visiting schools and teaching people about the effects of bad oral hygiene and how to prevent oral diseases. The most positive thing we can do as dentists is to share the knowledge we have and give people the ability to know how to take care of their own health. We can also hold more community events with dentists, informing parents and the general public of how to take care of their oral health. This will allow us to raise awareness and teach people the importance of maintaining good hygiene.

Analysis: Thinking critically identifies the problem and provides a solution. The candidate provides ways to overcome problems surrounding oral health and the potential impact of bad dental hygiene. They also mention some valid points on how to make people look after their own oral health and how empowering patients is useful.

Q18) Answer: The NHS is funded through tax, which relies on the UK economy. The NHS is one of the industrialised world's most efficient health care systems, although it has been struggling financially in recent years. We can help out the NHS by volunteering and helping out in the local community. This will provide support for the understaffed NHS. We should all provide feedback to the NHS when we use their services as this can help improve their care. The NHS's funding problem can be solved by increasing taxes paid by the public. Currently the UK pays significantly lower tax compared to neighbouring countries such as France and Germany. I believe the public would support this tax increase as long as the money is spent on the NHS. To do our part on the smaller scale we can make donations and help raise money for the NHS through charity events.
Analysis: This answer shows that the candidate has done their research and is aware of the current problems surrounding the NHS. The candidate identifies the issues and provides reasonable suggestions to help overcome those issues. This shows that the candidate has the ability to think critically and has produced a good response.

STATION 9: KNOWLEDGE

Q19) Answer: Plaque is a soft, sticky film that builds up on your teeth and contains millions of bacteria. The bacteria in plaque cause tooth decay and gum disease if they are not removed regularly through brushing and flossing.
Analysis: It is crucial for candidates to come prepared and know the key terminology used in dentistry.

Q20) Answer: Smokers develop more tartar on their teeth than non-smokers, which can lead to periodontal disease. Another way which smoking affects the teeth is that it can cause teeth to become stained to a yellow colour, while also causing bad breath. Smoking can also cause oral cancer and it interferes with blood circulation through affecting normal function of the gum tissue. The dentist can inform the patient of these risks associated with smoking, and follow the 'Very Brief Advice on Smoking' guidelines, to support patients who want to quit. Analysis: Interviewers know that you will not be an expert and so they don't expect you to know everything. However, they do expect you to have the basics covered so they can distinguish which candidate has researched in their own time, showing dedication prior to the course starting.

Q21) Answer: I have written an EPQ on 'Technology Advancements In Dentistry'. In my EPQ, I have included information about some of the latest technology being used within dentistry. During my research I was particularly interested in the use of 3D printing, which allows us to produce crowns very quickly as the dentist can make the crown by themselves. It is one of the most common applications of 3D printing in dentistry, making it possible to get a scan of the patient's teeth, model it and print the crown directly.
Analysis: Mentioning something you have written in your personal statement has the benefit of showing that you have genuine experience. If EPQ is mentioned in your personal statement you can still talk about it during your interview. However, not having done an EPQ does not put you at a disadvantage. The candidate makes use of what they have done and tells the interviewer in detail about their research. You can also mention anything that you have read in dentistry-related books, or things that you found out during your work experience or through your own research online.

STATION 10: COMMUNICATION
Q22) Answer: The information is presented in a table showing the number of patients requesting teeth whitening in the capital of England, London, in a 10-year period. In the left-hand column are the years 2009, 2015 and 2019. Listed in the right-hand column are the number of patients requesting teeth whitening in each of those years. We can see that in 2009 the number of patients asking for teeth whitening was 888,943, which is the lowest number of patients in the 3 years

given. The number of patients who asked for teeth whitening in 2015 was 1,892,750. Lastly, in 2019, the number of patients asking for teeth whitening jumped to 3,001,220, which is an increase of almost 1,000,000. The overall trend shows us that over the years the number of patients requesting teeth whitening has been increasing. This indicates a positive correlation between the two factors.

Analysis: This answer covers every piece of information which was presented in the table. The candidate uses the table well to form their answer. The structure of the answer was perfect because the candidate first mentioned the bigger picture and then went into the finer details and even quoted values presented in the table.

Q23) The trend of an increasing number patients requesting teeth whitening over the years could be due to more exposure in society to social media. In 2009, social media was not as popular and accessible as it was in 2019. Social media can play a significant role in patients wanting teeth whitening because of celebrities promoting teeth whitening brands, as well as more awareness being spread about oral hygiene, making people more conscious of their appearance.

Analysis: The candidate mentions relevant explanations for the trend shown in the table. It is key to back up your points with a good explanation. As long as you do this, the point you are making will be much clearer to the interviewer.

MOCK PANEL INTERVIEW

In this section we will give you a mock interview with suitable answers that you could use. The aim of this section is to give you an example of how the panel interviews are carried out and how the interviewers try to make the questions flow together.

Try answering the questions with personalised responses.

The following mock interview should be used for preparation purposes only and does not represent the exact dental school interview of any university. Candidates should spend 45 minutes answering the 14 questions.

Q1) Why do you want to study at Richardson?

Q2) Why do you want to study dentistry?

Q3) As you know, we teach dentistry here at Richardson with the traditional method. With this we teach with two years of solid background before you see patients in your 3rd year. Do you think this is a good method and are you suited to it personally?

Q4) Carrying on from this, in your first year you are taught anatomy and other topics regarding the rest of the body. Why do we teach you this when you would only focus on teeth in your daily career?

Q5) What would you do to help you get through dental school?

Q6) I'm sure you're aware that dentistry is a very stressful job. Could you list some negative aspects of the job and how you would manage them?

Q7) When have you completely failed at something and how did you fix it?

Q8) Have you ever been criticised and how did you cope with that?

Q9) Do you have any particular weaknesses that you are aware of?

Q10) We also notice that you play the piano. How do you think this could help you with dentistry?

Q11) You also say you volunteered at a nursery and care home. Do you think there are different skills needed for these two age groups and how this could relate to dentistry?

Q12) If you had to undertake an independent study how would you do this?

Q13) Do you have evidence of working in a team?

Q14) Regarding your work experience, it says you did 2 weeks at a general dental practice and one day at a community dental practice. Could you explain how you arranged this work experience?

‖ Answers & Explanations

Q1) Answer: When I attended your open day I was impressed with the friendly atmosphere. Your dental students were very caring and positive during the tours and I noticed that your dental society seemed heavily involved. I find the buildings and history of Richardson fascinating and I enjoy football so I was also excited to see the football stadium during my visit. As the university is right in the centre of the city I would enjoy being immersed in city life and culture.

Analysis: The candidate immediately mentions the open day, showing that they made the effort to visit the university in person. They also mention the dental students, society, and atmosphere – good points as all dental schools try to promote a positive and caring environment between their students. The candidate also touches on the type of university (campus or off-campus), showing they have done their research, and once again have considered how they could fit into the university lifestyle. Mentioning football could be another potential talking point in the conversation (providing they actually do watch football).

Q2) Answer: I want to be a dentist because I have had a lot of dental procedures myself over the years, which gave me an interest in dentistry. I was always impressed with the communication skills my dentist showed and how I was made to feel comfortable. I am actually quite intrigued that having such small changes to your teeth can increase your self-confidence. This coupled with my love of science and ability to use my hands made me decide this was the right career for me, which was reinforced when I did my work experience.

Analysis: This is the most obvious question you will be asked and one you will probably answer for the rest of your life. Although there is no perfect answer, the key is to try and make it as personal to you as possible. This candidate started off with their initial motivation and interest in dentistry. This is a fine way to start but the key is to expand on your answer. Talk about any particular instances that resonated with you, or anything your dentist did that you noticed portrayed the key skills dentists require. The candidate also noted the impact that dentistry can have on confidence. If you have had lots of treatment, that's something you could relate to yourself to personalise your answer. The candidate mentioned their love of science and practical skills, which was once again a good way of showing how they would be suited to the career. The interviewers can then expand on these statements. Finally, a good tip is to mention work experience. This shows that you have some practical experience of what the role of a dentist entails, plus it gives the examiners a nice way to ask you more questions about your work experience.

Q3) Answer: I believe this is a good method. Two solid years of background teaching will give us a foundation of the knowledge needed before going on to see patients. Dentistry is such a vast subject related to the whole body so it is imperative to be prepared and understand the basics before treating patients clinically. Although it could be argued that we should see patients sooner, I think this will suit me as I am the type of person who likes to understand things very well and practice before moving onto larger tasks.
Analysis: The answer you give should of course vary depending on particular dental schools and their teaching methods. The key point here is to show that you have done your research regarding the particular dental school and can explain how their teaching method will suit you. Try to give a balanced response and end on a positive note of the particular teaching method.

Q4) Answer: On a similar note to my previous answer, dentistry is a very broad topic that is not only focused on the teeth. Having extensive knowledge of all the structures of the body is important as they are all interlinked. As medical professionals we will need to know the implications that different structures in the body can have on the oral cavity. This will also allow us to be prepared in case something goes wrong in practice. Patients could also have underlying health conditions that are important to understand and be aware of – not just in relation to the oral cavity. Dentists also need to deal with any medical emergencies that could occur at the practice.

Analysis: This is a very good answer to a question that can trip up a lot of candidates. The key point is that dentists are medical professionals and you will be called Doctor when you graduate. With this comes responsibility in the eyes of the public so it's imperative that you appreciate the need to know more about the body than just the teeth. Dental schools expect you to realise that.

Q5) Answer: To manage the workload and prevent burnout, I would try to keep up the hobbies I currently pursue. I understand that studying for a degree in dentistry can be very stressful so it's important to keep your life varied and balanced as there is more to life than dentistry. I would love to join societies and keep up with my hobbies such as music and sports as well as socialising with my friends.

Analysis: There is no correct answer to this question. This would be your chance to mention any hobbies you have. The interviewers want to see from your answer that you are a varied individual with lots of interest and hobbies. They also want to see your personality as well as your understanding of the career itself. This is a good opportunity to mention things from your personal statement.

Q6) Answer: Like any job there are negative aspects, and I feel like there is a perception that dentistry has more than usual. Some aspects I can list off the top of my head would be persistent back problems, the stress that comes with the job, lawsuits and dealing with difficult patients. I think the most important thing is to stay organised and calm at all times. For back problems, although easier said than done, I would try to ensure that I keep a good posture when practising dentistry and perhaps take part in yoga classes to help me improve my posture. When dealing with difficult patients, I would try to ensure that I had good communication, and if I was overwhelmed by anything I would talk to people and ask for help. I would ensure to have a good work-life balance and keep up with my hobbies, such as playing music and team sports.

Analysis: In this question the key is to not only list the negative aspects but to expand on them and give good answers as to how you deal with them. There is no perfect answer, but you should try and talk about communication and organisation. The interviewers want to know how you would handle the pressure of dental school.

Q7) Answer: Unfortunately I didn't get a good grade in my Year 13 mock exam due to a lack of preparation and had to retake the test. To rectify that I asked my teacher for extra help and lessons and subsequently achieved a much higher mark the second time around. I learnt that I needed to be more organised but could also to ask for help when needed.

Analysis: The key is to think of a good example which you can relate to your experience and give solutions. Also mention any reflections you learnt from this experience. Dental school is very tough and there will be times when things won't go well, and you might not get the grades you want. The interviewers are looking to see how you would handle this.

Q8) Answer: During my music lessons I have been criticised for not playing my instrument correctly. I have learnt to take the criticism on board by asking for suggestions of ways to improve and then practicing even harder to become better.

Analysis: This question is similar to the previous one so you can answer it in a similar way. The key is to relate the answer to a personal experience and see how you learnt from it. Music, sport or an academic experience are good examples of things you can mention.

Q9) Answer: I think one particular weakness of mine is that I can take a while to do tasks, because I'm a perfectionist. This could be a problem with regards to dentistry as I am aware that you may have several appointments and be very busy during the day. Having said that, I still believe it is important to not rush work and to make sure that it is completed to a high standard. To solve this problem and in the future with regards to dentistry, I would try and practice frequently the tasks I am undertaking. With lots of practice I can improve my speed while also ensuring I produce optimum work.

Analysis: This is another good answer. Don't say that you do not have any weaknesses, and don't try to spin a potentially positive trait as a weakness (e.g. being too organised or too conscientious). Nobody is perfect and everyone makes mistakes. The interviewers are more interested in how you approach self-improvement. The candidate has mentioned their weaknesses while giving reasons for why they have them. They have then further expanded on things they can do to make improvements while relating it to dentistry.

Q10) Answer: Playing the piano requires manual dexterity and concentration to use hands and feet at the same time, which is similar to the coordination skills a dentist uses with a hand piece or dental instruments. The skills I have learnt from playing this instrument is very transferable and applicable to dentistry, I believe.
Analysis: This question is a chance to show off your manual dexterity and show how it relates to dentistry. The interviewers will note what you have said about manual dexterity in your personal statement and ask you questions related to that. You could use any example you like of playing musical instruments or other skills requiring manual dexterity. The key point is to convey that you have concentration and manual dexterity as a transferable skill to dentistry.

Q11) Answer: I believe dealing with different age groups requires certain skills, although the most important thing is still communication. Dentists deal with patients of all ages so must be equipped with these skills. From my experience, I think you have to be calmer and more methodical with elderly people as they may have underlying health conditions which have to be taken into consideration. With children, you also have to interact with the parents, so you have to ensure that you speak logically and have good body language. You also might have to change the terminology you use when explaining things to children. Children may also be more likely to be scared of the dentist, so you would have to employ techniques to get them more relaxed and used to the dentist. In terms of tone, whilst working at a care home, I understood the elderly like to be treated with much more respect as well as with a formal tone. This contrasted heavily to my experience tutoring children, where I found an informal and light hearted approach evoked more engagement.

Analysis: This is a very good answer. The candidate has mentioned communication skills first, as this is something the dentist requires regardless of the age group. With regards to elderly people, the candidate has realised that seniors have underlying health conditions which dentists have to be able to deal with. This also relates to the earlier question of why dentists are not just taught about the teeth. Regarding conversing with children, the candidate has realised the dentists have to deal with the parents, which requires another set of skills. They have noted that children are often scared of the dentist so different skills are used by the dentist to make the children relaxed.

Q12) Answer: I would firstly try to obtain as much research as possible by using online sources and the libraries. I would also try to get some advice from someone who has had experience in this type of project. Once I had done my research, I would make notes and try and obtain a rough layout and plan. I would then undertake the task after everything had been planned and organised.

Analysis: The interviewers are looking at how you can work independently as in university you will have to do written work such as essays, reports and case studies.

Q13) Answer: In dentistry you have to work in a team – working with dental nurses, therapists, practice managers and other healthcare professionals. I am part of a music ensemble and a member of my school football team. Through these I have learnt that having good communication skills is critical in making sure things run smoothly and efficiently. If we ever have any disagreements or if things go wrong, we always try to discuss our problems to sort it out.

Analysis: This is another personal statement question. Make sure you give a good personal example of working in a team while also noting how that relates to dentistry. Further expand on the answer by mentioning the things you do to work well in a team.

Q14) Answer: I sent emails to all the dental practices in my area asking if I could undertake work experience. Although some did not respond to me, I followed up by calling them directly and was lucky enough to undertake 2 weeks of work experience at one of the practices I spoke to. At this work experience I...

Analysis: The interviewers are interested in you taking initiative to organise work experience. This is then a perfect opportunity to expand on any work experience you saw.

CHAPTER 6

NON STANDARD
APPLICATIONS

INTRODUCTION

This chapter is dedicated to those individuals who are not following the traditional entry route to study dentistry. The majority of students applying for UK dental schools will be UK residents studying traditional qualifications such as A-Levels in science, International Baccalaureates, Cambridge pre-U or equivalence in Scotland or Wales. Many of these candidates will have known during their early studies that dentistry would be their likely career option. Based upon this, many individuals structure their education choices on the most obvious criteria for entry. However, there are other routes to study dentistry which are covered in this chapter.

In this chapter we discuss:
- Non-conventional routes to entry
- What to do if you have not done A-Levels
- Available options if you haven't chosen science subjects
- Students with disability/learning difficulty
- Studying abroad – how, where, when, why.

Non-conventional Routes

Various entry pathways exist to study dentistry in the UK for those individuals who have not taken a 'typical academic journey' or may not have attained the entry requirements to transit via a 'traditional routes'.

These pathways to entry include:

- Pre-dental courses / foundation programmes/ preliminary year of study/ gateway to dentistry courses

These programmes exist for those with proven academic ability in subjects other than science qualifications to apply to study dentistry directly. As such this is often an additional year of study (prior to the usual five year BDS degree) to prepare students for entering the five year degree programme.

- Access to Higher Education Diplomas

Access courses allow those who have been out of education for some time to gain the necessary qualifications to be considered for entry to dentistry. Each dental school has its own outlook on whether this type of course is suitable. Therefore, we recommend that you discuss your individual circumstances with the admissions team to determine your likely options. Some schools do not accept diplomas, so we suggest contacting the admissions team before you embark on starting these courses.

Access courses are unlikely to be suitable for entry for those who have failed to attain the necessary A-level qualifications. However, the university may consider an individual for whom extenuating circumstances have held them back in this respect.

When considering an access course you should determine the following:

1. Whether the university will first accept this course. If so, what are the scores and specific entry requirements (credits needed)?
2. Are there any other minimum requirements needed i.e. GCSE?
3. Is the course regulated by Quality Assurance Agency (QAA)?
4. What is the feedback of the course from previous students?

5. Does the course content satisfy the university's requirements?
   o Wider Participation Schemes

‖ Widening Participation Schemes

These schemes have been established to provide access to higher education opportunities to individuals from less represented backgrounds.

Eligibility is often specific to ensure the schemes benefit those who are most in need. These factors may include the performance of the school or college you study at, your household income, progression of your geographical area and other factors related to your environment. As such, it is extremely important to read through the exact criteria and contact the relevant university admission team with any questions. Recruitment for these courses often begins as A-levels start, so you need to be aware of application deadlines.

Universities offering this type of support for dentistry applicants include:

University of Aberdeen
https://www.abdn.ac.uk/iemds/study-here/widening-access-356.php

Newcastle University - 'Partners Scheme'
https://www.ncl.ac.uk/schools/partners/eligibility/#d.en.930521

University of Birmingham
Access to Birmingham (A2B) programme
https://www.birmingham.ac.uk/teachers/pupil-opportunities/post-16/Pathways-to-Birmingham-Eligibility-Criteria.aspx

University of Manchester
pre-dental course in Dentistry (contextual offer)
https://www.manchester.ac.uk/study/undergraduate/
courses/2020/00399/bds-dentistry-pre-dental-entry/
entry-requirements/#course-profile
https://www.manchester.ac.uk/study/undergraduate/
applications/after-you-apply/contextual-data/

University of Leeds - Alternative Admissions
http://www.leeds.ac.uk/info/128005/applying/33/
alternative_admissions

University of Central Lancashire
https://www.uclan.ac.uk/about_us/access-widening-participa-
tion.php

Queens Belfast
https://www.qub.ac.uk/directorates/sgc/wpu/

Bristol Gateway To Dentistry
http://www.bristol.ac.uk/study/undergraduate/2020/
dentistry/bds-gateway-to-dentistry/

Peninsula Pathways to the Healthcare Professions
https://www.plymouth.ac.uk/study/outreach/
medicine-dentistry-biomedical-healthcare

Cardiff -Contextual admissions
https://www.cardiff.ac.uk/study/undergraduate/applying/
contextual-data

Kings College London Enhances Support Dentistry pro-
gramme
https://www.kcl.ac.uk/study/undergraduate/courses/
enhanced-support-dentistry-programme-bds

Dundee - Reach
https://www.dundee.ac.uk/study/widening-access/in-demand/

University of Liverpool- Dentisination Dentistry
https://www.liverpool.ac.uk/dentistry/widening-participation/

University of Sheffield - Discover Dental professions
https://www.sheffield.ac.uk/schools/programmes/discover/dental

University of Glasgow
https://www.gla.ac.uk/study/wp/admissionssummary/

QMUL- Widening participation
https://www.qmul.ac.uk/teachers/teacher-resources/resources/medicine--dentistry-tips/
https://www.qmul.ac.uk/undergraduate/apply/entry/contextualised-admissions/

It is critical that you know the specific criteria for widening participation at each university. As such, we strongly recommend that you familiarize yourself with the most updated guidance from the universities listed.

Realising Opportunities

Realising Opportunities is a nationwide widening participation scheme in partnership with 16 research-intensive universities, many of which offer dentistry. The application criteria is similar to other widening participation schemes with the application process beginning in autumn of year 12.

The program offers several advantages such as a 'Skills 4 Uni' module, which is designed to give you an insight into university life, a mentorship scheme and a student conference.

Most importantly, upon successful completion of the program you will be entitled to an alternative offer, which can be up to two A-level grades lower than the typical offer. *

The partner universities will also give your application additional consideration. Another advantage of this scheme is that you are not limited to a university and its individual widening participation scheme. It essentially enables you to receive additional consideration and alternative offers from several universities.[3] *

Recognition guide 2021 entry: http://www.realisingopportunities.ac.uk/_assets/reports/RO_Recognition_Guide_2021_Entry/files/assets/common/downloads/RO%20Recognition%20Guide%202021%20Entry.pdf

Determining which entry routes are most suitable for you depends on your individual scenario and circumstances.

Use our entry tables and flowchart to determine which course maybe best suited for you:

Links to graduate entry table

Links to Standard entry table

---

3   However, it is important to note that recognition of Realising Opportunities can vary depending on each university. Some select universities, King's for example, may not give an alternative offer. Instead you will be eligible to apply for the enhanced support dentistry programme, which does include a reduced offer. Offers vary from year to year so make sure you read the latest annual recognition guide published by Realising Opportunities for the most up-to-date information.

'Non Standard Entry' pathways shown diagrammatically below

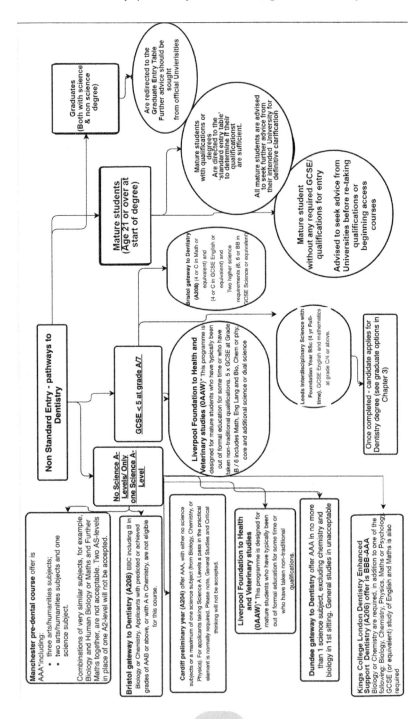

Disabilities/ Special Needs

Universities are very supportive of students with disabilities and learning needs. It is likely that whichever university you are applying to it has a dedicated advisory and support service for this for occupational health and other such special requirements.

If you have such needs, contact the relevant team early on to discuss your personal situation. Furthermore, universities offer accessible and inclusive services to ensure that higher education is provided without discrimination.

Importantly for dentistry, the GDC stipulates in its health self-certification guidance that it is important to be aware when 'your health condition impacts your ability to work safely with patients or affects your ability to carry out your job. In many cases, registrants with a disability or health condition can practise safely.' Your personal health related matters should be discussed with the university prior to submitting an application and will likely be monitored by the disability service and occupational health services throughout your course.

Once you have established the university you intend to apply to, it's important to disclose all your relevant personal health information on UCAS. See Chapter 2 for more details on how to successfully complete this.

CHAPTER 7

NEVER GIVE UP

INTRODUCTION

Have you lost hope after being rejected from dental school?

This chapter should inspire you not to give up and move ahead. We'll cover the following:
- Pathways if you are unsuccessful in gaining an offer
- Re-applying to dental school
- Retaking qualifying examinations
- Retaking UCAT & BMAT
- Re-applying as a graduate
- Real student stories
- Gap years and deferred entry
- Studying abroad
- Managing stress

Common pathways if you are unsuccessful in gaining an offer

It's harrowing to think that your efforts may have not yielded an offer or you have fallen short of the conditions of your offer but it's not the end of the world.

We want to shine the spotlight on 'never giving up'. Dealing with rejection is a subject we feel is neglected. It leaves many feeling lost or at a loose end but guidance for individuals in these situations is hugely valuable yet rarely discussed.

When you experience failure, having the right mind set is of paramount importance.

Here are 3 key thoughts you should remind yourself of in the face of failing to secure a place.

One
80% of Applicants Don't Succeed

The sheer volume of applicants applying for the same courses means many don't even get through to the interview stage. Only a few applicants will actually secure a place and it's common to be unsuccessful in the first round. The vast majority of those chosen are equipped with all the necessary academic requirements plus experience from a lot of extra-curricular activities. An estimated 60% of applicants are rejected before interview and only about 50% of those interviewed are offered a place to study dentistry.

Two
Don' Take Rejection Personally

Not succeeding in the application process is not a reflection of your intelligence or capabilities. It's more a reflection of the limited number of places each dental school has to offer.

Three
Time is on Your Side

There are people of all ages with various experience doing dentistry. Many of them old enough to already have a degree and some married with children. Whilst not swiftly transitioning to university immediately after college is frustrating to say the least, a huge number of multi-talented students don't get in at 18 years old and so begin their studies slightly later – often looking back with no regrets. Many of them will have taken gap years or pursued other degrees before embarking on dentistry.

Now that we have honed in on the realisation that you will not be the only one in this quagmire, let's look at the different possibilities which may have led to your current situation.

No Interview Attained		
Schematic showing different routes leading to re-application to dental school		
Grades for entry NOT achieved	1.	Take a year out to focus on enhancing your overall experience including strength-ening your personal statement, re-taking UCAT/BMAT, re-taking qualifications and then re-apply to dental school.*
	2.	Commence an alternative pathway via an appropriate under-graduate degree, then, if feasible, tailor your modules and gain insight into a career in dentistry.**
Grades for entry achieved	1.	Consider calling the universities that interviewed you to deter-mine whether they will accept you.***
	2.	Take a year out to focus on enhancing your overall experience including strengthening your personal statement & re-taking UCAT/BMAT and re-apply to dental school.*
	3.	Commence an alternative pathway via an appropriate under-graduate degree.** Then, if feasible, tailor your modules and gain insight into a career in dentistry**
Dentistry Interview Attained		
No offer but grades attained for entry i.e. AAA	1.	Consider calling the universities that interviewed you to deter-mine whether they will accept you.***
	2.	Take a year out to focus on enhancing your overall experience, including strengthening your personal statement & re-taking UCAT/BMAT and re-taking qualifications and re-apply to dental school.*
	3.	Commence an alternative pathway via an appropriate under-graduate degree. Then, if feasible, tailor your modules and gain insight into a career in dentistry**
Offer made but grades NOT at-tained for entry	1.	Consider calling the universities that interviewed you to deter-mine whether they will accept you.***
	2.	Take a year out to focus on enhancing your overall experience, including strengthening your personal statement & re-taking UCAT/BMAT and re-taking qualifications and re-apply to dental school.*
	3.	Commence an alternative pathway via an appropriate under-graduate degree. Then, if feasible, tailor your modules and gain insight into a career in dentistry**

*You should familiarise yourself with whether the university considers those who have re-taken qualifications. You should call the university to discuss your individual circumstances.

**Before embarking on an undergraduate degree, you should strongly consider whether your chosen degree will satisfy requirements for graduate entry into dentistry. Additionally consider whether you have the other required qualifications such as A-levels and GCSEs.

*** Calling the University on the day of results is not a guaranteed method of entry. It's more of a last chance saloon. Due to the nature of dentistry, only universities that have interviewed you are likely to offer you a place. As a rule, universities make more offers than actually exist to compensate for those who do not attain the stipulated conditions and those who choose a different university.

There are several actions you can make depending on your individual situation (please note this advice is from our personal views and based on anecdotal information, not official advice or representative of UCAS or the schools' official guidance.).

Results Day

Below are our suggestions for individuals in the following situations:

- Those who may have received offers but narrowly missed the grades.
- Those who were interviewed and achieved the necessary grades but have not received an offer.
- Those who have sufficient grades but did not secure a university interview.

Place Offered

If you received offers but narrowly missed the grades, have close to hand the contact details for the universities you applied to so you can be the first to telephone the universities and ask for advice. You'll probably be put through to the secretary but ask to speak to the Admissions Tutor directly.

No Offer

If you haven't received any offers but do meet the entry grade requirements, UCAS is the first place you should check as they will display any available places.

After checking that, you may also want to contact the dental schools directly to check whether they have any openings. If they do, you may be required to have a mini interview over the phone on the day, and may also be asked to attend a face-to-face interview at the university at a later date. Having good interview skills will put you in a stronger position.

If you are unable to get through by phone, you may wish to email the school as well. It must also be mentioned that universities may not accept telephone enquiries to prevent being bombarded with calls from students. As such, we advise that you follow the information given by the individual universities. We strongly advise contacting the university ahead of results day to determine your action plan.

Although this is by no means a guarantee, especially as universities issue more offers than places, contacting the universities will give you some guidance on the availability of spaces or openings, for example, through clearing or adjustment.

DEALING WITH STRESS
Results day can be stressful to the point of being overwhelming. You might have life-changing choices to make on the day. Avoid making any rash decisions by having a plan to identify the options available so you can make an informed decision.

Whatever happens, keep your chin up, maintain composure, and work through your options. Keep two phones; one to call universities and the other to receive calls so you can be sure not to miss any calls.

Having a friend or family member nearby can help you navigate through what can be a stressful day. Remember, you are not alone. There will be countless others going through the same experience as you. It can be a very emotional time, which is why you need to be guard yourself against making a rash decision that you could later regret.

Also remember that you don't have to go to university that year. You don't have to accept your 5th option. It could be your chance to take a gap year or retake your A-levels. You can always re-apply to dental school (you must first note which schools consider retakes – discussed later on).

Take time to consider all your options, carefully, and pick the one that best suits you.

I have been unsuccessful this year in gaining a place to study dentistry. What are my options?

If you have exhausted the avenues above and are certain that you cannot gain entry through clearing or adjustment you still have a few other options:

TAKING A YEAR OUT OR 'GAP YEAR' THEN RE-APPLYING		UNDERTAKING ANOTHER DEGREE THEN RE-APPLYING FOR DENTISTRY
GRADES **NOT** ATTAINED RE-TAKING* QUALIFICATION AS NEEDED. RE-TAKING UCAT/& BMAT	GRADES **ATTAINED** RE-TAKING UCAT/& BMAT	SUCCESSFULLY COMPLETING AN APPROPRIATE DEGREE** AND LATER REAPPLYING TO DENTAL SCHOOL MUST RETAKE THE UCAT/& BMAT

*Candidates are strongly advised to consider what requirements particular universities have for re-taking qualifications and those re-applying. We suggest you find out by contacting the relevant university directly.

**Before embarking on an undergraduate degree you should be absolutely sure the degree will satisfy entry requirements for graduate entry into dentistry. Also consider the other required qualifications you should have such as A-levels and GCSEs. Again we strongly recommend that you contact the official dental school before undertaking a degree course.

For those re-applying, refer to the crucial ways you can further your career insight and strengthen your application mentioned in Chapter 2.

CONSIDERING DOING ANOTHER DEGREE BEFORE RE-APPLYING TO STUDY DENTISTRY?

As mentioned earlier, it's important to check the entry requirements of each university. The individual institutions may have differing opinions, and may still have certain requirements for your A-level subjects and grades, in addition to your degree classification. Here are some examples as a guide:

- **Biomedical Sciences Degree.** This makes up a large amount of the initial theory which dental students are required to know and use throughout their course. Completing this allows for application onto 'Accelerated Graduate Dentistry' courses (at time of writing). For this reason it's a popular course to have as a fifth choice.

- **Dental Hygiene and Therapy Degree.** This may also be competitive to get onto but will provide many transferable skills between what you learn on this course and what you will be doing as a dentist. It is arguably the closest subject choice to dentistry.

- **Dental Material Science Degree.** If Maths and Physics are your strong points, then this will give an insight into the engineering aspect of dental materials and will allow you to finish with a Bachelors of Engineering, which can open other avenues for jobs, should you change your mind or be unable to obtain a place at a dental school.

In actual fact, provided your A-level subjects and grades satisfy the university entry requirements, you can apply for a range of degrees (for example Law and Sports Science) but remember to ensure that your degree choice will allow re-application to dentistry.

For further information on which degrees are accepted we advise you to browse our table 'Graduate Entry Dentistry'. Be sure to contact the prospective schools for definitive advice before making any concrete decisions.

Re-applying to Dentistry

First Let Us Reflect

If you have been unsuccessful in your application for dentistry, there are a few things to ask yourself before re-applying:

- What is it that makes you want to pursue a career in dentistry?

Being unsuccessful can cause a huge blow to motivation and can cause you to forget what you liked about dentistry in the first place.

- What do you think attracts you to the career path?

Make a list of these and remind yourself of the passion you have towards dentistry. Sometimes we need to be reminded of our motivation.

- Do you think that any other career can give you what you want from life other than dentistry?

This is an important question to ask yourself, because if you don't think that any other career can give you what you want (e.g. use of refine motor skills, helping people when they're in pain etc.) then you shouldn't give up on it.

- Do you think that this is a realistic goal?

Probably the hardest question to ask yourself is whether your goal is realistic and achievable.

Do you have the academic requirements for this course and if not, what can you do to rectify it? If it is something that can be rectified then yes, it's a realistic goal!

- Do you have the passion and stamina to go through the application process again?
- Do you know what may have caused you to be unsuccessful?

Obtaining feedback from these dental schools is valuable as you can reflect on where things could be improved. Submitting another application without fully understanding what went wrong would be unwise.

Was is your UCAT score; did your personal statement lack key elements; or was your interview technique off?

Learning where you can improve will dramatically enhance your chances of succeeding the next time.

I WANT TO RE-APPLY. WHAT SHOULD I DO?

If you are possessed with a relentless drive to achieve entry to dental school, you first need to determine where your application can be enhanced. If you attained an offer but simply did not meet the grades, improving your academic achievements is a must.

You should seek guidance on which universities allow re-take of academic qualifications. Some of this information can be found in our Standard Entry table. (see Key Resources).

However, if you did not receive an interview invitation, it could have been several factors, including: Predicted grades; personal statement; UCAT and/or BMAT score; or references.

If you gained an interview but were unsuccessful in attaining an offer:

Was it your interview techniques?

Did you buckle under the pressure?

Did you know your personal statement well enough?

If any of these scenarios resonate with you then you should ask why this has occurred. Look for objective feedback and see where you can improve.

Secondly, make sure you remember to carry out all the appropriate requirements:

Register a new application on UCAS

Re-sit the UCAT/BMAT

Update your personal statement

Rework, improve and add to your personal statement. During a second application, you should be able to talk about what you have done since you last applied, especially work experience, any volunteering opportunities and maintaining an interest in dental developments.

Thirdly, familiarise yourself with the admissions criteria. Entry criteria changes frequently. Don't rest on your laurels assuming that the entry criteria won't have changed. Search through the official university website and create a table of the criteria and the exact requirements to ensure you satisfy them all.

When it comes to the interview stage, don't be frightened that people may know you are re-applying. It's not a negative thing. In fact it's to your advantage as you'll have more to talk about, especially if you have done something productive in the meantime.

Re-taking Academic Qualifications

Getting into dental school is highly competitive. Preparation is key – and it starts early! When making your final selection for your UCAS application, you need to have done your research on the nuances of the admissions criteria for your preferred universities – especially understanding your options if the worst happens and you don't get a place.

You need to understand which universities will accept students who retake their A-levels; whether you need to have applied to them first time around; and whether they need to have been your first choice, among other factors.

Mention any mitigating circumstances in your personal statement and universities will be more likely to consider you.

When choosing your backup option, you may want to research which degrees are most favourable when applying to dental school as a graduate. Going the extra mile to research this helps you make a better informed decision. And you'll be better prepared on results day with a much stronger understanding of your options.

Some information can be hard to find online.

Tip: contact dental schools directly.

Secondly, consider whether you'll need the help of a school/college for your retakes: Does your school have a Year 14?

Would you have to change schools/colleges and retake a year while in attendance?

Can you retake by yourself at home?

Furthermore, you need to make sure that you are registered to re-sit the exams, which may have a cost if you are doing so privately. You also have to check where you will be sitting them, so you are organised.

Another thing to ask yourself is whether you think you can do better the second time around. Are you willing to put in the work?

Consider what went wrong the first time around and make the appropriate changes, whether that requires support from a tutor, changing your exam technique, going back to school or just stress or time management.

The final thing to consider is what to do if you do not succeed the second time. What are your back up options?

Which other courses besides dentistry would interest you?

Naturally you may experience some anxiety or stress when retaking A-levels. You need to find the right stress relief techniques that work for you.

Retaking UCAT and BMAT

Unfortunately, for those re-applying to dental school, re-sitting the UCAT and/or BMAT assessments are mandatory.

Although this may seem frustrating, you will be at an advantage to those sitting the test for the first time. You know exactly how the assessment runs and you would likely have had more time to revise.

Looking at the UCAT, this assessment was sat by over 29,000 candidates in 2019. Analysis of the results illustrate how individuals faired in the different sections.

The mean scaled scores of the **cognitive subtests** are below:

	2019
Number of candidates	29,375
Verbal Reasoning	565
Decision Making	618
Quantitative Reasoning	662
Abstract Reasoning	638
Total Cognitive Mean Scaled Score	2483

We can note how the verbal reasoning and decision making sections were the weakest whilst the quantitive reasoning was the strongest. In addition, the majority of individuals scored Band 2 in the SJT component.

Decile Rank	2019 Final Scores	2019 Actual percentile
1st	2170	10th
2nd	2280	20th
3rd	2360	31st
4th	2420	40th
5th	2480	50th
6th	2540	60th
7th	2610	70th
8th	2690	80th
9th	2800	90th

	2019
Number of candidates	29,375
Band 1	17%
Band 2	40%
Band 3	33%
Band 4	10%

Using this data and your own strengths and weaknesses, you can tailor your revision strategies to optimise your results.

For those re-taking the BMAT for entry in Leeds Dental Institute, a detailed breakdown of the 2019 results can be found at https://www.admissionstesting.org/Images/563514-bmat-explanation-of-results-2019.pdf.

For any assessment, candidates are strongly advised to begin preparing 6-8 weeks ahead of the assessment. Undertaking questions with timed mock tests in exam simulated conditions have been shown to be beneficial for those who have performed well in these assessments.

Re-applying as a Graduate Applicant

As previously discussed, the first step is to gather objective feedback from the universities you applied to. You should use the time during your first degree to build on any skills you may have lacked when you first applied. Undertaking an analysis of the skills, experiences and insight you gained into dentistry on your first application and making a comparison table can objectively show how you have improved.

A concern you may have is that you missed your predicted A-level grades in school and are now worried about being unable to attain the required degree classification to re-apply. It is important to note that the approach to university examinations is often very different to A-levels, and the grades you achieve at A-level don't determine your final university degree classification.

In terms of applying to dental school, it is key to make sure that you continue to gain work experience in dental settings if possible; perhaps in the university summer holidays as many dental schools like to see that you have recent work experience within the past few years of applying.

Undertaking work experience outside of dentistry is also not a bad thing. Doing so allows you to consider another line of work. It may also give you evidence that you have been drawn into dentistry from wider experiences. If anything, work experience will allow you to reaffirm your decision to study for an additional 4 or 5 years to become a dentist.

No matter what degree course, universities provide a great environment to do a range of extracurricular activities. It's equally important for your application to maintain these or take up new activities. Your degree is just one aspect of your application. Being well-rounded and having other interests is key to a good dentistry application. (You should refer to Chapter 2 for more information of how to make your personal statement stand out).

Keep practising for the UCAT and/ or BMAT, especially if that was a weaker point in your initial application. Each dental school differs on how they use this in their application process but getting to know the format of the exam and what techniques work for you can go a long way to improving your score.

Further advice on how to benefit as a graduate in detailed in Chapter 3.

Although it may seem overwhelming, you must stay focused and have belief. Here are some tips from a dental student who failed to get in first time:

1. Don't stress. All you can do is be prepared. Getting stressed will not help the situation. If anything, you'll put more pressure on yourself, which can really affect your health. Just remember that whatever happens, you tried your hardest and everything happens for a reason. Don't let it get you down. Try and look for the positives in everything. These 'setbacks' will only make you grow as a person and the skills you learn from dealing with them will help you to become a better dentist!

2. It's a risk but don't give up. Anything you do is a risk – whether it be retaking, re-applying or doing a different degree in the hope of getting into dental school. But without taking the risk, there is no way to know if it would have paid off. A career in dentistry is a marathon and not a sprint. Even if it takes you longer than you initially planned, if you're really committed to dentistry, taking the risk may work for you.

3. You are not alone. If you are unsuccessful in gaining a place at a dental school, don't think you're the only one. There will be many people in the same position. Also, re-applying does not mean that you are a failure or that people will think any less of you when you get to university.

People often fear that they will be the oldest or stick out like a sore thumb. That's really not the case. On a course such as dentistry, everyone is united by their passion to be a dentist rather than by age! Many current dental students have all taken different paths to get there; some longer than others. No one judges you on how you got there. The important thing is that you did it for yourself and can say that you are glad you stuck in there to do something you really enjoy.

4. Don't rush to plan your alternate route. Consider all your options, whether that be retaking some A-levels, taking a gap year or doing an alternative degree. Just make an informed decision that is completely yours. It's important to get advice from parents and school teachers. However, what you decide to do next should ultimately be your choice.

5. It could be a blessing in disguise. Taking a gap year or doing a different degree is not a negative. It can be a time for growth. For me that time allowed me to gain more independence and confidence without being thrown into an intense situation like dentistry. It helped me grow as a person and made it easier for me when I did eventually join dental school as I had more experience. You become more resilient and more open to change, which will help you in dealing with situations in the future.

6. Surround yourself with positive people. If you have people around you that support you and believe in you, it really helps make the experience a positive one. It drives you to do better and helps with your personal mentality.
7. Believe in yourself! Missing your A-level grades or not getting in first time doesn't define you!

Listen to the stories of these two dental students who didn't get into dental school easily. Click the link to read their unique journeys into dentistry. Scan QR codes to hear their stories.

Real student stories

Khushbu's story   Jasleen's Story

Gap Years & Deferred Entry

There are many reasons for taking a gap year (as shown diagrammatically below). The most common are either to take a break from academic studies or to re-apply to university, possibly because you were unsuccessful in achieving the grades, or because you didn't achieve any offers.

OFFER NOT ATTAINED (RE-APPLYING)	GRADES NOT ATTAINED (RE-APPLYING)	DEFERRED ENTRY (NOT RE-APPLYING)

If the rationale behind taking the gap year is to put you in better stead for your subsequent application then fortunately there are many things you can do during this time.

STRATEGIES FOR SUCCESS

First undertake some work experience. It gives you a more realistic insight into dentistry and is also one of the most useful talking points in both your personal statement and your interviews. It will demonstrate your interest and commitment to pursue dentistry. It's also a great way to confirm whether dentistry is the right career choice for you and gives you a chance to talk to qualified dentists so you can understand their journey.

Secondly, do as much research into dental courses and universities as you can, and consider your back-up options. You can use this time to visit different universities and go to open days. Taking a gap year gives you more time to choose the right course and right university.

Also consider getting a job. This is not a necessity but can be helpful in many ways. It can really help you improve your organisational skills, professionalism and work ethic, all of which are transferable to dentistry and can also provide useful examples for your personal statement and interviews. It is also a great way to earn a bit of money!

Another very popular route is joining a gap-year scheme. There are many different options for aspiring dentists to consider, including: medical-based schemes; charitable organisations; volunteering; or a scheme you have to pay for, abroad or at home. There are many organisations offering a wide variety of schemes. You'll be able to find out more from your school/college or by searching online. But! Make sure you do your research and use a reputable provider.

You could also use this time to volunteer or learn a new sport or skill. This is an ideal time to work on yourself and find new interests. It may be something that can improve your manual dexterity such as cross stitching (warming your hands up for dentistry) or it may be something involving public speaking, which really helps build confidence and communication skills (making interviews a lot easier).

Volunteering, particularly in the healthcare field, gives you better insight into patient care and shows your drive to help others. It can give you real life eye-opening experiences of the rewards and challenges in working in a healthcare profession. Participating in sports can also hone leadership, teamwork and communication skills.

Another salient point is to stay on top of dental news. Read different dental articles and stay in the loop as dentistry is constantly evolving. It shows good initiative in your personal statement and you are likely to find this useful as some universities may ask at the interview about recent developments in dentistry.

Finally, some of the time in a gap year can be put aside for relaxing and seeing friends (and possibly travel). Life is not all about dentistry and work. Use the time to work on yourself and reset. Don't burn yourself out before you even get to university. If you are going to meet friends who are at university, it's worth having a look around and getting a feel for different places and figuring what you like and don't like.

‖ Deferred Entry

WHAT IS THIS?

Deferring your dental school entry simply means you wish to take time out before commencing dentistry. This is where you get your place to dental school confirmed and they await you to start the following year. So for instance, those applying for dentistry in 2020 may defer entry until 2022. Usually you can only defer entry to dental school by one year but some schools don't consider deferring at all.

WILL I BE ALLOWED TO DEFER MY ENTRY?

Certain dental schools warmly welcome deferred entry. In fact, most schools do consider deferred entry, however it's important to ensure that you discuss your individual circumstances with your prospective school.

Our standard entry table lists some details related to schools accepting deferred entry.

Your confirmed decision to defer entry should be listed on your point of application via the UCAS form. Be aware that requesting deferral after receiving an offer is not usually be considered.

HOW MAY MY APPLICATION DIFFER IF I WISH TO DEFER?

Some schools may demand a clear plan of action detailing how you wish to use this year productively with some indications embedded into the personal statement.

It's important to note that it should not dissuade the judgement of the admission team should you wish to defer entry.

You will need to ensure that you meet the conditions of your offer at the time of application. For instance, if you receive a conditional dentistry offer in 2019/20 to start a course in 2021, you must have the academic qualifications to meet the conditions of your offer (i.e. AAA) by 31st August, 2020 (unless the School informs you otherwise).

WHY DEFER?

Deferring can have many benefits, especially for those students who are finishing college or school.

Embarking on a 'gap year' can offer the first 'academic break' for students who have been in education since secondary school. This can be a chance to recharge and refresh. Many students actively engage in travelling, volunteering and pursuing hobbies. For others it allows time to gather financial reserves to begin their studies or engage in personal commitments prior to starting.

Final Considerations
If you are committed to taking a year out, you should think about exactly how the year will be utilised. As discussed earlier, universities may wish to see clear forward thinking about how this time will be used to enhance your career aspirations. It may be worth contacting the schools to determine exactly what they require and how you can evidence this – should detailing this in the personal statement suffice?

Be sure that dentistry is for you!
By accepting the offer and deferring, you are committed to embarking the subsequent year. In this time you will not be able to re-apply to other courses until the university agrees to withdraw your place. With dentistry being so competitive, you should aim to relinquish your place should this not be for you so the opportunity can be offered to someone else that's keen to gain a place.

How to Defer Your Dentistry Application

1. You are strongly advised to first contact the university to ascertain the eligibility and details for deferral.
2. Once you have established the prospective schools that allow this, you will need to log in to your UCAS application and select to defer your start date for dentistry by a year.
3. In order to do this you will need to select the 'deferred entry start date' when adding your dentistry choices on your application.
4. In your personal statement, you may need to give indications why you wish to defer, and plans for the year out. These will be taken into account by dental admission when assessing your application.
5. Your application will then go through the same process at the same time as those applicants wishing not to defer and to start in 2020.

6. As with a normal application, you can use UCAS to track your status and you will undergo the same admission process as those who do not wish to defer.

Studying Abroad

Every year thousands of students in the UK are unsuccessful in securing a place at a UK dental school. As touched upon earlier, this is due to the immense competition for entry. Some schools receive more than 10 applicants for every space available. Without an offer, students may be left in a quandary and with their dream of studying dentistry still alive, look to alternative entry routes such as studying abroad in English.

Studying abroad has become a popular option over the past decade. The reasons for this may include the following:
- Increase in the UK university tuition fees to £9,000 a year and high UK living costs
- Unsuccessful in gaining an offer to study dentistry in the UK
- Not having gained a good score in the UCAT, BMAT or GAMSAT
- Not having the correct entry criteria such as GCSE grade requirements or A-level subjects
- Keeping a 'back-up' option if they were unsuccessful in gaining entry to a UK university (hence applying in the UK and also abroad during the final year of A-levels).

IMPORTANT CONSIDERATIONS
Studying abroad is a huge decision and should not be taken lightly. Since there is no central body such as UCAS governing the application process, you are left on your own to find out information about the universities, the application process, application deadlines and the differences in the courses available.

Here are a few questions you should consider when thinking of applying abroad:

Where can I find more information?

- Searching online to 'study dentistry abroad in English' will give you a plethora of information which you will have to sift through. This is a good starting point.

Should I go through an agency/representative or directly to the university?

- You will come across many representatives or agencies that work with universities abroad that will help you go through the application process. However, they often put a charge on top of the application fee. Sometimes going through an agency will help make the process easier (as each university has its own application process) and you may be able to have an interview arranged in the UK.
- An agency can also put you in touch with students they have helped in the past from the UK so that you can get first-hand experience of what studying in that university is like.

What factors should I consider when looking to study abroad?

GDC RECOGNITION

Look at how you can obtain General Dental Council (GDC) registration in the UK upon graduating. Is the course recognised by the GDC?

Look at the GDC website for more information https://www.gdc-uk.org/contact-us

Please note: EU rules and regulations are fast changing due to Brexit. DO NOT START A COURSE IF IT IS NOT RECOGNISED BY THE GDC ALREADY as you will not be allowed to work in the UK and most probably many other countries.

LIFE AFTER GRADUATION

It's a known fact that UK graduates are given preference over international students in terms of foundation job allocation. This makes gaining the anticipated post graduate job even more challenging.

COST

You will need to determinate the financial implications incurred by studying abroad. We recommended first looking at the cost of the annual tuition fee and estimated living costs in that country. For dentistry there may be additional costs in year 3-5 for clinical materials. Note that these are private courses and no government funding will be available.

LANGUAGE

When you chose a country of study, most likely you will have to learn the language to a basic level to speak to patients. All universities will help you with this by giving you language classes alongside the dental course. All the international students will be in the same boat as you.

VISA REQUIREMENTS

Some countries may require you to have a student visa (new rules due to Brexit). Find up-to-date information on each country's government website.

COURSE STRUCTURE

Most courses abroad are 5 years in length. The first two years are pre-clinical years to learn basic sciences and also the language. Third to fifth years are clinical years, during which you will see and treat local patients.

APPLICATION DEADLINES

WHEN IS THE DEADLINE TO APPLY?

You can find this on the individual university or agency website. If you are applying during the final year of A-levels then you may not want to take a gap year. Look carefully at application deadlines and interview dates.

Dental School Entrance Exam / Interview

Each university will be an international university, whereby they have their own entry requirements and interviews (as every country does not follow the UK system of doing GCSEs and A-levels). Look carefully at what they require and at what level. There may also be a written paper as well as an oral exam.

The best way to prepare for a specific university's entrance exam is to speak to students in the past year who are studying there. Try contacting past students through an agency or social media platforms such as Facebook groups, YouTube or Instagram.

When should I visit the university?

- You can visit before you apply to see where you are applying, alternatively and more sensibly, after the interview. Once you have been accepted it may make more sense to visit before starting. Otherwise you may visit places that you did not get accepted to, which can be a costly exercise.
- If you have been accepted you will be asked to pay a seat reservation fee (deposit) prior to paying the tuition fee. Visiting will give you a good idea of the location, place, people, student entertainment, cuisine and general living conditions. You will be living there for 5 years so it is important to get a good feel for the place. Organising a meet-up with current students is a good starting point.

Distance from Home

- You may want to consider the distance you will be prepared to travel if you study abroad. There may be times when you want to visit home for a weekend or for special occasions. If the distance is too great, you may not be able to travel both ways in a weekend.

Speak to current students at the university

They are the only ones who will give you an unbiased perspective of student life, examinations and life in that city. You may want to ask students from different years on the course as not every first year student will be able to answer your questions. Here are some of the questions you may want to ask:

Please note, it is wise to get multiple opinions from current and former students from the same university. Each student may have had a very different experience. Gathering multiple views will help you form your own opinions.

ENTRANCE EXAM
- What did you do to prepare for the exam?
- Did you go through an agency or a representative?
- Were there any hidden costs?
- What year did you do the exam (has the process changed)?
- What was asked in the exam?
- Was doing A-levels sufficient?
- What evidence/certificates did I have to bring to the interview?
- Did you take a gap year before applying?
- Dental School
- What facilities are there at the dental school and how modern are they?
- What is the course structure?
- What is their teaching style?
- Do you feel confident treating patients?
- What is the examination process?
- How many students start the course each year?
- How many students fail each year (some universities are notorious for accepting lots more students than they can accommodate for in clinical years)?
- Is the exam system fair?
- If students fail what is the process for repeating?
- How many students graduate each year from the course (If the starting number is very different to the finishing number, find out why)?

- Have students graduated and got jobs in the UK and can you put me in touch with any?
- What is the process of graduating and getting a job in the UK (ask final year students this)?
- Did graduates have to do another exam to go back to the UK?
- How established is the course and what year did they start taking on international students?
- When did the university course get GDC recognised?

Social / Other
- What is the university social life like?
- Which country are most other students from?
- What range of restaurants / bars / clubs are available?
- Are my dietary / religious requirements met there?
- How often do you go home?
- How much does it cost to rent a modern flat / house near the university?
- What is transport like?
- Is the university close to an airport?
- What sports facilities are available?
- Is the language hard to learn?
- Are there many UK students there?
- Do you have university societies?

Studying dentistry abroad has many advantages and disadvantages. It will teach you another language, allow you to make friends with others from different countries, and you will be more open-minded towards others from different backgrounds to yours.

However, studying abroad can be difficult and it's not for everyone. It does require you to adapt to a system and culture that you may not be familiar with. It also requires academic perseverance, which your fellow UK peers may not face to the same scrutiny. Ultimately, studying abroad is an option to consider in order to achieve your dream of studying dentistry.

Managing Stress

It's important to make sure you don't get so caught up in university applications that you neglect to spend time pursuing other interests and general downtime to relax.

Having a good work-life balance from a young age will bode well for you both now and as you grow older and become a healthcare professional.

STRATEGIES BUSTING STRATEGIES

Try to find activities which de-stress you and build them into your routine, rather than only doing them only when you feel overwhelmed and can't cope. This strategy prevents you getting to that point of being overstressed. Intense stress can have very powerful physiological effects such as nausea, lack of sleep and tension headaches, so it is important to learn how to manage your stress levels.

You could also combine de-stressing activities with something that adds to the value of your university application. For example, it is very easy to pair a relaxing activity with something that also improves your manual dexterity, such as model making, painting, playing an instrument, henna painting and so on.

Meditation and slow breathing exercises are good ways to deal with high stress levels – inhaling and exhaling slowly to reduce your heart rate.

Trying to find small things in life which bring you joy is also nice to include into your routine such as reading, walking or listening to music.

Staying organised to prevent burnout is crucial. So is having a life outside of academia. You can achieve this by making to-do lists and being realistic with targets and goals that you set yourself.

Make sure you know your deadlines well in advance and pace yourself through studying. Take regular breaks when studying for long periods. If you have a busy schedule and struggle to find time to study, try and be innovative in how you approach your learning. For example, if you have a fairly long commute, try listening to videos/audio or take flashcards with you. As social media is often a large distraction from studying, it is also best to switch off your phone when revising to eliminate distractions. Alternatively, use an app that rewards you if you do not use your phone for a set amount of time. Keeping your room and study area clean, tidy, and well-ventilated is also important to put you in the right frame of mind for studying.

LEARNING TECHNIQUES

When it comes to learning techniques, try and find out what works best for you. Different people learn in different ways. Four main groups of studying techniques having been identified: visual, kinaesthetic, oral and reader.

Which group you fall under determines how you should be learning. For oral learners it's best to learn by talking, such as teaching someone else a topic, or reading your notes out loud and listening back to them.

Take care of your body as well as your mind throughout your application journey. Living healthily can largely be achieved by having a balanced diet, staying hydrated and exercising. These things are also very important in allowing you to study in an effective manner.

COPING STRATEGIES

If you do feel like you are struggling to cope with the pressures of university applications, be sure to talk to someone about how you feel, such as a family member, teacher, friend or a mental health charity.

It is also good to be conscious of those around you as your university applications can also be stressful for close family members. They also wish to see you succeed and achieve your goal of becoming a dentist but it's nice to spend quality time with your friends and family

NEVER GIVE UP

rather than shutting yourself away to study constantly. It is important to think positively about your future.

Although at some point or the other everyone does doubt themselves, envisage attending your 'dream' university to study dentistry motivate yourself and give your confidence a boost. You can essentially train your mind to think in a calm and positive manner, even if thinking about exams fills you with dread.

Successful sports players use visualization techniques. Before a game they know will be particularly difficult they have already visualised themselves scoring the winning goal. Try to have this same positive mind set when studying, such as imagining opening up your exam paper and knowing the answer to every single question! Then match this mind set by putting in the hard work necessary to achieve these results.

Finally, try to not compare yourself to others who are also going through the university application process. It's important to remember that everyone will have different pathways leading up to starting a career as a dentist. The only person you should be competing with is yourself in order to achieve your very best in all that you apply yourself to.

FINAL WORDS

This idea of this book was born through the struggles that many students have faced, before, during and even after their application to dental school. With so many individuals embarking on this journey, we wanted to create a clear, comprehensive and actionable guide to help those applicants.

The core aim of 'I Want To Be A Dentist' is to support those considering applying to dental school at every stage.

We hope that this resource has given you knowledge, clarity and most of all belief that you are able to pursue dentistry as a career.

We wholeheartedly wish you the best of luck with your application!

Next Steps
Take action and visit our website for more free information to help with your journey to dental school.

www.iwanttobeadentist.com

Claim your FREE BONUS RESOURCES

As a thank you for purchasing this book we'd like to offer you some exciting bonus resources.

1. Free 'Dental School Checklist' Spreadsheet
This downloadable checklist is an excellent resource when it comes to deciding between universities. Although you only have four choices, making these choices can be difficult. As such, we have created this table for you to use. By objectively scoring each criteria, we hope to help make your decision easier when selecting a dental school.

2. Free Access to UCAT & BMAT Online Module
We understand that you are committed to maximising your chances of gaining an offer to study dentistry at university.

As part of our pre-interview resources, we have developed a unique online UCAT & BMAT mastery course. Developed with the UK's leading tutors and mentors, these courses help you achieve scores of 700 + in UCAT and gain top marks in the BMAT.

Here's your free link to access each course now for FREE (scan the QR code or click the links)

UCAT FREE module

(https://www.iwanttobeadentist.com/ucat-free-module-sign-up)

BMAT FREE module

(https://www.iwanttobeadentist.com/bmat-free-module-sign-up)

3. FREE PDF – PERSONAL STATEMENT MARK SCHEME

We want to do everything we can to make a beneficial impact on your application. A key determinant of the UCAS application is the personal statement. By using a well-structured, well-written and cogitative statement you can drastically impact the strength of your application in its entirety.

We've designed this useful mark scheme to help you think like an assessor. Using this you can see where your statement can be strengthened.

FREE personal statement mark scheme

4. 10% OFF CODE FOR OUR ONLINE COURSES

In addition to this book, we also have our online pre-interview and interview packages as discussed earlier on.

For all book readers, we are giving you a 10% gift voucher to be used exclusively on our website www. iwanttobeadentist.com with any of our packages.

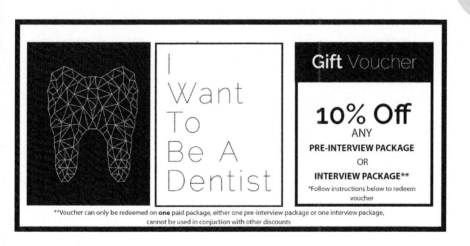

I Want To Be A Dentist

Gift Voucher

10% Off
ANY
PRE-INTERVIEW PACKAGE
OR
INTERVIEW PACKAGE**
*Follow instructions below to redeem voucher

Voucher can only be redeemed on **one paid package, either one pre-interview package or one interview package, cannot be used in conjuction with other discounts

What can I use the voucher on?

You can get 10% off the total fee on any one of our pre-interview or interview packages.[4]

---

4   Please note that this voucher cannot be combined with any other offers.

Find out more about our packages below:

Pre-interview Packages

https://www.iwanttobeadentist.com/
pre-interview-dentistry-applicant-preparation-packages

How to Get the Discount

You can get your unique voucher code in 4 easy steps

Step 1: Take an image of this book in your hands (if it's an ebook take a screen shot of your confirmed purchase)

Step 2: Share the image on Instagram and tag us: @iwanttobeadentist. Use hashtags #IWTBAD #iwanttobeadentist

If you don't have Instagram then tag us on Facebook @iwanttostudydentistry #IWTBAD #iwanttobeadentist

Step 3: Send us a direct message on Instagram or Facebook with this image

Step 4: We'll send you a discount code to use

THE AUTHORS

Raza Ahmed

 @RA0440

Raza is a first year dental student at The University of Leeds. Having recently gone through the UCAS and admissions process whilst on a gap year, Raza secured his place for dental school. He is one of the few selected individuals who gained an offer into dental school on the second attempt. From an early age, Raza knew that the dental career was the one for him. From attending lectures at the University of Birmingham to initiating opportunities independently, Raza was able to meet renowned dentists such as Dr Mark Tangri and was further inspired to accomplish his goals.

Completing his GCSEs at Lordswood Boys School, Raza became the Head boy in 2017 out of 60 students. He was an active contributor in developing the school, whilst consistently being a role model for his peers. Soaring in his academic performances, Raza continued his

education and moved to Hillcrest Sixth Form to study for his A-levels. Just like any student, Raza also found it difficult to cope with the demands of higher education and after just a month of sixth form he was informed of the teachers' decision to remove him from his subjects as they believed he wasn't going to progress further. Hitting rock bottom and realising that this would limit his chances for a career in dentistry, Raza took it upon himself to move to Windsor Sixth Form, where he completed his A-levels in two years.

Unfortunately, after not receiving any offers on the first attempt, Raza was unable to progress to University. This didn't stop him from trying again and working even harder to achieve his dream. Taking a gap year was a pivotal point in his life. Deciding not to give up, Raza reapplied to study dentistry at university. Being an opportunist, he used this year to strengthen his application, travel and work at Specsavers as an Optical Assistant. On the second attempt Raza applied for a place at Leeds University.

He undertook both the UCAT and BMAT exams. He received an invitation for an interview at Leeds whilst practicing for the MMI, during which time he met Dr Kalpesh, who mentored him further. After successfully passing the interview and selection process, Raza received an offer to study dentistry at the University of Leeds for September 2020. At the age of just 19, Raza Co-Founded 'I Want To Be A Dentist' with Dr Kalpesh to provide the ultimate resource for prospective dental students and to aid them throughout their application to dental school. The platform was designed to guide students and support applicants wishing to apply to dentistry. Raza's application journey is a reflection of his determination and willingness to succeed.

"To be the best, you must learn from the best."

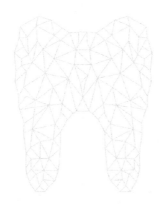

Dr Kalpesh Prajapat BDS (Liverpool)

@DrKPUK

Kalpesh graduated from Liverpool Dental School in 2016 with distinctions in Restorative Dentistry and Oral Health. He was awarded several prizes while an undergraduate and during his early postgraduate career; the most recent being 'Best Young Dentist - Highly Commended' for the Midlands Region. Kalpesh owes his career inspiration and passion for education to his mentors and teacher, to whom he is forever grateful.

Following graduation, Kalpesh secured his 1st choice foundation post at Cambridge and then followed a formal training pathway. He currently works part-time between Birmingham Dental Hospital and three private clinics; providing mainly restorative, oral surgery, sedation and minimally invasive cosmetic dental treatments. Kalpesh continues his learning from world renowned clinicians in the UK and internationally.

Kalpesh is a self-published, bestselling Amazon author with his books 'Foundation To Dental Core Training' and 'Dental Associate Interviews' becoming 'No 1 sellers' in the Dentistry book category. Kalpesh is passionate about self-growth and personal development. His motto is, 'I'd rather suffer the pain of discipline, then suffer the pain of regret'.

Kalpesh co-founded 'I Want To Be A Dentist' with Raza Ahmed to develop a universal educational platform to help dentistry applicants with their journey to dental school.

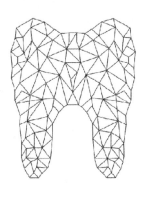

I
Want
To
Be A
Dentist

 iwanttobeadentist.com

 iwanttobeadentist
iwanttostudydentistry

Printed in Great Britain
by Amazon